GOLD, OIL, AND AVOCADOS

GOLD,

OIL, *and*

AVOCADOS

A RECENT HISTORY
OF **LATIN AMERICA** IN
SIXTEEN **COMMODITIES**

ANDY ROBINSON

MELVILLE HOUSE
BROOKLYN • LONDON

Gold, Oil, and Avocados

First published in 2020 by ARPA

Copyright © Andy Robinson, 2020
Translation © Andy Robinson, 2021

This new and revised edition has been prepared
especially for English language publication.

First Melville House Printing: August 2021

Melville House Publishing
46 John Street
Brooklyn, NY 11201

and

Melville House UK
Suite 2000
16/18 Woodford Road
London E7 0HA

mhpbooks.com
@melvillehouse

ISBN: 978-1-61219-935-1
ISBN: 978-1-61219-936-8 (eBook)

Library of Congress Control Number: 2021938500

Designed by Euan Monaghan

Printed in the United States of America

1 3 5 7 9 10 8 6 4 2

A catalog record for this book is available
from the Library of Congress

In the colonial and neocolonial alchemy, gold changes into scrap metal and food into poison.

– Eduardo Galeano, *Open Veins of Latin America*

CONTENTS

Introduction   1
  Itaituba, the Battle for the Future

PART ONE: EXTRACTION

Chapter One   17
  Iron (Minas Gerais, Brazil)
  The Brutal Force

Chapter Two   40
  Niobium (Brazil)
  The Fetish of Jair Bolsonaro

Chapter Three   58
  Coltan (Gran Sabana, Venezuela)
  The Mines of Nicolás Maduro

Chapter Four   71
  Gold (Colombia; Central America; Utah; Nevada)
  El Dorado in Salt Lake City

Chapter Five   103
  Diamonds and Emeralds (Diamantina, Brazil)
  The Other Side of Paradise

PART TWO: CONQUEST

Chapter Six   117
  Bananas (Honduras)
  Banana Republic, Twenty-First Century

Chapter Seven   132
  Potatoes (Puno, Peru)
  From *Chuño* to the Potato Chip

Chapter Eight   155
  Copper (Apurímac, Peru; Atacama Desert, Chile)
  Two Press Conferences and a Revolution

Chapter Nine   183
  Lithium (Potosí, Bolivia)
  Coup on the Salt Flat

Chapter Ten   205
  Quinoa (Uyuni, Bolivia)
  The Rise and Fall of the Miracle Grain

Chapter Eleven   218
  Silver (San Luis Potosí, Mexico)
  "Racers" and the Fourth Transformation

PART THREE: DEPLETION

Chapter Twelve   231
  Avocados (Michoacán, Mexico)
  Hot Dog with Guacamole

Chapter Thirteen   247
  Soy (Pará, Brazil; Bahia, Brazil)
  Cargill and the War of the End of the Planet

Chapter Fourteen   266
  Beef (Pará, Brazil)
  The Capital of the Ox

Chapter Fifteen   280
  Oil (Venezuela; Brazil; Mexico)
  Petrosocialism and Counterattack

Chapter Sixteen   319
  Hydro (Pará, Brazil)
  The Maps of the Munduruku

Itaituba, the Battle for the Future

How would Eduardo Galeano write his classic *Open Veins of Latin America* today? It seemed the right question to ask during a visit to the boomtown of Itaituba on the banks of the Tapajos River in the Brazilian Amazon. The Workers' Party was still in power and I had traveled from Rio de Janeiro to assess whether the controversial Growth Acceleration Program championed by President Dilma Rousseff would prove compatible with the survival of the planetary lung and, more immediately, of the thirteen thousand citizens of the Munduruku indigenous community who lived along the banks of the Tapajos. Under the scheme, the Munduruku's millenary lands would be flooded by the gigantic hydroelectric project of São Luiz do Tapajos, planned to generate electricity for the new Amazonian metropolises as well as the megamines and soybean plants.

After a thirteen-hour passage upriver aboard a Fitzcarraldian ferry boat from Santarém, the jungle capital, itself a seven-hour flight from Rio, the last thing I expected to encounter were five Jet Skis equipped with 2,600cc engines. But there they were, zigzagging before a wake of white foam. After millennia of silence, broken only by the shrieks, howls, and buzzing of the deep jungle, perhaps Itaituba felt the need for deafening noise and breakneck speed. "Jet Skis are all the rage here. You will see fifteen or twenty a weekend;

mine reaches one hundred and five miles per hour," said Bruno, eighteen years old, as he coupled his Yamaha to a 4x4. While we spoke, a riverboat plying the Tapajos from Santarém two hundred miles downstream docked and unloaded five "quad"-motor tractors, ideal for racing along the newly opened jungle trails.

Bruno explained he had bought his Jet Ski for twenty thousand reais (more than $7,000) with his wages as a construction worker paving the Trans-Amazonian Highway that would bring forth a new phase of uncontrolled deforestation. But there were other ways to make a quick buck in Itaituba. Teeming with banks and gold merchants–and a population that was growing explosively–the frontier city was the center of all extractive activities in the western Amazon state of Pará (most of them illegal) from panning for precious metals and stones to clearing the rain forest for timber. Not to mention the soybeans loaded at the terminal built by the multinational agribusiness corporation Bunge. Another boost to the economy was expected with the construction of the megadam thirty miles upstream in Munduruku territory and the new waterways for the transport of soy, minerals, and timber.

"Has Itaituba changed much in recent years?" I asked Bruno, the son of impoverished migrants from the outskirts of Brasília who had chanced the move to the Amazon thirty years earlier in search of wealth or at least two plates of beans and yuca a day. He looked to one side and pointed to seven black vultures–*urubú* in Portuguese–perched on a pile of garbage, wings spread like funeral curtains: "You think there are a lot of urubus over there, right? Well, in the old days there were many more."

The scene in Itaituba seemed to illustrate the contradictions of the Latin American left's economic development project. Taking power at the beginning of the new century, the so-called pink-tide progressive governments rightly perceived a crucial need to accelerate growth in order to eliminate poverty and extreme inequality, burdens that the region had shouldered from the first era of mass enslavement, in the gold and silver mines in the sixteenth century, and the second, that arrived in chains from Africa to toil in the plantations of the first commodity crops–sugar, bananas, coffee–for the new global market. Brazil's former president Luiz Inácio Lula da Silva, or, as he is affectionately known, Lula, was justifiably proud of lifting forty-two million previously excluded Brazilians into what he called the new middle class.

Achieving and maintaining the support of Latin American workers like Bruno required constant improvements in the population's material well-being, and the fastest way to achieve this without triggering an external debt crisis was through exports of raw materials–minerals, monoculture cash crops like soy, and meat–and the foreign exchange that these would generate. In a time of diminishing resources and the rise of China as a superpower, raw materials were valued as never before and the temptation to rev up the extraction machine was difficult to resist. A race for ever-more-scarce resources in a quasi-cold war between China and the United States made the model even more seductive.

But how could the strategy prosper without committing the same atrocities as in the classic epochs of the plunder of Latin America, captured so vividly in Galeano's great book? Environmental destruction and accelerating deforestation in the Amazon, after all, was not only hastening planetary climate change and bringing catastrophic droughts to the Andes and Central America. It had also raised the risk of

GOLD, OIL, AND AVOCADOS

killer pandemics as the slaughterhouses and feeding lots of the new Latin American meatpacking industry became the biggest in the world and the pathogens of wildest nature were released into the slums of jungle metropolises. Burgeoning Amazon towns like Itaituba, with poor sanitation and chaotic urbanization, had already become breeding grounds for Zika, the mosquito-borne virus that threatened to spread throughout Brazil, terrifying athletes due to perform at the 2016 Rio Olympics.

Then there were the political problems generated by the model. If Bruno was typical of this new "aspirational" middle class (with aspirations to consume more, perhaps even more Jet Skis . . .), how could it uphold the principles of equality and environmental protection that progressive governments from Brazil to Ecuador had championed? The problem would soon be confirmed by the defeat of the Workers' Party in Brazil and its replacement by a ruthless, extreme right-wing government under Jair Bolsonaro that was closely allied to mining and agribusiness. The new middle class had destroyed its creator, a fate shared a year later by Evo Morales in Bolivia, though Morales's Movement Toward Socialism, staged an impressive comeback.[1] As the rivalry for access to natural resources between China and the United States intensified, Latin American progressive governments also became vulnerable to Washington-led regime-change policies, threatening a return to the years when Galeano wrote his masterpiece and most of the continent was governed by brutal pro-US military regimes.

In this book, a collection of chronicles based on a range of raw materials extracted in Latin America, from soy to

---

1 André Singer, *O lulismo em crise* (São Paulo, Brazil: Companhia de Letras, 2018).

niobium, beef to gold, and oil to avocado, I try to reflect on this dilemma as well as analyze the dramatic events–coups d'état soft or hard in Honduras, Bolivia, and Brazil; extraordinary popular uprisings in Santiago de Chile, Quito, and Bogotá; and the likelihood of more social unrest after the devastation caused by COVID-19–that have shaken the region in recent years. Some of Galeano's destinations are revisited: icons of colonial plunder and pillage such as Potosí, Minas Gerais, and Zacatecas, where I have tried to update his bold thesis, based on the dependency theories of Immanuel Wallerstein, Celso Furtado, and Andre Gunder Frank, that in "a world of powerful centers and subjugated outposts," "we Latin Americans are poor because the ground we tread is rich."[2]

Open Veins of Latin America, written when Galeano was only twenty-eight years old, was the bible of a generation of the left that came to power in Latin America at the beginning of the new century, from Lula to Evo Morales, Rafael Correa to Hugo Chávez. (Chávez even gave a copy of the book to a skeptical Barack Obama.) But of the two main messages in Galeano's argument–the need to break the ties of dependence with the ex-colonial powers and their multinational corporations while steering the economy away from dependency on the export of raw materials–only the first has been heeded.

The dependence on the export of commodities remained in many countries and when, inevitably, the supercycle of high international prices of minerals, oil, and basic foodstuffs ended in a second wave of the great financial crisis,

---

2 Eduardo Galeano, *Open Veins of Latin America: Five Centuries of the Pillage of a Continent*, trans. Cedric Belfrage (New York, NY: Monthly Review Press, 1997), 285.

the failure would prove costly for a leftist project that appeared to have found the magic formula to redistribute income and, at the same time, stay in government. The pink tide receded and the left fell from power in Ecuador, Brazil, Chile, Argentina, and, briefly, in Bolivia, while, in Venezuela, a catastrophic socioeconomic crisis weakened Chavism to a point unimaginable ten years earlier and an unresolved problem of dependence on oil exports heightened Venezuela's vulnerability to US-sponsored coups. Reassessed, the spectacular social conquests of the left's decade in power seemed chimeras, the unsustainable windfall of a bubble in the commodities market.

Ironically, Galeano contributed to the crisis of ideas on the left by renouncing his very own book in 2014 at the literary biennial in Brasília, calling it simplistic, the work of a young man with no grasp of economics, infected by the dogmatism of the old left. "I wouldn't be capable of reading this book again; I'd keel over," he joked, a year before his death. Galeano's mea culpa gave way to a round of back-slapping by the usual suspects of the Latin American right. Álvaro Vargas Llosa, whose book *Guide to the Perfect Latin American Idiot* was a crude caricature of *Open Veins*, celebrated the intellectual defeat of the left. Michael Reid, the Americas editor for *The Economist*, declared the definitive retreat of the pink tide and dubbed Galeano's book "the work of a propagandist, a potent mix of selective truths, exaggeration and falsehood, caricature and conspiracy theory," a description better suited, in my view, to Reid's magazine than to Galeano's masterwork.[3]

During my travels in Latin America as an itinerant

---

3 Michael Reid, *Forgotten Continent* (New Haven, CT: Yale University Press, 2017).

reporter for the Barcelona-based newspaper *La Vanguardia*, I came to a different conclusion than Reid. The young Eduardo Galeano, far from exaggerating the destruction caused in Latin America by the forces of global capitalism allied with local elites, had underestimated the damage. Looting has occurred not only in the economic sphere of the extraction of raw materials but also in the extraction of the soul from peoples whose cultures–and that Quechua philosophy of *sumak kawsay*, or "good living"–are being annihilated in a remorseless process of commodification. Maybe the latest open veins are more subtle, and certainly more environmental. The conversion of Peruvian ceviche into a symbol of international gastronomic status, cited by International Monetary Fund (IMF) managing director Christine Lagarde as an inspiration for their programs in Latin America, while an island of plastic floats in the Pacific. The new tourism of exotic experience embodied in the trains of the Andes–privatized by the Peruvian state and sold to Belmond, a subsidiary of the global luxury branding company LVMH–whose transparent carriages allow travelers to Machu Picchu to contemplate poverty from a safe distance on a parched altiplano now bereft of glaciers.

The difference now is that many governments of the left–without belittling the colossal social gains that they have achieved–have been complicit in the same material and spiritual pillage as those that preceded them. "What has been done here is bullshit, now we have soy, soy, and more soy," remarked Edilberto Sena when we met in Santarém. The charmingly foul-mouthed Franciscan monk was one of the followers of liberation theology who helped found the Workers' Party in Amazonia three decades before. It was not only a lament for the thousands of campesinos forced by the latest cash crop to move to the city but for the disappearance of a rich and complex culture based on the staggering biodiversity of the Amazon.

In a broad swathe of countries from Brazil to Ecuador, Venezuela to Chile, I witnessed fierce debates between those appalled by the pink-tide governments' embrace of "neoextractivism" and those who dismissed the anti-extractivists as romantic dreamers, unaware of the urgent need to raise growth rates as a means to combat poverty and generate development.

"Oil and mining helped us avoid the Chinese path of inhuman wages and precarious labor conditions," said Fausto Herrera, finance minister of Ecuador under Rafael Correa, whose frustrated attempt to leave millions of tons of oil in the Amazon subsoil was a model for the environmental movement . . . until Correa backtracked. Correa's critics, led by Alberto Acosta, another former minister, opposed extractivism and defended new means to measure welfare inspired by *sumak kawsay*.[4] The same splits occurred in Bolivia, where some members of the environmental movement went so far as to support the coup against Evo Morales because of his turn to mining and agribusiness. These chronicles support a position that will please no one: that common ground has to be found between the two schools of thought.

These are issues of universal concern, but things are more clearly focused in Latin America, a region in which "computers coexist with the most archaic forms of peasant culture and . . . with all modes of production in history," to quote the US philosopher Fredric Jameson's article on *One Hundred Years of Solitude* in the *London Review of*

---

4 Alberto Acosta, *Sumak kawsay, el buen vivir* (Barcelona, Spain: Icaria Editorial, 2016).

Books.[5] The surviving remnants of these past worlds, their inhabitants still protected in mind and body from the forces that destroy the rest of us, turn the region into a key actor in the struggle to defend the planet. This lesson is being learned fast in Colombia, where ex-guerrilla Gustavo Petro's innovative humanist project rejected all aggressive extractivisms and placed climate change at the heart of his bid for the presidency in the elections he came close to winning in 2018. The same ideas drove some of the mass mobilizations against the conservative government of Iván Duque that filled the streets of Bogotá, Medellín, and Barranquilla in the autumn of 2019, and the protests in Chile and Ecuador, where signs emerged of a new movement committed to a different way forward.

Latin American experts at international think tanks and in the global media, from Reid to Alma Guillermoprieto and Monica de Bolle, a Brazilian economist based in Washington, were deeply pessimistic about the 2019 protests. "Far from hope, the discontent in Latin America in past weeks has been driven by what we might call a post-commodity bubble syndrome," wrote de Bolle in an article for the Peterson Institute.[6] But Washington has never been a place to feel optimistic about Latin America. The Andean altiplano told a different story. When I ambled through the baroque center of Ecuador's capital, Quito, in October 2019, surrounded by Quechua street vendors visibly encouraged by the success of their rebellion against the Lenín Moreno government, another more positive reading

---

5 Fredric Jameson, "No Magic, No Metaphor: Fredric Jameson on 'One Hundred Years of Solitude,'" *London Review of Books*, June 15, 2017.

6 Monica de Bolle, "The Spring of Latin America's Discontent," Peterson Institute for International Economics, October 29, 2019.

of events emerged. This time, the agenda of social transformation, forged in huge popular mobilizations, would have a more solid foundation than the price of oil, copper, or soy on the Chicago commodity market.

Although the immediate cause of the protests in Ecuador was a rise in the price of gasoline after the IMF-designed withdrawal of energy subsidies, the presence of so many pollera-clad indigenous women bravely defying the rubber bullets of the anti-riot police suggested that the defense of the *Pachamama* (Mother Earth) would be a central element of the next stage of struggle. Proof came in the inclusion of the principles of *sumak kawsay* in the alternative plan to the IMF's shock therapy, which was drawn up by the Confederation of Indigenous Nationalities of Ecuador (CONAIE) and presented to the government at a tense ceremony at the Catholic Episcopal Conference in Quito, which I attended. The left's young candidate in the 2021 elections, Andrés Arauz, seemed more open to reconciliation with the indigenous project than his mentor, Correa, although divisions remained and Arauz finally lost to the millionaire banker, Guillermo Lasso.

In Chile too the multicolored flags of the Mapuche became a ubiquitous emblem of mass protest against the most successful model of neoliberalism in Latin America, eulogized by think tanks, market analysts, and oligarchs alike but despised by everyone else. Perhaps the rebellions would be a new link in the alliance between the Latin American left and the emerging global movement against climate change. While the COVID-19 pandemic exposed Latin America's continuing social inequality and failing health systems, it also demonstrated once again the capacity of favelas, slums in Brazilian megacities, or ranchos in Venezuela to organize collective self-protection.

After rereading *Open Veins of Latin America* during long trips by plane, bus, and, on occasion, riverboat, far from bored by the leaden prose of the pedantic left, I felt inspired once again, as I had been in my youth, by the young Galeano's desire to write "about political economy in the style of a novel about love or pirates."[7] In these vignettes, I have tried to follow that example.

Each chapter reflects on the end use of raw materials in a world of ostentatious consumption, extreme inequality, and dwindling natural resources. The diamonds extracted by the Brazilian *garimpeiros* in an inferno of mud and violence, processed in Surat, India, and bought in Swarovski stores in Dubai. The prototypes of hypersonic missiles assembled in California or Shenzhen with the niobium extracted close to indigenous territories in Amazonia, now the target of mining companies allied with the new Brazilian ultraright led by Bolsonaro. The soy from a deforested Amazon that supplies industrial chicken plants in Europe, which then churn out a billon Chicken McNuggets. Or the vast herds of melancholic zebu in Amazonian latifundia, grazing in the wake of chain saws and forest fires to supply Burger King. The conversion of the potato, the sustenance to the great pre-Columbian civilizations in the Andean highlands, into the addictive potato chip of Frito-Lay (PepsiCo), and its contribution to an epidemic of obesity in Latin America. A global fashion of guacamole that has turned the Mexican region of Michoacán, cradle of the Purépecha Empire, a more complex society than the Aztec's, into a monoculture of avocado run by organized crime. A visit to San Luis Potosí in Mexico uncovers how the indigenous Huichol's success in avoiding the reopening of a nineteenth-century silver mine

---

7 Galeano, *Open Veins*, 284.

has been clouded by an invasion of tourists, many keen to try the hallucinogenic properties of the peyote cactus.

Chapters on oil and iron ore discuss how overdependence on raw materials has sown the seeds of disaster for progressive governments in Venezuela and Brazil, causing an economic crisis that persuaded broad swathes of society to support US-driven coups d'état. The Mexican president Andrés Manuel López Obrador's bid to repeat the petronationalism of Lázaro Cárdenas is also discussed. In Bolivia, a visit to the Salar de Uyuni, the largest lithium deposit in the world, shows how Evo Morales's socialist-indigenist government's attempt to industrialize extraction with new battery plants ended in a rebellion of the middle class and, in November 2019, a coup d'état. In the rarefied atmosphere of the Bolivian altiplano, another existential question is posed. Which is worse? A lithium mine or ten thousand tourists posing for selfies against the sunset?

In the chapter on gold, a trip from Colombia and Central America that ends in Utah links record gold prices and the rush to open mines after the 2008 global financial crisis to conservative thinking in the United States and then back to impoverished gold prospectors in Colombia. In its own perverse way, the twenty-first-century El Dorado is another example of a new era of "open veins." A search for the safe haven of gold in the metropolis unleashes yet another destructive invasion by thousands of *garimpeiros* and *barequeros* (artisanal miners) in the Amazon and the Andes.

A terrible irony emerges too from the plan for a global transition to a zero-emissions economy to avoid catastrophic climate change. As Jason Hickel notes in his new book *Less Is More*, trying to meet this challenge without questioning capitalism's growth imperative will require massive increases in the extraction of materials such as copper, cobalt, silver, lithium, and the elusive rare earths. "Mining has already become a big driver of deforestation, ecosystem collapse and biodiversity loss around the world. If we're not careful, growing demand for renewable energy will exacerbate this crisis significantly," he writes. "Parts of Latin America, Africa and Asia are likely to become the target of a new scramble for resources . . . and new forms of colonisation."[8] Grotesquely, Latin America may see its veins opened further by a corporate-friendly plan for a market-driven green economy.

A new development model in Latin America will require a radical change of philosophy, beyond the simple extraction of raw materials and beyond the old formulas of industrialization oxidized in the lost world of Fordlandia, the industrial city of rubber that Henry Ford tried to found three hours by boat from Itaituba, now overgrown by vines and *ipê* trees where macaque monkeys scamper across the rusting processing machines. Without abandoning the advances and social goals of the decade of the left in South America, it is now the time to devise new systems of pro-duction on a smaller scale and linked to an eco-economy, a radical redistribution of income, and less destructive consumption. Instead of centralizing power in one person and co-opting the social movements that cleared the route to power, it is crucial to broaden and deepen democracy. If the left is given another opportunity in Latin America–a seed perhaps already sown in the spectacular citizens' movements in Santiago, Bogotá, Quito, and even Lima–it is essential that alternatives are considered.

Inspiration may come in part from the indigenous

---

8 Jason Hickel, *Less Is More: How Degrowth Will Save the World* (London: William Heinemann, 2020).

philosophy of the *sumak kawsay* regarding models of society compatible with the protection of the environment and culture. This is not a romantic longing for a society of hunters and collectors in a Rousseauean state of *bon sauvage*. As is explained in the final chapter, which describes the Munduruku's epic struggle against the São Luiz de Tapajos hydrodam, the Amazon's past is a relevant lesson in development. Two millennia ago, long before the arrival of the Europeans, Amazonia housed a society of eight million inhabitants that built roads and managed the forest in a sophisticated and sustainable way. Its inhabitants even practiced genetic modification to ensure food security through crops such as cassava. Fish were farmed and urban parks stretched along the banks of the Amazon's mighty rivers. "We are the guardians of the jungle," Jairo Saw, one of the leaders of the Munduruku in Itaituba, told me in a statement of fact, not pretense, during my visit to the Tapajos. The Munduruku understand technology. They have delimited their lands using GPS to demonstrate with scientific accuracy their territorial rights to defend the jungle. When we spoke next in Rio de Janeiro, Jairo Saw was on his way to Los Angeles to meet a group of General Electric engineers and try to persuade them to abandon the hydrodam project. "If they do not listen, there is no future for them or for anybody else," he said as he headed off in a yellow Rio taxi to Galeão International Airport.

PART ONE: EXTRACTION

CHAPTER ONE

Iron (Minas Gerais, Brazil)
The Brutal Force

Bento Rodrigues is a town that no longer exists. Six months after the collapse of the main containment dam at the Samarco iron mine and the sudden death of the river Doce–the "sweet river"–some might think it never did.

"Make a right down the dirt track," they told us at the last gas station in Mariana, where the young *mineira* girls, perhaps sensitized to the devastating power of fate, lined up to have their palms read by the local fortune tellers. "But, beware, it is forbidden to go!"

The road was as red as rusted iron and three *urubú* vultures flew on ahead through the dense jungle of the Mata Atlântica like angelic guides in a journey to hell. Little was left of the town. The sole remnant was a wooden sign erected by the state tourist authority, somehow untouched by the deadly wave. It marked the ancient camino real where the Portuguese transported gold and diamonds from the mines that gave their name to the Brazilian state of Minas Gerais (General Mines).

IN BENTO RODRIGUES, TRY OUR AUTHENTIC *MINEIRA* DISHES, read a sign describing the delicious pork and yuca *feijão tropeiro*, and chicken with *quiabo* (okra), that would surely attract tourists from the moneyed capital, Belo Horizonte, in a bid by the historic Paraopeba mining towns to shake off their dependence on iron ore. But not anymore. On the other bank, only three or four houses poked out above the mountains of mud, lit under the mining company's spotlights like a Belém nativity scene as dusk thickened.

Bento, a small town of some six hundred inhabitants, was the epicenter of the largest environmental disaster in the history of Brazil–though no one would have thought it given the lack of interest from international media, which focused instead on the Zika viral epidemic, gang warfare in Rio's favelas as the Olympics approached, or Neymar's latest haircut. Having erased Bento from the map, a tsunami of fifty million tons of mining waste material, equivalent to twenty-four thousand Olympic swimming pools filled with toxic mud, crashed downriver as far as the port city of Espiritu Santo five hundred miles away where the Rio Doce meets the Atlantic, destroying everything in its path. Amazingly, only nineteen people were killed, two in Bento Rodrigues. But the damage to the river, the second-biggest in Brazil after the Amazon, was catastrophic. The cause of the collapse, according to an initial investigation by the Brazilian federal police, was a rise in water content in the sludge of waste material piled up against the dam. This was compounded, said the police report, by the negligence of the technicians at the Samarco mine owned jointly by two giants of the global mining industry: the Brazilian corporation Companhia Vale do Rio Doce and the Anglo-Australian BHP Billiton. A small seismic movement was the trigger for the catastrophe.

When I visited the area during Easter week of 2016, five months after the disaster, more than a million people lacked drinking water and fishing was banned along the full length of the river, depriving 1.4 million people of their principal means of subsistence. Some of the worst affected were the Krenak, an indigenous community that stretched for hundreds of miles along the river whose main source of nutrition were the eighty-plus species of fish that had populated the river before the disaster, eleven of them unique to the Rio Doce's ecosystem. All eleven were now in danger of extinction.

"The river is irrevocably altered. The sediments have moved. It is now another river with a completely different morphology," said Marcelo Campos, director of the Brazilian Institute of the Environment and Renewable Natural Resources (IBAMA) in Belo Horizonte, who appeared shocked by his own diagnosis of the disaster. Vale do Rio Doce and BHP Billiton insisted that there were no toxic elements in the waste material that had washed downriver. But it was well known that the chemical agent ether amino was used in the separation process to obtain the iron ore at Samarco and the other Mariana mines.

In a technical report on the toxicity of ether amino Montal 800, the Swiss company Clariant, which had doubled production of the agent during the Brazilian mining boom, warned of the "dangers to aquatic life" of a "non-biodegradable" toxin. The Doce River was effectively dead, and that Easter week in Minas Gerais no one dared to venture how long the wait for resurrection would be.

"A generation will be born and raised on the banks of a forbidden river," said Ailton Krenak, a Krenak philosopher and author of the essay *Ideas to Postpone the End of the World*. "It is a terrifying vision of the future of the planet."

* * *

Brazil's vast reserves of iron ore are the key to understanding a decade of US intervention at the beginning of the Cold

War, culminating in the 1964 coup d'état designed with the interests of US Steel and Hanna Mining Corporation in mind. In fact, as Galeano dryly notes in *Open Veins of Latin America*, the Minas Gerais mines were of such importance to Washington's strategy in the region that the US embassy in the then capital of Brazil, Rio de Janeiro, created a new diplomatic post, the mineral attaché, who "had at least as much work as the military or cultural attachés—so much, indeed, that two mineral attachés were soon appointed instead of one."

The Cleveland-based Hanna, chaired by the then US treasury secretary, George Humphrey, had in the years prior to the coup made seats available on the company board for no fewer than five Brazilian ministers in its bid to win the concession for what was now known to be the world's largest iron deposit in the valley of Paraopeba. It was a generous offer, but the wave of developmental nationalism sweeping across Latin America had reached Brazil, and a showdown was inevitable.

When Getúlio Vargas, Brazil's iconic developmentalist president, committed suicide in 1954 after nearly two decades in and out of power, relations with the superpower were already frayed. Vargas was keenly aware that, as Galeano noted, "steel is produced in the world's wealthy centers, iron in the poor suburbs," and he had created a state-owned national steel company to ease dependence on exports of ore in its crude form. He had even persuaded Roosevelt to build the first Brazilian steel plant, in exchange for permission to set up a US military base on the northeast coast during the Second World War. As we shall see in chapter 15, Vargas's tragic demise was more closely related to his decision to nationalize the oil industry. His successor Juscelino Kubitschek sought a Solomonic arrangement with the US mining giants by trying to condition Hanna's and other multinationals' concessions to his plans for state-driven industrialization. But pressure mounted from an increasingly active workers' movement to take more radical measures. When the socially conservative economic nationalist Jânio Quadros took over in 1961, he went a step further and cancelled Hanna's mining licenses in Minas Gerais to make way for Brazilian industry.

The reaction was immediate. "Terrible forces rose up against me," lamented Quadros, who resigned four days later. The leftist vice president João "Jango" Goulart, a loyal follower of Vargas's state-directed nationalism, took the reins and upheld the withdrawal of Hanna's license. The Brazilian Supreme Court backed the president and rejected an appeal by the US company's lawyers to have the concession restored.

In March 1964 half a million God-fearing anti-communists, mainly women, paraded along Avenida Paulista in São Paulo and Nossa Senhora de Copacabana in Rio in the so-called March of the Family with God for Freedom, calling for an armed intervention to overthrow the rebellious government. The nation's generals obliged days later with a full-blown military coup, initiated not coincidentally in Minas Gerais.

General Castelo Branco was sworn in as president with the support of a compliant Congress in the gleaming new modernist capital of Brasília, beautifully conceived by the architect Oscar Niemeyer but tragically distanced from the population centers where the coup might have been resisted. Castelo Branco arrested between five thousand and twenty thousand dissidents and then promptly attended to the needs of the US iron seekers. "The revolt that overthrew Goulart last spring arrived like a last minute rescue by the First Cavalry," commented *Fortune* magazine.

Galeano describes what happened next: "After it tired of throwing the books of Dostoevski, Tolstoy, Gorky, and other Russians into bonfires or into Guanabara Bay, and after it had sentenced countless Brazilians to exile, prison, or the grave, the Castelo Branco dictatorship got down to business: it gave away the iron and everything else."

Hanna received its license on December 24, 1964, a "Christmas gift" that gave it exclusive access to the Paraopeba deposit as well as permission to build a new export terminal in Rio. The generals would remain in power until 1984.

Galeano's account of the geopolitics of Brazilian iron made essential rereading during my visit to Minas Gerais that Easter of 2016, because historical revisionism had spread like a plague across Brazil's hyperactive alt-right social networks. Leading the charge was the esoteric guru of the Brazilian neocons, Olavo de Carvalho, and his most faithful disciple, a former army captain and little-known member of the Brazilian Congress by the name of Jair Messias Bolsonaro. A former Marxist and reporter at Brazil's most influential newspaper, *Folha de São Paulo*, de Carvalho had taken up astrology and homespun philosophy, written a couple of bestselling books littered with provocative axioms, and relocated from Brazil to Virginia. From there, sporting a lumberjack shirt and a cowboy hat, he video-streamed the wildest of conspiracy theories while rewriting Brazilian history.

For de Carvalho, the generals who had staged the 1964 coup were not brutal murderers spinelessly representing US designs on Brazil's natural resources. They were, rather, saviors of a Brazilian "patria" then, as now, threatened by communism and what de Carvalho called "cultural Marxism." Castelo Branco had actually been far too soft. The real national hero was General Carlos Alberto Brilhante Ustra, commander of the dictatorship's unit of repression that tortured thousands of dissidents, including future president Dilma Rousseff, who at twenty-two years old had joined the armed struggle against the generals.

As he surfed a wave of conservative fury directed at the Workers' Party (PT) buttressed by a growing population of conservative evangelicals that would carry him to the presidency, Bolsonaro often closed his political rallies with a collective shout of "*Ustra vive!*" (Ustra lives on!). As if rebranding a mass torturer as a national hero were not sufficient to excite the Bolsonaristas, de Carvalho called on Brazil's burgeoning neofascist movement to take to the streets and demand another coup d'état, so toppling the communist dictatorships disguised as the governments of Rousseff and Lula da Silva, whose electoral victories, needless to say, had been the most resounding in the history of Brazil's short-lived democracy.

Thereafter, every week in São Paulo, a thousand or so incensed anti-Dilma protesters paraded past the street artists and the evangelical preachers on bustling Avenida Paulista, shouting slogans like "Military intervention now!" accompanied by a thirteen-foot-high inflatable doll of a soldier in combat gear holding a machine gun, which some of the protesters believed to represent Brilhante Ustra himself. "If the military doesn't act, Brazil will soon cease to exist!" shouted a Bolsonarista when I asked why he had climbed on top of a stool to wave a flag that announced in English, ARMED FORCES SAVE BRAZIL. De Carvalho, an occasional guest of Donald Trump's Machiavellian onetime adviser Steve Bannon, was the addled brain of this disturbed movement. And he was also, for the record, one of its most visceral haters of *Open Veins of Latin America*, which he had called "a real shit of a book."

Perhaps Galeano had exaggerated the role of the United States in the 1964 coup. After all, as Marcelo Miterhof, an economist at Brazil's state development bank, BNDES, pointed out to me as history threatened to repeat itself in Brasília, "the Brazilian elite is perfectly capable of organizing its own coups d'état." Those "terrible forces" that had forced the resignation of the messianic Jânio Quadros might not only have been the CIA or the State Department. The short-lived president had made enemies all over Brazil due to bizarre polices such as banning bikinis on Copacabana Beach and cockfights in the favelas now creeping up the mountains behind Rio. Besides, the control over iron deposits was just one of the objectives of the coup against his successor, "Jango," whose government had terrified the Brazilian elite and middle class by promising land reform and a mass campaign to combat illiteracy, which in 1964 affected more than half the Brazilian population.

That said, Washington's support was crucial to the success of the coup. Roosevelt's noninterventionist Good Neighbor policy had given way to Cold War paranoia, and fears grew that Brazil could become a Latin American version of Maoist China. Quadros had recognized Fidel Castro's revolutionary government in Cuba and had even invited Che Guevara to Brasília. Both Kennedy and Johnson openly supported military action against Goulart. So as the Brazilian generals brought the tanks out into the streets of the big cities in the spring of 1964, the US Navy launched Operation Brother Sam, placing aircraft carrier *Forrestal* and the rest of the Caribbean fleet on alert in case the Brazilian generals needed support. Iron was undoubtedly at the center of US concerns, just as the raw materials of other Latin Americans coups, successful or attempted, would be copper (Chile) or bananas (Guatemala) or, decades later, oil, in Venezuela.

Brazilian iron ore was a strategic resource in times when all that was good for General Motors was good for America.

Augusto Azevedo Antunes, a powerful business leader in São Paulo who had helped Pennsylvania-based Bethlehem Steel buy a manganese mine in the Amazon, became an instrumental figure in the 1964 coup. This helped Bethlehem set up its own iron ore mining operations in Paraopeba alongside Hanna. US Steel, meanwhile, won support from the generals for a joint venture with the Brazilian state mining enterprise created by Vargas in 1942 to generate export revenues directly for the government and supply the new Brazilian steel industry: Companhia Vale do Rio Doce.

The twenty-year suspension of Brazilian democracy that was triggered, at least in part, to guarantee US access to the Minas Gerais iron ore deposits, left a deep scar on Brazil's national pride. Opposition to Washington grew, aided by the work of Galeano himself and Brazilian pioneers of dependency theory, such as the economist Celso Furtado and the young and brilliant sociologist Fernando Henrique Cardoso. Both had analyzed underdevelopment in the context of unequal relations between a former colonial center (Europe, the United States) and a subjugated periphery (Latin America). The plunder of Latin America's resources was the most obvious result of the centuries-long asymmetry between North and South.

Ironically, Cardoso, elected Brazilian president in 1995 and moderated by age, power, and the harsh conditions imposed by the United States to resolve the Latin American debt crisis, would privatize Companhia Vale do Rio Doce and rename the company Vale, pronounced "valley," to make it less of a tongue twister for Wall Street brokers. It was floated on the stock market in 1997 and sold off for a song. As the commodity boom advanced, Vale's profits multiplied by thirteen in eight years and it became Brazil's biggest exporter. When the left finally came to power after Luiz Inácio Lula da Silva's historic victory in 2002, measures were taken to avoid a second episode of humiliation at the hands of Uncle (or Brother) Sam.

Although Lula would not dare renationalize Vale, its national credentials were strengthened by increasing the stake held by BNDES, whose lending portfolio was now bigger than the World Bank's as it became a key instrument of Brazilian industrial policy. Lula's economic adviser, Nelson Barbosa, was placed on the board, although he later told me "this was more representation than orientation." Vale would be a Brazilian "national champion" financed with private capital but a key player in a state developmental project. From that point on, the iron mined in Minas Gerais and elsewhere would help build the foundation for a new model of democratic consumption and redistribution under Lula's governments. That at least was what appeared in the Workers' Party electoral manifestos and Vale's annual reports. The international environment was favorable. China had emerged as an inexhaustible source of demand for the most useful of all metals. What's more, trade and investment relations with Beijing would not be those of that vampire neocolonialism denounced by Galeano. They would be more egalitarian relations of trade and commerce on a south-south axis. Driven by Chinese investment in manufacturing and construction, the demand for iron grew, prices soared, and iron ore became Brazil's primary export.

Staking the future on iron and other commodities was not exactly the approach recommended by the Latin American left's best brains. At the end of the 1940s, economists at the United Nations Economic Commission for Latin America and the Caribbean (CEPAL, by its Spanish initials) had warned of the so-called "curse of natural resources." It was essential, they said, to reduce the dependence on the exports of raw materials, because of an inevitable decline in their price in comparison with manufactured goods. This would lead to a deterioration of Latin America's terms of trade vis-à-vis the industrial north and cause balance-of-payment crises. Moreover, the prices of commodities such as oil, iron, or soy were characterized by their extreme volatility and boom-and-bust cycles. These ideas drove the agenda of developmentalist industrialization in Latin America from the 1950s until the violent arrival of the neoliberals in the 1970s, commencing in mass torture not so far from CEPAL's head office in Pinochet's Santiago de Chile.

But now in the new Chinese century CEPAL's old fears seemed exaggerated. The rising Asian manufacturing superpower showed a voracious hunger for Brazilian iron ore and other raw materials. Iron fed the giant steel plants from the island of Caofeidian in Beijing to Baoshan in Shanghai, which supplied steel for the unstoppable Chinese-manufacturing locomotive and the most ambitious modernization of hard infrastructure in the history of humanity. China now produced half of the world's steel and scoured the world for stable sources of iron ore. CEPAL's fear of deteriorating terms of trade seemed to be contradicted by trends in prices. Globalization had set off a long-term decline in the price of manufactured goods while the prices of raw materials soared in a world of diminishing resources. Mexico, which had chosen a development path diametrically opposed to Brazil by focusing on exports of manufactured goods assembled in the low-wage *maquiladora* assembly plants on the US border, was not prospering. The Mexican economy grew more slowly than Brazil and failed to reduce poverty after two decades of stagnant wages.

Thanks to Chinese demand, the violent swings and volatile fortunes of external dependency seemed to belong to the past. The price of iron ore had quintupled during Lula's first presidency in 2003–2010 from $30 to $150 per metric ton and the dollar value of Brazil's iron ore exports was up 500 percent too. This did not appear to be a short-lived windfall from an inevitable boom-and-bust cycle in the commodities market like those that had led to disaster in Latin America on so many occasions. It was a supercycle that drove prices ever upward and showed no signs of exhaustion. Iron appeared to have forged a rock-solid foundation for the Workers' Party project. Vale's prodigious exports, along with others in basic foodstuffs such as soy and beef, generated billions of dollars of foreign exchange which, in conjunction with Lula's redistribution polices, made spectacular increases in the wages of the low income working class possible. Through Lula's landmark anti-poverty subsidy program, Bolsa Família, cheap consumer credits for the poor, and successive increases in the minimum wage, thirty-six million Brazilians emerged from poverty in the first decade of the new century and forty-two million joined what Lula called the new Brazilian middle class.

Some economists, like Luiz Carlos Bresser-Pereira, a former minister under Lula's predecessor, were skeptical. The Brazilian real had appreciated to a historical record of 1.65 reais per dollar, 30 percent above its long-term value according to Bresser-Pereira. This would have dire consequences, he said. It was a classic symptom of "Dutch disease," a term coined first by *The Economist* to describe the nefarious effects of an unexpected resource boom, named after the discovery of gas in the Netherlands in the 1950s that ironically caused a manufacturing slump and recession.

"Exchange rates become overvalued because raw materials like oil, soy, or iron ore can be exported when a currency is strong without affecting the profits of its exporters, but this appreciation damages the competitiveness of the manufacturing industry. There's the distortion," said Bresser-Pereira during an interview we held in his sumptuous modernist villa in São Paulo. The result had been a process of premature deindustrialization that began under Cardoso and accelerated under the Lula governments and those of his successor, Dilma Rousseff.

But nobody paid much attention. The left defended the strength of the real as a means to contain inflation and raise the wages of the most needy, boosting consumption without rising prices. In Bresser-Pereira's reindustrializing alternative, wages would have had to be kept much lower, as they had been in Mexico. The markets, meanwhile, adored the Lula model, which had sent the stocks of companies like Vale and the state oil producer, Petrobras, racing toward the stratosphere. The "super real" also attracted billions of dollars in external capital flows, as did Brazil's high interest rates. Brazil was the most dynamic and sexy of the BRICS (the biggest emerging economies: Brazil, Russia, India, China, and South Africa, according to Goldman Sachs's enthusiastic acronym). *The Economist*, its groundbreaking analysis of "Dutch disease" now forgotten, joined the general euphoria with a 2009 cover in which the iconic *Christ the Redeemer* statue on the top of Mount Corcovado in Rio had lifted off like a rocket under the headline: "Brazil Takes Off."

* * *

The scene recalled those euphoric years of the commodity boom. A conveyor belt loaded with thousands of tons of iron ore crossed a rickety metal bridge over stagnant pools of rust-colored water. The iron was headed toward Ponta da Madeira, Vale's terminal in the port of São Luís on the Atlantic coast of Brazil's historically underdeveloped northeast. The ferrous rock had come by freight train from the biggest open-cast iron mine in the world, nearly four hundred miles west in the now deforested region of eastern Pará in the Amazon jungle.

An enormous wound in the tropical forest, the Carajás mine had been designed by the military government after the 1967 discovery by US Steel of the most extensive iron ore deposits on the planet, twice as large as the Paraopeba reserve in Minas Gerais. Vale do Rio Doce, still state-owned at the time, would team up with the US multinational to exploit the deposits of iron, bauxite (a mineral essential for aluminum production), gold, copper, magnesium, and the tin oxide casserite. The military government had also ushered in a dozen pig-iron producers that built their furnaces along the railway from the Carajás to São Luís, cutting down millions of trees over eight hundred thousand hectares to be used as fuel. Soon the east of the state of Pará would be a large patch of scarlet in the otherwise green maps of Amazon deforestation.

Other mining concerns in the iron and aluminum business followed. Eike Batista, the son of Vale's chairman born in Minas Gerais during the military dictatorship, reached number eight in the *Forbes* billionaires list thanks to his mines in the Amazon. The US giant Alcoa was another new arrival in the jungle.

In need of power for their mining operations, Vale and Alcoa lobbied for the construction of the Tucuruí hydroelectric project built in the late 1970s, which flooded thousands of square miles of indigenous reserves and forced whole communities to abandon their homes when Agent Orange was employed to deforest the land. Years later, Vale would also participate in the controversial Belo Monte hydroproject in Altamira as it searched for more energy sources to fuel its vertiginous growth. The enormous dam would flood one thousand five hundred hectares of forest, dry up a river vital for the livelihoods of several indigenous communities, and displace tens of thousands of people, many ethnic Kayapo, others poor migrants from the northeast.

It was the summer of 2016 when I gazed upon the clanking belt that carried the ore to the Ponta da Madeira terminal. The Carajás mine was breaking records of production, beyond even the astronomic levels of 2011 when the price of iron had torn through the previous maximum to nearly $190 per metric ton. Vale had even opened a new iron mine in the S11D complex in the Carajás. The iron ore that crossed the bridge would soon be loaded onto one of the gigantic Valemax cargo ships, the biggest merchant vessels in maritime history, 328 yards long and with the capacity to transport 360,000 tons of iron—enough to build three Golden Gate Bridges. These colossal vessels were now unloading in Chinese ports just as they had in the days of the bonanza.

But appearances deceived that day under the scorching sun of the parched Brazilian northeast. The scene in São Luís was not a picture of success but failure. The supercycle had ended with an epic screeching of brakes, and the new record of production was in fact Vale's reaction to the collapse of the price of iron, now only forty dollars a ton—a decline of nearly 80 percent. Chinese growth was now at just half of the spectacular rates of 2007. Vale, the champion of the PT's extractive development model, now resembled a scene from *Alice's Adventures in Wonderland*: In this country, says the Queen of Hearts to Alice, you must run as fast as you can just to stay in the same place. Vale was producing ever more iron ore just to stay afloat.

The third phase of the great crisis of globalized capitalism had now reached Brazil and the rest of Latin America. It had started in 2007–2008 in the US financial and mortgage sector and crossed the Atlantic to the eurozone in 2010. Now the third tremor of the earthquake, late to arrive but no less lethal, was shaking the emerging economies–particularly those that exported raw materials. The key to understanding the dynamics of the megacrisis was China.

After the collapse of world trade in 2009 and the deep recession in the United States and Europe, Beijing responded with a massive recovery package pumping half a trillion dollars into public investment both in infrastructure and real estate. The result was even greater demand for commodities than before the crisis, especially construction materials such as iron and copper. This lengthened the commodity supercycle despite the world recession in 2009. The Chinese boom further pumped up a bubble in the commodities markets already inflated by billion-dollar speculation where traders bought and sold tons of iron, bushels of wheat, and barrels of oil as if they were financial derivatives or high-yield bonds. Investors the world over sought out assets that offered returns to compensate for the collapse in the stock markets and interest rates that had fallen to zero. The financial crisis appeared to accentuate the shift in fortunes which had fed the euphoria during the rise of the BRICS. Big commodity producers like Brazil posted spectacular growth rates as higher interest rates sucked in capital at a time when returns in the Global North's half-frozen debt markets evaporated. Europe and the United States, meanwhile, struggled to pull out of their recessions.

The dynamics of the "open veins" went briefly into reverse gear. The curse of the wealthy economies appeared to be a blessing for the poor ones. Some spoke of a decoupling of the Global South from its former masters in the north thanks to the resilience of the Chinese economy and its inexhaustible demand for raw materials. While the United States sunk into its most serious recession since 1929, Brazil grew by 7.5 percent in 2010, helping Dilma to romp home in the presidential elections the same year. While their counterparts in the advanced economies deleveraged and downsized, big corporations in Latin America and other developing regions (Vale was just one example) could hardly resist such easy access to credit and capital markets. They loaded up on debt, often denominated in dollars. The 2008 crisis, joked Lula, was a rich man's problem provoked by "the irrational behavior of white-skinned, blue-eyed people." It was a glorious moment. But the crisis of globalized capitalism would soon redirect its fury toward those of dark skin and brown eyes. Who could have imagined otherwise?

The *mundo al reves*–the world upside down–would last just a summer. China was burdened with its own imbalances and could not be a permanent lifeline. The decoupling thesis proved to be a fantasy. When commodity prices crashed in 2013 and 2014, the Brazilian economy fell off a cliff. Vale, with $24 billion in debt, stared into the abyss and was downgraded by those courts of financial final judgment, the rating agencies Moody's and S&P.

The frenetic extraction of iron throughout boom and bust had accelerated beyond all expectations the rate of depletion of the Carajás iron deposit, which the geologists at US Steel believed would last for centuries. On the latest estimates it would be entirely gone by 2035. But the years of bonanza and spectacular profit-making had not been used productively to industrialize or create more sustainable activities with greater added value in the mining zones of Minas Gerais or the Amazon. Just as in the era of classical colonialist pillage that Galeano had described, the railway that transported iron ore from Carajás to the port of São Luís passed isolated villages, leaving behind a part of the Amazon in which 42 percent of the population still lived in poverty. Carajás had become rich, but its inhabitants were still poor. The municipal district registered the highest GDP per capita in the state of Pará but life expectancy was the lowest and inequality most extreme. While 20 percent of the Amazon had been deforested since the 1970s with a massive loss of biodiversity, the Amazon region's share of Brazilian GDP remained at 8 percent. As if Amazonia were a semicolony, "the more it exports the poorer it becomes," declared Gilberto de Souza Marques in his book *Amazônia*, a compelling critique of the failed attempt by Lula and Dilma to change the model of extraction.

The subsidies of Bolsa Família had stabilized poverty in the Amazon, but the extraction did not drive development. Robert Freitas, an economist with CEPAL in Brasília, summed up the irony during the presentation of the Brazilian edition of a book I had written on the Davos global elite and the crisis of 2008, *Un reportero en la montaña mágica* (A Reporter on the Magic Mountain). It was spring of 2014. I had suggested that the apparent collapse of the neoliberal Davos paradigm would perhaps lend more credibility to the economic alternative represented by the Latin American left. "Don't you realize?" he replied. "We have been exporting rocks, repeating the errors of the past."

The political impact of the abrupt change in the commodity supercycle was seismic in Brazil. The economy was not nearly as dependent on commodity exports as Venezuela, Chile, Bolivia, or Peru. But the export of raw materials, minerals, and foodstuffs had been crucial for the left government's bid to generate consumer-led growth without risking inflation and balance-of-payments crises.

The sociologist André Singer, Lula's former spokesperson who had identified the Workers' Party's magic formula for economic and political success in the first decade of the century, concluded that it had all been propped up by an unsustainable bubble in the market for raw materials. "The Lulaist miracle was sustained by a phase of strong world growth and the boom in the price of commodities. The 2008 crisis would bring the end of this cycle, which would materialize in Brazil three years later," he wrote in his second book, *O lulisme em crise* (Lulaism in Crisis). The collapse of the Brazilian economy in 2015 and 2016 would be the death sentence for the Workers' Party in power, aided by a corruption scandal in the state oil company, Petrobras, investigated selectively by intrepid US-trained prosecutors who had little sympathy for national champions like Vale or Petrobras and even less for public banks such as BNDES.

Brazil would soon enter the worst recession in its history while the rapid depreciation of the real set off a wave of inflation. The purchasing power of the working classes shrank drastically after a decade of improving living standards. *The Economist*, always a late echo of the boom-and-bust psychology in the financial markets, published a new cover in which *Christ the Redeemer* plummeted to earth in a trail of black smoke. Another issue instructed Rousseff, reelected only a year before, to resign, under the headline "Time to Go." The outraged conservative middle class echoed the sentiment and now filled the avenues of São Paulo and Rio in huge demonstrations that demanded Rousseff's impeachment and the imprisonment of Lula. Apart from the yellow shirts of the Brazilian football team, de rigueur for the new generation of privileged Brazilian discontents, the protests were eerily reminiscent of that March of the Family with God for Freedom of April 1964. Although the twenty-first-century God, for millions of Brazilians, was now evangelical.

* * *

It soon became clear that the death of the Rio Doce was a consequence of Vale's fateful decision to ramp up exports and increase iron production even while the crisis forced draconian cuts to costs at the Samarco mine. A report from the Inter-American Commission on Human Rights concluded that cost-cutting and the relaxation of environmental controls had led to a greater risk of rupture in the containment dams in Minas Gerais. A Samarco engineer confessed that "we had no instruments to detect earth tremors; they didn't care about lives, just profits."

"This must bring about a change in mentality," said Marcelo Campos at IBAMA as we stared at the now useless maps of a river that was no longer the same river.

But, far from learning the lessons of the Bento Rodrigues disaster and the dramatic end of the commodity supercycle, Brazil appeared to have returned to Galeano's classic era of open veins when multinationals "exercised their right" to Latin America's natural resources.

In the midst of a grave economic crisis, the new government of former vice president Michel Temer, a centrist wheeled into power after Rousseff's impeachment, announced its commitment to attract foreign capital and remove restrictions on mining investment. Just as in 1964, the coup would open the path to the pillage of the past. Investment in mineral and oil extraction would no longer be made by the national champions of Lula and Dilma but by mining multinationals from Toronto or Big Oil from Houston.

Lula, imprisoned with little evidence for alleged crimes of corruption and money laundering, was barred from competing in the 2018 elections, despite being the most popular candidate. He charged that the judicial and media campaign against him and his party had been designed precisely so that the United States could once again exploit Brazilian natural resources, particularly oil. Perhaps it was conspiracy theory. Perhaps not. What was undeniable was that the dependency on commodity exports had intensified the Workers' Party governments' vulnerability to the volatile supercycle and to Washington's geopolitical goals.

In its place, the return of the old neoliberal Washington consensus would leave wide swathes of the Amazon open for business. The same Inter-American Commission for Human Rights report warned of conflicts of interest in mining concessions, since the parties now in control of Congress had received generous donations from the mining companies. In spite of the low price of iron and the environmental disasters in Minas Gerais and the Amazon, the new government offered even more incentives to the mining corporations.

The lesson was not even learned in the area of Minas Gerais that had been wiped off the map in 2015 by that tsunami of toxic mud. Pressure was growing to resume operations at the mines in Paraopeba. WE WANT WORK! OPEN THE SAMARCO MINES! demanded the banners of the miners' union, Metabase, draped at the roadside on the outskirts of Mariana. The danger of a repetition of the catastrophe was obvious and, like another chronicle of a death foretold by Gabriel García Márquez, in 2018 a second containment dam collapsed at a Vale-run mine in Brumadinho, only sixty miles from the now inexistent municipality of Bento Rodrigues. Once again thousands of tons of mining waste spilled out, this time into the river Paraopeba. Two hundred and forty-eight people were killed and twenty-two disappeared without a trace, their bodies never recovered. Vale warned of the danger of collapse of other dams in Minas Gerais, though it categorically denied suggestions that a similar catastrophe might occur in the Amazon.

* * *

What emerged from the ruins of Bento Rodrigues and the rubble of the Workers' Party's ambitious project for social transformation was a biblical desire to punish the political class. It was palpable during the Easter celebrations of 2016 in Minas Gerais.

A couple of hours by car from the disaster zone in the Paraopeba, Ouro Preto, the jewel of Brazilian baroque and the epicenter of the eighteenth-century gold fever, prepared for its yearly execution of Judas. A group of young locals placed a life-size rag doll representing the treacherous disciple on top of a white pony. The effigy would be hung from a scaffold later that day just as Tiradentes, the hero of Brazilian independence, had been hanged in Rio in 1792. A brass band whose musicians wore helmets made of old chamber pots bleated out a mournful dirge. Once more, the *mineiros* felt betrayed by the false promises and fleeting profits of an ephemeral bonanza, by the sudden economic collapse and the death of the Rio Doce. But nobody knew for sure who had betrayed whom.

"Who should Judas represent this year?" I asked an Afro-Brazilian security guard who looked on while the dummy swung from the gallows.

"Well, I would say Dilma," he replied after pausing to recall the betrayed electoral promises in Rousseff's 2014 election manifesto. Some said Judas should be Dilma's former vice president, Michel Temer, who was briefly serving as president with an approval rating below 5 percent. Others were convinced that the rag doll, bearded and with large forlorn eyes, must be Lula. "When they were dressing the doll, I saw one of them bend a finger so you couldn't see it, like Lula's," said José Eduardo, who was throwing sweets from a bag to the children that scampered around the square. The joke referred to Lula's index finger, amputated in a lathe accident when he worked for a motor plant in São Bernardo do Campo before starting his rise to power in the autoworkers' union. The only politician that nobody in Ouro Preto accused of being Judas was that ex-army captain, an apologist for the crimes of the military dictatorship and the deaths and torture of the 1964 coup. The house member Jair Bolsonaro, misogynous, homophobic, racist, contemptuous of the environment, whose incendiary speeches always included an impassioned defense of the right to extract all that remained in the depleted veins of Minas Gerais and the promising subsoil of the Amazon.

CHAPTER TWO

Niobium (Brazil)
The Fetish of Jair Bolsonaro

"Once upon a time, maybe thirty years ago, a group of strangers appeared. They set up camp, dug a huge hole in the earth, and took out several blue stones. If they had any value, they said, they would return later and pay us. Then they left."

The person telling this story was Marcio, fifty-six years old and grandfather to a family of numerous Macuxi, whose members resided in an adobe-brick house with a palm-leaf roof in the Guariba community of the Brazilian Amazon, about forty miles from the Venezuelan border.

That encounter with the latest of an endless procession of mineral pillagers from the other side of the Roraima Mountains had taken place before the historic recognition in 2005 of the indigenous territory of the Macuxi, Wapichana, Ingariko, Tuarepang, and Patamona peoples of the northern Amazon. That landmark year, Marcio and his people won back control of over 1.7 million hectares of land known as Raposa Serra do Sol, a landscape of spectacular waterfalls dominated by the breathtaking Mount Roraima.

On this mysterious tropical plateau Arthur Conan Doyle set his novel of Victorian tourist fantasy, *The Lost World*, in which a journalist keen to prove his worth sets out, accompanied by the eccentric zoologist Dr. Challenger, to write the definitive adventure reportage. After scaling the mountain, a pinnacle of rock "like a broad red church spire" with a chasm in front, the two Englishmen chance upon an authentic Jurassic Park on top of the plateau inhabited by giant dinosaurs. A century later, the vertical two-thousand-foot-high granite walls of Mount Roraima still proved an irresistible challenge to intrepid reporters and tourists intent, just like Conan Doyle, on leaving nothing undiscovered, no stone left unturned. At nearly nine thousand feet, Mount Roraima was the highest mountain in Brazil, although other statistics were more relevant to Marcio and his family. In Macuxi mythology, the plateau was the axed trunk of the tree of life, from which flowed the essential elixir: water.

The so-called demarcation of Raposa Serra do Sol was one of the most important victories in the history of indigenous struggles in Brazil. The Macuxi and their sister-peoples had had to fight pitched battles with rice growers who had tapped those very same Roraima springs to cultivate the water-guzzling cereal. Other battles were fought with thousands of *garimpeiro* gold and diamond miners, who sought a chimeric fortune in the Northern Amazon's tributaries. The 1988 constitution, written during an explosion of democracy after the military dictatorship relinquished power in 1984, was one of the most progressive in history and, for the first time, gave unequivocal support to indigenous claims to their land. Lula's first government from 2003 to 2010 was another ally in the fight.

Since then, the twenty-three thousand indigenous people in the region had been relatively protected from the activities of Brazilian agribusiness and mining. Marcio and his neighbors were poor, but they had learned new techniques for raising livestock, for growing cassava, corn, and sweet potatoes, and they had installed a fish farm in the river, full of huge, local species such as the *tambaqui* and the *pirarucu*, whose meaty flesh was deliciously combined with the unclassifiable tastes of the Amazon's infinite vegetable biodiversity.

They had built a small school where the children learned Portuguese, Spanish, and Macuxi. There were, of course, the inevitable problems of alcoholism in the community, a proven method to subdue America's original peoples. Marcio had already downed several cachaças when we spoke at eleven in the morning. When I asked him if he feared the arrival of other pillagers, he smiled as if to say, "And you, friend from a distant land, what do you think?" before pouring himself another mug of Brazilian rum.

Despite the early hour, I accepted his offer to share a drink of solidarity and toast in the hope that the Lost World of the Macuxi remained definitively lost. Because, as Marcio and Eduardo Galeano knew so well, the extractivist lobbies in Latin America would never give up. Roraima, after all, was an area of rich pasture on the surface for those immense flocks of zebu cattle, white, humpbacked, and sad-eyed, that would end up finely ground in a Burger King Whopper, but not before they had left a disastrous trail of Amazon deforestation.

The subterranean treasures were far more enticing. Below the granite rock caps of Raposa Serra do Sol lay vast deposits of gold, diamonds, amethysts, bauxite, titanium, uranium, and the most coveted of all . . . niobium. As I had managed to glean from a 2018 report of the United States Geological Survey, this metal of unequaled durability and resistance when alloyed with steel was an essential material for the automobile industry and a critical mineral for the energy transition with promising applications in redox-flow batteries for electric cars and zero-emissions wind and solar power plants. It was a key component too for electronic microcircuits and for the aerospace industry, principally for rockets, space vehicles, fighter bombers, and missiles. The SpaceX rockets, for example, the most powerful in history, used large quantities of niobium. And, since during my visit to Roraima a new generation of hypersonic missiles were the breaking news in international defense magazines, I should add that niobium was a key component of these terrifying weapons, rockets that would reach a velocity of more than three thousand miles an hour, taking about seventy minutes to reach Beijing from Seattle.

"Planes cannot be built without aluminum, and aluminum cannot be produced without bauxite: the United States has almost no bauxite," mused the young Eduardo Galeano in *Open Veins*. Fifty years later, many believed that the same was true of the niobium in Raposa Serra do Sol.

In Brazil, which owns 98 percent of the world's reserves, some considered niobium to be a shamefully underexploited national treasure. The more imaginative resource nationalists fantasized that the value of its deposits—including the similarly critical tantalum always found together with niobium—could be worth as much as $22 trillion, more than the entire US GDP and ten times that of Brazil's. Niobium—metallic gray in its pristine state, blue after oxidization—was one of the thirty-five elements considered critical to the future growth of the United States, according to the US Geological Survey, whose reports Galeano correctly identified as an implicit program of planetary hegemony after the Second World War.

To date, the exploitation of Brazilian niobium had been exclusive to Minas Gerais, where the Salles family, owner of the powerful Banco Itaú, had become a multimillion-dollar dynasty thanks to the largest niobium mine in the world. Walter Salles, an acclaimed filmmaker and director of *Central Do Brasil* and *The Motorcycle Diaries*, owed his fortune to niobium.

During decades of neoliberal consensus, the Salles family and their company, CBMM, appeared to have easily enough niobium in their mine to satisfy all the industrial needs of Thomas Friedman's contented "flat world" where the presence of a McDonald's in two rival countries ensured that they would never go to war. But a decade later, despite all those confident forecasts of permanently benign globalization, a paranoia was growing in Washington and Beijing worthy of a bad remake of Stanley Kubrick's *Dr. Strangelove*. Geopolitical tensions had arisen between the two powers that were hitherto barely imaginable at least since Nixon and Kissinger flew to Beijing in 1972 and invited Mao to join the "family of nations."

Almost fifty years later, a race was intensifying to gain control of waning resources. Minerals like niobium, tantalum, and bauxite, buried underground in Raposa Sierra do Sol, were now perceived by apocalyptic minds as strategic reserves for a new cold war. Chinese investment had been poured into Brazil and Latin America, even in the crisis years. China was now Brazil's number-one trading partner and destination for 35 percent of its exports, mainly raw materials such as iron, soy, oil, beef, and chicken. Mining concerns from the Asian giant also bought 30 percent of Brazil's niobium and had invested billions of dollars in the Minas Gerais mines, acquiring a minority stake from the Salles company. Then, in 2016, the Chinese company China Molybdenum bought a mine in Roraima. Strategists in the Pentagon and neoconservative think tanks eyed the Chinese advance nervously. After all, as Michael Klare noted in his gripping study of the scramble for the world's last remaining resources, *The Race for What's Left*, niobium was deemed to have a high degree of "criticality" because it is "both irreplaceable and vulnerable to supply disruptions."

Slate noted in an article headlined "This is the Dawning of the Age of . . . Niobium?" that the national strategy of the US Department of Defense had characterized the "long-term strategic competition" of China as a more dangerous threat than post-9/11 terrorism. "Welcome to the Critical Mineral Age," announced the online magazine.

After the fall of Dilma Rousseff in that soft parliamentary coup d'état, Washington foreign-policy hawks set out to reestablish the anti-communist Washington-Brasília axis that had marked the era of the generals and would now be adapted to the task of countering the rise of the new Asian superpower.

Meanwhile, Brazilian mining and agribusiness lobbies were working hard to reassert control over the Amazon and roll back the indigenous demarcation that had gained such momentum after the victory in Raposa Serra do Sol in 2005. They had powerful allies in the Brasília Congress, such as Romero Jucá, senator and governor of Roraima, one of the architects of the impeachment against Rousseff. Jucá, whose daughter was a leading partner in the Boa Vista mining company, had spent years trying to legislate mining access to indigenous lands. A close ally of Dilma's successor, Michel Temer, he had been the proverbial fox in charge of the chicken coop when appointed president in 1986 of the National Indian Foundation (FUNAI), a federal body created in 1967 to protect the interests of indigenous people.

Jucá had used the post to encourage *garimpeiro* gold miners and loggers to seek their fortunes in the millennial territory of the twenty-five thousand Yanomami who inhabited the dense forests in northwest Roraima where niobium and other critical minerals are also present. In 1988, the demarcation of nine million hectares of Yanomami lands, making them the largest protected indigenous territory in Brazil, had helped detain the invasion. Jucá, never one to throw in the towel, attempted to fragment the constitutional protection by creating nineteen demarcated areas, each separated from the others, balkanizing the Yanomami homeland. Aware that they had an ally in the Senate, Brazilian and multinational mining companies requested concessions in 55 percent of those areas in the hope that Jucá or some other politician close to their interests would someday reopen the gate. They could not have imagined then that the man of their dreams would be a mediocre former army captain who railed against democracy from his solitary seat in Congress where few paid him any attention.

The constitutional right to demarcate indigenous lands was a landmark achievement not only for the original peoples of the forest, but also for the survival of the planet. After all, the nine hundred thousand indigenous citizens of Brazil, spread over 254 ethnicities, most of them inhabitants of the vast Amazon forest, with 20 percent of the world's fresh water, were the true guardians of the great planetary lung. Much more so than James Cameron, the director of *Avatar*, whose attempts to help the Xingu people's struggle against the Belo Monte dam had been criticized as a rich man's indulgence, or Al Gore, who ended up alienating local public opinion with statements such as "Contrary to what Brazilians think, the Amazon is not their property, it belongs to all of us." Protesting deforestation was now a public-relations must for global celebrities, centrist politicians, and corporate CEOs as climate change threatened the future of all.

Advised by their marketing consultants, multinationals now defended the redesign of their global supply chain to eliminate raw materials–minerals, but more importantly, food commodities–sourced in deforested areas of the Amazon. At other corporate headquarters in New York and London, experts with MBAs drew up complex systems by which companies would buy up "virgin areas" of the jungle and so offset their own CO_2 emissions. But in Brazil everyone knew that the most effective way to stop deforestation was much more straightforward: demarcate indigenous territories. The rate of forest destruction on indigenous-governed lands was ten times lower than in the rest of the Brazilian Amazon. "Deforestation in demarcated indigenous areas is infinitely lower than in the rest of the Amazon," explained Danicley de Aguiar, from Greenpeace in Brasília. Demarcation accelerated under Lula's governments and, by the end of the first decade of the new century, 43 percent of the Brazilian Amazon was protected as indigenous territory. This was a key component of policies that had led to a spectacular reduction in average yearly deforestation from 10,695 square miles in 2004 to 1,698 in 2012, a fall of 80 percent.

However, the alarm bells were ringing. The demarcation rate had already begun to slow during the second Lula government and it fell sharply under Dilma. A defender of the fast-growth developmental model, Rousseff had approved fewer demarcations than any other president since the Brazilian Constitution was ratified in 1988. Under interim president Temer, a wheeler and dealer from the clientelist Brazilian Democratic Movement, nicknamed the "party for hire", the situation became critical. There were almost thirteen hundred open demarcation processes, but only 30 percent were progressing. More than five hundred requests had not even received an official response. Predictably, deforestation ticked up, threatening the gains of the Lula years.

With the support of his friend Senator Romero Jucá, Temer tried to force through a presidential decree that would give the mining industry access to an enormous swathe of protected forest in the Amazon, an area of eighteen thousand square miles that included six indigenous territories. The interim president had to back down due to protests from environmental groups, but the plan was kept under the table.

At the same time, a bill had been introduced that would allow the Brazilian Congress, so malleable under pressure from the agricultural lobbies, to assess new demarcation requests instead of the National Indian Foundation. Temer was especially receptive to the so-called ruralist *bancada*–members of Congress who financed themselves through agribusiness and mining lobbies–because he depended on their support to avoid being prosecuted in the anti-corruption probe sweeping through PT leadership. While Lula was tried and sent to prison on flimsy charges of corruption, Temer escaped prosecution despite a recording in which he was heard giving the green light to bribes from the president of JBS, one of the beneficiaries of cattle-driven deforestation in the Amazon that had become the largest meatpacking company in the world. Congress's decision to protect the interim president from the prosecutors was a quid pro quo from the food and mining lobbies in return for access to the Amazon jungle. The impunity did not stop at the interim president. The annual average of indigenous people murdered in disputes over demarcation had risen from sixty to one hundred in three years, mainly in states such as Mato Grosso, Rondônia, Maranhão, and Amazonas, where ranchers and loggers seemed emboldened by government measures. Very rarely did the murderers face trial.

But the worst was yet to come. Jair Bolsonaro, so unashamed in his racism and misogyny that even Donald Trump felt briefly uncomfortable when discussing him, was a remorseless enemy of indigenous demarcation. His relationship with the indigenous Mother Earth was perhaps best summed up by his remark to a Workers' Party congresswoman during the vote to impeach Dilma: "You are not worth raping." He would not say the same of the mineral-laden indigenous lands of Raposa Terra do Sol.

The former paratrooper had been advised by members of the Miami-Washington lobby, specifically neoconservative senator Marco Rubio, who was now effectively in charge of Donald Trump's Latin American strategy. Rubio, who met with Bolsonaro in Miami during the 2018 Brazilian electoral campaign, was increasingly concerned by Chinese presence in Latin America. That same year, at the eighth Summit of the Americas in Lima, the senator warned that the United States would take note of any country that gave easy access to Chinese companies in strategic sectors. Rubio emphasized the importance of reserves of the so-called "rare earths," vital minerals for new technologies whose biggest reserves, to the profound chagrin of the Cuban-born American senator for Florida, were mainly located in China.

The concern deepened with the 2020 pandemic as plans to use the COVID-19 crisis to cut supply chains to Asia and nearshore manufacturing in the Americas were undermined by the shortage of rare earths and critical minerals in the United States. The Trump administration's concern regarding Chinese presence in Latin America was such that the national security advisor, the walrus-mustached war hawk John Bolton, had confessed to CNN that "we're not afraid to use the phrase 'Monroe Doctrine,'" in reference to the nineteenth-century strategy of the emerging US power, devised by then President James Monroe (1817–1825), to act militarily against his colonial rivals. Rex Tillerson, briefly secretary for state after heading Exxon for two decades, and with an eye on the offshore oil fields in the Brazilian Atlantic, also evoked those days when Latin America was "America's backyard."

Bolsonaro, even when sporting the Brazilian football strip at press conferences, was quite prepared for Brazil to be a five-billion-square-mile backyard. He would soon lend an important hand in nominating the next president of the powerful Inter-American Development Bank. Mauricio Claver-Carone, an ex-blogger from the radical anti-Castro fringe in Florida who helped Rubio design Trump's strategy to keep China at bay in the region, was tapped.

The new relationship soon bore fruit. In the fall of 2020 Trump signed an executive order warning of a "national emergency" due to dependency on "foreign adversaries for the critical minerals that are increasingly necessary to maintain our economic and military strength in the twenty-first century." Within a week, the new International Development Finance Corporation set up by Trump a year earlier had taken a stake in a mine owned by TechMet in Piauí in the northeastern Brazilian savanna that would produce the cobalt and nickel essential for the manufacture of smartphones, solar energy generation, and electric vehicles. Niobium, now on a list of twenty-five critical minerals issued by Trump in an executive order, was discussed as the next target for the new US security strategy.

While democratic presidential candidate Joe Biden toned down the rhetoric, his stance on China was as hawkish as Trump's, and it seemed safe to assume that his interest in Brazilian minerals would be no less keen despite voter-friendly calls to save the Amazon. Meanwhile in Europe, preparing for a resource war with China was now official strategy as the European Commission issued a commitment in September 2020 to create "diversified and undistorted access to global markets for raw materials" and augmented its list of critical minerals to thirty. The coronavirus pandemic had shown "just how fast and how deeply global supply chains can be disrupted," it added. The report included a map in which Brazil was highlighted in green under the label: niobium.

Bolsonaro was an addict of sinophobic theories that surpassed even those of Marco Rubio and Mauricio Claver-Carone for sheer crazed paranoia: those of Olavo de Carvalho, who you'll recall had settled in Virginia where he would be close to the Pentagon and the cheerleaders of the American alt-right.

"Everything that comes from China is contaminated," he posted during the COVID crisis. "The contagion is a work of engineering." De Carvalho was the president's Rasputin and Bolsonaro swallowed each and every word of his conspiracy theories. As the virus swept the country, turning Brazil into the second worst-affected nation after the United States, the president told his aghast health minister, Luiz Henrique Mandetta, that the "Chinese ambassador in Brasília, Yang Wanming, was intent on bringing his government down, and that the virus was part of the plan."

The same paranoia would drive Bolsonaro's policies on niobium and other critical minerals. In order to avoid the seizure of Roraima's underground wealth by the Chinese, it was necessary to open concessions and give preference to Brazilian mining concerns or, failing that, to the extractivists of the free world.

"We cannot deliver niobium to a single country. It has to

be ours, for a Brazilian company," Bolsonaro insisted with patriotic verve. Months later, after unsuccessfully pitching his own son Eduardo for the post of ambassador to Washington, he modified his position. Brazil was now looking for partners in "the first world" to exploit the wealth of Raposa Serra do Sol and other mineral-rich territories. "That is why I am approaching the United States," explained Bolsonaro.

In fact, the former captain had abandoned his beliefs in resource nationalism months before winning the elections when he agreed to a radical program of privatizations and the sale of Brazilian assets to multinational corporations under the tutelage of the financial billionaire and Chicago school disciple Paulo Guedes, who would become Bolsonaro's all-powerful finance minister.

De Carvalho and Bolsonaro adored niobium as passionately as the Macuxi adored the sacred water of Mount Roraima. For the two ultraconservatives, it was a quasimystical mineral which in its elemental composition condensed all the frustrations and neuroses of the new Brazilian right. A communist conspiracy, in alliance with environmentalist NGOs, had forced Brazilian patriots to leave this national treasure underground. All to keep a few backward Indians happy or, even worse, to give it away to the Chinese.

The secret powers of Nb, element 41 of the periodic table, seduced the most esoteric admirers of de Carvalho, who from his laboratory of delusions assured that niobium "would give a *grana preta* (black nugget) to the Brazilians" (in reference to the best gold from the famed gold-mining capital, Ouro Preto). Bolsonaro recorded a video during a visit to Araxá at the beginning of the presidential election campaign, in which he sang the virtues of the most Brazilian mineral, ignored by the elites of cultural Marxism.

"Niobium is a taboo . . . but I have nothing to hide," he

asserted, insinuating one of the conspiracy theories on which the Bolsonaro bases were fed. "Brazil could be the most prosperous country in the world. You've heard of Silicon Valley; well, I see in the future of Brazil a Niobium Valley," he proclaimed, and no one in the audience thought it worth mentioning that there is no more silicon in Silicon Valley than in any other part of the world.

For the Bolsonaristas, niobium would provide a historic opportunity to the heroic Brazilian *povo* (a collective subject not satisfactorily translated as "people"). All that was needed was to let Brazilians exploit the hidden treasure. In his tirades against anti-mining controls and the protection of the Amazon, Bolsonaro appealed to the frustrations of a million desperate *garimpeiros*, heroes of the mythologized Brazilian fortune seeker. Although the truth was that the most desperately poor would never vote for him. Niobium became the cover story of magazines such as *Superinteressante*, and the Bolsonaro social networks clogged up like the open sewers of Rio de Janeiro with fake news about its powers. The ex-captain's admirers swallowed it all and joined the adoration of $_{41}$Nb. The miracle mineral became the most sought-after gem in Bolsonaro's incendiary electoral speeches. Of course, to achieve the dream, the territories of the Macuxi and Yanomami would have to be reclaimed for mining.

"These lands have a lot of niobium, which may be more important than oil," declared presidential candidate Bolsonaro during a visit to Boa Vista in 2018 at the end of the campaign. "But they have demarcated them! They are killing Roraima's economy." He added: "The Indian does not speak our language, he has no money, he is a poor wretch. He must be integrated into society, instead of growing up in a millionaire's zoo."

The speech delivered excellent results in the second

round of the October 2018 elections, which launched Bolsonaro like a human cannonball to the presidency in a political earthquake that made Mount Roraima tremble. The former captain and his allies swept to power in the state of Raposa Serra do Sol and immediately arranged for a new battle against the Macuxi on behalf of niobium. The new mining secretary, Admiral Bento Albuquerque, announced that mining companies would be allowed to enter indigenous lands demarcated as Raposa Serra do Sol, despite the fact that the 1988 constitution expressly prohibited it. New legislation allowing mining activity on all indigenous land was put to Congress, though opposition prevented its enactment at least for the moment. Bolsonaro appeared on television with a handful of indigenous leaders who had accepted the offer to participate in reaping the profits from soy and mining on their lands.

"The Indians want to be Brazilian. Keeping them in their present state is a utopia," said former general Augusto Heleno, one of a handful of soldiers in the government, as if being indigenous excluded being properly Brazilian.

Bolsonaro soon announced that power over demarcation policy would be transferred to the Ministry of Agriculture, where the agribusiness lobbies had the first and last words. Congress would block the proposal but the Bolsonarista agenda advanced on other fronts. The president appointed a military officer as the new president of the federal body that protected indigenous rights, the National Indian Foundation (FUNAI). When he resigned after accusing a senior Agriculture ministry official of "salivating hatred against indigenous people", he was replaced by a top official for the federal police who had requested "persecutory measures" to be taken against the indigenous peoples.

As expected, deforestation in the Amazon soared. A surface area equivalent to three thousand soccer fields was now being destroyed on a daily basis, more than double that of previous years, as loggers, *garimpeiro* miners, cattle ranchers, and monoculture farmers, emboldened by Bolsonaro's rhetoric, ventured deeper into the forest. More than thirty thousand fires were detected in the Amazon eight months after the ex-military's inauguration, 60 percent more than in previous years, and huge clouds of ash darkened the skies over São Paulo. That the fires were provoked seemed obvious, since in the high-humidity rain forest spontaneous combustion was impossible.

Bolsonaro even suggested that the NGOs and their alleged sponsor Leonardo DiCaprio had started the fires in order to shame his government. "They used to say I was the chain-saw captain. Now they say I am Nero starting the fire!" remonstrated the president.

Up to twenty thousand artisanal miners invaded the Yanomami indigenous reserves in search of gold and other minerals, as in the days of Romero Jucá, and now were encouraged by Bolsonaro's passionate defense of the rights of the *garimpeiro*. The big mining companies prepared to follow in their footsteps. In a Waiapi reservation in Amapá State east of Roraima, fifty *garimpeiros* stormed a village and stabbed community leader Emyra Waiapi to death. *A queda do céu* (The Sky Is Falling) is the title of an extraordinary book by the Yanomami writer Davi Kopenawa, an apocalyptic vision that turns the Amazon into a microcosm of a threatened planet. And so it was. The invading *garimpeiros* brought with them COVID-19, the latest killer virus to threaten the Amazon Indians forty years after generals had declared bacterial warfare, releasing measles, smallpox, and tuberculosis onto the defenseless

Waimiri-Atroari tribe that had dared to block the construction of the Trans-Amazonian Highway.

By the end of 2020, twenty-six thousand indigenous Amazonians were infected, from 150 different peoples, and seven hundred had died. But in some sense, perhaps with poetic justice, the threat of genocide by virus had reversed course as deforestation and the growth of urban slums in the Amazon was now linked to the spread of potentially pandemic-contagious diseases such as dengue, Zika, and chikungunya while industrial beef and chicken processing on the fringes of the degraded jungle threatened to release other virulent pathogens. Bolsonaro insisted that the indigenous Amazonians, far from being victims, would benefit from mining, agribusiness, and meatpacking activities on their lands. They could even participate directly in the exploitation of niobium. "They can't carry on being prehistoric men," theorized the former army captain, now president of the largest country in Latin America. The newly elected indigenous congresswoman, Joênia Wapichana–her alma mater in law the Federal University of Roraima–replied succinctly in a public statement. The indigenous people of Raposa Serra do Sol did not wish to profit from a mining bonanza. They had other priorities: "To enjoy a life without being threatened, a stable climate, demarcated lands, a protected culture, and respect for our community."

Bolsonaro's fetishistic fantasies regarding niobium and the growing paranoia in Washington with respect to a new cold war would soon shatter the peace of the sacred Mount Roraima.

The Macuxi, Wapichana, Ingariko, Taurepang, and Patamona prepared for a new battle in defense of their lands and water. But behind the rhetoric of niobium, a tragicomic secret was concealed. In this new phase of open veins, there were many reasons to believe that the war for niobium was unnecessary even for those concerned about scarce resources and the Chinese threat. Other more readily available metals–tantalum, molybdenum, vanadium, and tungsten–served many of the same functions. A glance at the latest report from the United States Geological Survey left little room for doubt. In its 2017 edition on niobium and tantalum, it stated that estimated existing reserves of niobium "appear more than sufficient to meet global demand for the foreseeable future, possibly the next 500 years."

There was only one scenario in which the niobium could conceivably run out. According to a presentation by John Hebda, niobium engineer at Allegheny Technologies Incorporated in Pittsburgh, "it would take a strong external driver to bring about a significant increase in the use [of niobium]; for example a threat to international peace setting off a corresponding rearmament process . . . with applications for hypersonic flights."

CHAPTER THREE

Coltan (Gran Sabana, Venezuela)
The Mines of Nicolás Maduro

While Jair Bolsonaro prepared to turn back the clock on indigenous rights in Raposa Serra do Sol, surprising events were unfolding on the other side of the Roraima mountain range. In an even more fantastic setting of cloud-forested plateaus and deafening cascades of crystalline water, the Bolivarian Revolution was frantically searching for a way out of its own crisis in the subterranean veins of the Venezuelan Gran Sabana.

Huge open-cast mines had been excavated. Thousands of impoverished young Venezuelans, many malnourished as the food scarcity crisis deepened in the big cities, had descended upon the area in search of work and a wage paid in gold or other minerals, which would not lose its value overnight in the firestorm of hyperinflation that was laying waste to the Venezuelan economy. News reached Caracas of clashes between the Bolivarian military police and indigenous Pemon protesters, a strange foretaste of the violence that seemed inevitable over the border in Brazil. How had *chavismo*'s twenty-first-century socialism ended up accompanying Bolsonaro and his *garimpeiros* in an invasion of destructive mining in the lands of the Macuxi, the Yanomami, and the Pemon (an ethnic group which included the Tuarepang over the border in Roraima)? To begin to answer this question, let's pan away from the lost world of the Venezuelan Great Savanna to Trinidad and Tobago and the historic fifth Summit of the Americas in the spring of 2009.

* * *

The comandante's gesture was even better designed for pure dramatic effect than that unforgettable moment in 2006 when Hugo Chávez stood exactly where George W. Bush had just addressed the UN General Assembly and, after recommending Noam Chomsky's *Hegemony or Survival* to the gathered diplomats, declared with a mischievous smile: "Here it smells like sulfur!"

By the time of the Trinidad event three years later Bush was gone but Chávez had not lost his sense of humor or occasion. In his first encounter with Barack Obama at the summit, where Venezuela's allies outnumbered Washington's for the first time, Chávez mocked the empire once more. This time the theatrical prop was a copy of Eduardo Galeano's *Open Veins of Latin America*, which he handed to the young Democratic president. Newly elected and apparently prepared to seek a modus vivendi with the Latin American left, Obama understood the message: after a century of neocolonialism, unequal exchange, and bloody interventionism, Latin America was demanding a different relationship with Washington.

It was an ephemeral moment of mutual understanding. Six years later, Obama would announce a slew of minor sanctions against Venezuela that would be the first step toward the oil embargo that Donald Trump implemented in 2019, turning already disastrous shortages of food and medicine into a humanitarian catastrophe. In a surrealist inversion of power relations, the Obama administration had announced that Venezuela now constituted a threat to US security. Perhaps with hindsight Galeano's *Upside Down: A Primer for the Looking-Glass World* would have been a better gift at the presidential encounter in Trinidad.

The audacious gifting of *Open Veins* crowned a fantastic year for Chávez. Just as in Brazil, the global financial crisis of 2008 shattered confidence in the model of neoliberal globalization and debunked those elegant theories of efficient markets, benign multinationals, and mutually beneficial international trade so skillfully dismantled by the young Galeano forty years earlier. With their hyperindebted economies built on the quicksands of speculative finance, the United States and Europe had become the epicenters of the global economic earthquake, while large emerging economies, including Venezuela, appeared to have emerged largely unscathed. The Venezuelan economy grew 4.8 percent in 2008, less than the spectacular 8.4 percent of the previous year, but an impressive rate nonetheless given the great freeze starting in the advanced economies. Soon after the global shock, commodity prices, and Venezuelan oil income recovered. Chávez, too, believed they had dodged the rich man's crisis thanks to the emerging Chinese superpower and its insatiable demand for raw materials.

But it was only a matter of time before the shock waves reached Latin America. When the price of oil fell from $120 in 2014 to $35 in 2016, Chávez was already dead, victim of a sudden and lethal cancer that Chavista conspiracy theories immediately attributed to the CIA. Nicolás Maduro, hand-picked by the dying president for loyalty, would take control of Bolivarian petrosocialism at the very worst moment. As the second wave of the crisis hit Latin America, progressive governments would fall like pins in a bowling alley and the historic project of social transformation came to a shuddering halt.

Although Maduro–a "tough cookie" as Trump called him in his moments of candor–clung to power, shortages of basic goods plunged the majority of Venezuelans into poverty. Oppositional protests within the privileged strata of Venezuelan society had been a constant since Chávez's first electoral victory. But now the unrest threatened to spread to some of the ranchos, the poor neighborhoods that climbed the mountains around Caracas where only brutal police repression was now preventing an uprising. (As the criminologist Keymar Ávila reported, Venezuela outstripped even Brazil in deaths at the hands of the police.)

Foreign exchange, essential to buy food and medicines in an economy dependent on imports, was perilously short due to the collapse of oil output (the story of Venezuela oil is told in full in chapter 15). A devastating economic depression would destroy more than 40 percent of GDP in five years.

In 2019 the Trump oil embargo made a bad situation horrific. In a bizarre variation on regime-change strategies, Washington had recognized the self-proclaimed president Juan Guaidó, the young majority leader of the national assembly, as the legitimate head of state. The bungled attempt to create a parallel government only deepened the chaos. Shortages worsened and four million Venezuelans, out of a population of thirty million, fled the country. As the world forecast his imminent downfall, Maduro glimpsed an alternative to the petroeconomy in other mineral resources deeply embedded in underground rock formations of the Orinoco Basin and the Gran Sabana.

The Orinoco Mining Arc was created in 2015. It covered an area of some forty thousand square miles that cut across territory of enormous environmental value from the Orinoco River to the Brazilian border, home to thirty indigenous communities and vast biodiversity. But more important to the Venezuelan authorities at a time when sheer survival was now the only policy imperative was what lay underground: the second-largest gold deposit in the world, in addition to diamonds, silver, copper, and a range of other perhaps even more valuable metals. Gold was now considered the key income source to compensate for the collapse of crude oil output by more than 50 percent in three years, exacerbated by Trump's embargo. As the inflation rate reached a million percent, the legendary solidity of the glittering metal had become a last resort for the Bolivarian Revolution. Maduro hoped to reach annual gold production of almost 26 million troy ounces by 2025.

There was ample reason to sympathize with Maduro's plight. US sanctions had become a collective punishment targeting the Venezuelan population in clear violation of the Geneva Convention. Guaidó and his allies in Washington spoke openly about a military invasion to remove the Venezuelan president from power. The British government had become an accomplice in the humanitarian crime by withholding thirty-one tons of gold bars worth more than a billion US dollars that had been held for decades by successive Venezuelan governments in the vaults of the Bank of England. Perhaps there was no alternative to mining Venezuela's own gold to generate foreign exchange to help palliate the shortages and stave off a full-blown humanitarian catastrophe. Turkey was a reliable customer despite US sanctions. But extracting gold in a region of such breathtaking biodiversity in order to resolve the structural crisis in Venezuela's petroeconomy seemed a classic case of the old refrain, "When you're in a hole, stop digging."

Gold was not the only mineral that Maduro hoped to

extract in his bid to save the Bolivarian Revolution. Another metal of great strategic value in the flat-topped mountains of the Gran Sabana was thorium, a radioactive element used by the nuclear industry and in aeronautical construction. Then there were the rare earths, those quintessential minerals for the new economy of 5G smartphones and military drones that Marco Rubio, in his ever-more-paranoid resource war with China, was so keen to exploit in Bolsonaro's Brazil. However, the most important mineral in the Venezuelan Gran Sabana at a moment of rising geopolitical hypertension that had brought the politics of the coup d'état back to "America's backyard" was coltan. In the state of Bolívar, south of the Orinoco, geologists had discovered a huge deposit, valued at tens of billions of dollars, of "blue gold," a mineral highly prized for use in cell phones, GPS systems, and satellites.

Like niobium, coltan was an excellent conductor of electricity, even in adverse weather conditions, thanks to its extraordinary resistance and a melting point of 3,017 degrees Celsius. Ground into powder, it was the essential building block for the capacitors that regulate the flow of electricity from battery to screen. Without coltan, smartphones, tablets, DVD players, video-game platforms, laptops, and many more gadgets would not exist. The metal was also another key to the green economy thanks to its ability to boost the energy efficiency of solar panels. But what most concerned Washington about the coltan deposits in the Orinoco Mining Arc was the metal's key role in the construction of turbo propulsion engines, bombs, and intelligent missiles. After all, many of the companies Maduro had invited to tender for concessions in the Orinoco Mining Arc were Russian or Chinese–the United States' adversaries in the Cold War version 2.0.

When I visited Venezuela in the spring of 2019, a few days after the latest of a series of failed coup attempts headed by the hapless Guaidó, I sought out Gustavo Márquez Marín, minister in the first Chávez government and now a prominent dissident Chavista and critic of the mining project. We met at the Rómulo Gallegos Center for Latin American Studies in the upscale Altamira neighborhood of Caracas. After the power outages that had literally blacked out the entire country a few weeks earlier, there was not even running water in the cafeteria restrooms. Like most Venezuelans, Marín had lost a lot of weight since his days as minister and ambassador in the halcyon days of the first Chávez governments. But he spoke to me with great clarity, highlighting the close relationship between the opposition's violent support for a coup and the growing authoritarian mood of the Maduro government. This, in turn, had prompted the 2016 decree that created the Orinoco Mining Arc, a project that in Marín's view violated Venezuela's progressive constitution enacted by the newly formed constituent assembly in 1999 at the start of the Chávez decade.

The plan for large-scale mining of such a vast area of Venezuela's most biodiverse region (12 percent of national territory, equivalent to the surface area of Cuba) had convinced Márquez and other dissident Chavistas of the need to build a democratic platform and demand a referendum to decide the future course of policy. Taking a difficult middle ground between the pro-coup opposition and the beleaguered Maduro regime, their aim was not just to avoid US military intervention but to prevent a further authoritarian drift by the Maduro government.

"In 2016 Maduro began to act outside of the constitution. He created a state of emergency in order to enact economic measures by decree. This included the creation

64

of the Orinoco Mining Arc and opening up access to oil in the Orinoco Belt. Deals were done with mining companies with no checks by the National Assembly or by anyone else. He has deepened Venezuela's dependence on extractivism and granted generous mining concessions to foreign multinationals that have sold out the Venezuelan state," said Marín. Maduro had announced investments of some $5.5 billion involving 150 multinationals. These would form joint ventures with Venezuelan mining companies, most of them owned by the military. "What you have in the Orinoco Mining Arc is what Harvey calls accumulation by dispossession," Marín continued, referencing the New York University geographer and twenty-first-century Marxist guru David Harvey. "This bears no relationship whatsoever to the Bolivarian revolutionary process."

* * *

I had hurriedly toured the Gran Sabana a year or so before, from the abandoned steel and aluminum plants of Puerto Ordaz and Ciudad Guayana to the Brazilian border. At that time, the Venezuelan exodus to Brazil was turning into a stampede, and when I reached the border town of Pacaraima, on the Brazilian side, I came across a hundred or so indigenous Warrau who had abandoned their territory on the Orinoco delta four hundred miles north in search of food in Roraima, although their final destination was the Amazonian capital of Manaus.

They were camped out next to the bus terminal, their clothes piled up on the wasteland surrounded by mounds of trash. The ashes of a bonfire where they had prepared a meager dinner the night before had scattered in the wind. Young mothers pleaded with me to buy necklaces made from beans and seeds while they breastfed tired and sickly babies. It was a graphic image of starving refugees from the Maduro dictatorship, which CNN Español might have called the naked, undeniable truth. These Warao seemed to confirm the degeneration of the Chavista commitment to right the historical wrongs committed against indigenous peoples in Venezuela. Yet, when I asked them about their political allegiances, the answer could not have been more surprising. "We are one hundred percent Chavista! We are revolutionaries, we do not want the opposition," said Marcelino, a thirty-something spokesman for the Warao refugees in Pacaraima. The women gathered around and nodded their heads in emphatic agreement. They blamed neither Chávez nor Maduro for the hunger that had driven them from the delta, but rather the governor of Amacuro, who had banned fishing. It was yet another indication that in Venezuela, despite the uniform narrative of most Western media, nothing was what it seemed.

Before reaching the Brazilian border I passed close by the mines of El Callao, the most active area of the Orinoco Mining Arc. I witnessed the black-market gasoline sellers, who would later sell the fuel to the miners at vastly inflated prices, waiting in endless lines at the service stations. But here I must make a confession, given the implicit commitment in this book to adhere to the journalistic principles of Francisco de Goya in his famous etching *Yo lo vi* (*I Saw It*) in his *Disasters of War* series. Despite being so close to the gold-and-coltan belt, I did not dare to venture further on my own into the mining territory. This was because of the macabre testimonies I had heard from multiple sources, namely accounts of the presence in the mines of Colombian organized crime, from the National Liberation Army (ELN) guerrilla who specialized in cocaine trafficking to sadistic paramilitary mafias. According to several NGOs, Venezuelan and Colombian gangs were extorting money from the miners and from other companies, with the apparent approval of the Venezuelan military. The paramilitary groups and the guerrillas collected a *vacuna* (extortion money) from the miners, generally paid in gold. Meanwhile, the Venezuelan military charged criminal groups and miners their own revolutionary tax, an amount that could be as much as six hundred and forty Troy ounces of gold (about $800,000) per month. That, at least, is what a report by the International Crisis Group alleged, citing intermediaries in the Venezuelan gold business. Miners who refused to pay the *vacuna* were murdered or worse. The most gruesome crime reported at that moment was that of a group of thugs who had gouged out the eyes and cut off the tongue and hands of a miner who refused to pay. He was found alive. One hundred and seven miners had been murdered between 2016 and 2019.

I chose not to confirm in flesh and blood such chilling reports. After all, I was not traveling in an armor-plated corporate 4x4, nor was I clad in a bulletproof waistcoat with three armed Blackwater guards, like those reporters from Fox News and CNN who would soon descend upon the Venezuelan-Colombian border for Richard Branson's Venezuela Aid Live concert. Bulletproof vests to see reggaeton artist Luis Fonsi perform "Despacito" seemed excessive. But visiting the Arco *minero* on my own did not seem advisable either. In any case, I was comforted to read that Goya's *Yo lo vi*, an image of a mother urging her reluctant child to come to her arms as she fled, just as the Warao mothers must have done on leaving their homes, was almost certainly not exactly what the great painter saw.

So, like Goya, I would have to rely on witnesses. And, they soon appeared once I reached Manaus, the mythical metropolis in the Brazilian Amazon, seven hours by road from the Venezuelan border. The migrants from the Orinoco Mining Arc soon confirmed the stories of hell.

"In my town, last week, a guy was decapitated. They left his head in the plaza," said Jeison Brito, a seventeen-year-old Venezuelan youth who had worked in a gold mine in Callao to pay for his passage to Brazil. What was it like working in the mine? I asked him. He replied enigmatically, as if metamorphosed into a character from a Kafka novel: "Imagine yourself entering a house made of rock. You enter a room and in that room there are other smaller rooms, and you enter one of them and there you find other smaller rooms and finally you find the last one, which is very small and you cannot breathe and there you have than to chip away at the wall with a pickax." For every four bags of rock he excavated, he received one as payment. Three rocks were then ground down and the minerals separated in a nearby town using mercury and other separators. The mines were surrounded by swamps where diseases such as dengue and malaria were endemic. Gold was already the only valid currency in the mining area, said Brito. It was a perfect means to buy real estate in Puerto Ordaz. The problem was that "you only usually find very small nuggets," chipped in his brother, another young immigrant who now played the accordion in front of the Teatro Amazonas, the Manaus opera house where a century earlier the rubber barons listened to Verdi while their laborers died of dengue and exhaustion.

Maduro's mining decree was implemented "without environmental or sociocultural impact studies to assess the dangers to indigenous communities in the mining areas and, of course, it [would] be disastrous for the environment because this [was] where the water comes from that feeds into the Orinoco and where the subterranean aquifers are so important," said Marín. "To extract all these minerals, you have to remove the entire top layer of the rock and excavate everything to a depth of over a mile. The whole lot is removed and then broken up and crushed with cyanide," he continued. "With the old mining techniques of the last century, they drilled into underground seams. But with these huge open-pit mines, for them to be profitable, they have to destroy everything: the fauna, the rain forests. The rivers, too, because they need a lot of water. So, I mean that with Maduro we are going back to the savage extractivism that prospered under the dictatorship of General Juan Vicente Gómez in the 1930s."

If any readers doubt the environmental impact of opening a coltan mine in the Venezuelan Gran Sabana, they might try reading *Coltan* by Michael Nest, a short book that describes the "blue gold" fever in the Democratic Republic of the Congo, a new *Heart of Darkness* for the age of 5G smartphones. In order to assess the impact of the mines on fauna in a mining area near the Okapi reserve, the miners were asked what they ate, and they answered that they hunted elephants, gorillas, chimpanzees, buffalo, and antelopes. Two years later, the same questionnaire was distributed and the diet had changed. They only ate turtles, birds, small antelopes, and monkeys because there were no longer any specimens of the great species left in the area.

It wasn't only local gangsters who stalked the frontier economy of the Venezuelan mining arc. One of the multinational companies that received a concession was the American-Canadian company Gold Reserve, which ran the huge Las Brisas-Las Cristinas mine in the state of Bolívar. Hugo Chávez had expelled Gold Reserve from Venezuela before the crisis in order to give priority to national companies. But the mining company filed a lawsuit with the World Bank Administrative Tribunal, the International Centre for Settlement of Investment Disputes, which, as is usually the case, ruled in favor of Gold Reserve against Venezuela and forced Caracas to pay $700 million in compensation. To avoid disbursing that money, Maduro created a joint venture and handed Gold Reserve 45 percent of the mine.

Gustavo Márquez Marín, who like all the pioneers of *chavismo* had *Open Veins of Latin America* etched in his revolutionary DNA, had no doubt that the governments of the Latin American pink tide, despite their achievements in the battle against poverty, had repeated the mistakes that Galeano had catalogued: "To a certain extent, the progressive governments ended up continuing and even intensifying the pillage. And there is a clear reason why: they did not change the political model," he explained. At the beginning, he added, "the project was aimed at deepening democracy, promoting participation and diversifying development to get us out of the primary-export extractivist model that Galeano denounced and that has been the curse of the last few centuries in Latin America. But, unfortunately, the old model returned: stay in power via a state based on patronage and handouts, with ultraleadership dependent entirely on oil revenues."

It was a devastating criticism of the Maduro government and others in Latin America. But anyone who thought that Juan Guaidó's young neoliberals would save the Gran Sabana suffered from delusions. When I spoke to Marco Aurelio Quiñones, a young National Assembly representative from Guaidó's party, Voluntad Popular, he cursed a "dictatorship that has destroyed Venezuela." Then he added: "This is a rich country. I mean, look, we have underground deposits of coltan worth $100 billion."

CHAPTER FOUR

Gold (Colombia; Central America; Utah; Nevada)
El Dorado in Salt Lake City

The quest for El Dorado had always been an enterprise of greed, delusion, and destruction. And, though the latest generation of conquistadores were multinational mining corporations headquartered in Vancouver with Machiavellian departments of corporate social responsibility, or desperate fortune seekers from the megaslums of Bogotá, Lima, or São Paulo, the twenty-first-century gold rush trod the same paths as those first frenzies of extraction and death behind Columbus, Cortés, or Pizarro half a millennium before.

But perhaps something else could explain the latest variant of gold fever that I had witnessed in rivers tainted with blood and mercury in the megamines of Central America. In years of crisis, gold was the safest haven from a wave of fear that spread like a virus from Wall Street across the planet. Impoverished artisanal miners, *barequeros* in Colombia and *garimpeiros* in Brazil, waded deep into Latin American's muddied rivers in search of their fortune or at least a tiny nugget to buy a plate of beans. But in the Global North, gold was sought in a neurotic quest for financial and psychological security. Gold has justified the most atrocious acts and the most extraordinary human resistance. Why? Because it "annihilates uncertainty," mused Peter Bernstein in his book *The Power of Gold*. More directly, the financial blogger Masa Serdarevi quipped, "gold is all about fear."

And in the decade after the outbreak of the epic crisis in 2008, fear was not a scarce commodity in a world traumatized by financial contagion and viral pandemics. The price of a troy ounce (460 grams) had remained stable for decades at around $500. But when the financial system froze and panic gripped the markets in the fall of 2008 it soared to $1,900. The destruction of trillions of dollars of stock market value (though it would soon recover to restore the fortunes of the global plutocracy) heightened the appeal of the glittering yellow metal in the Global North.

An unprecedented monetary expansion, and interest rates that plunged to zero or lower, hastened the flight to the golden bunker. Yet fear was not the only driver of the boom. In a society of globalized ostentation and extreme inequality so perfectly personified by Donald Trump and his towers in the form of giant ingots, gold reflected a universal desire to boast vulgarly of social status. Demand soared from the nouveau middle classes of India and China, buyers of goldsmithed jewelry in the Swarovski boutiques of a thousand identical luxury-brand malls, to the "ladies only" LVMH stores of kitsch theocracies in Dubai or Doha. And, like other symbols of the age of bling, gold entered the decadent world of contemporary art, overtaking bronze as the chosen metal of globally branded artists such as Damien Hirst, whose skeleton of a mammoth cast in pure gold, *Gone but Not Forgotten*, sold for $15 million. Marc Quinn's gold statue of fashion model Kate Moss in a tortuously contorted yoga asana, *Siren*, was commissioned by the British Museum for $2 million. Or the pièce de résistance, a gleaming 18-carat-gold WC sculpted by Maurizio Cattelan that the Guggenheim in New York dispatched to Trump for the White House bathroom instead of the Van Gogh that the president had ordered.

Gold also became the core business of organized crime, which competed (and sometimes partnered) with the mining multinationals listed on the Toronto Stock Exchange. The most prized metal was a reliable and increasingly liquid financial asset, perfect for laundering the illicit income of the McMafias. Millions of dollars were extorted from impoverished prospectors and autonomous miners who provided no less than 20 percent of global output. Intermediaries in remote outposts of the Andes or the Amazon rain forest paid up too, and after taking their own share of the booty exported the gold to the civilized world. To Switzerland, mainly, whose four refineries in the Alps processed 50 percent of world production of gold. In each link of this most lustrous supply chain, billions of dollars of dirty money were quickly laundered. But the *garimpeiros* and the *barequeros* or the corrupt officials who turned a blind eye to the illegal gold trade, even the paramilitaries who spread terror in the mines, were just symptoms of a wider malaise. The underlying disease was extreme inequality, the plague of the twenty-first century's predatory capitalism, of which the international gold business became a quintessential symbol like Wagner's ring.

"I have visited the La Rinconada mine, at an altitude of sixteen thousand feet in the Peruvian Andes. Sixty thousand artisanal miners work there and live in shacks made of scrap metal; they die before reaching fifty because the oxygen content of the air is barely 50 percent; there are no police, but there are four thousand prostitutes, almost all slaves," the Swiss lawyer Mark Pieth, author of *Gold Laundering: The Dirty Secrets of the Gold Trade*, whom I had first met in Davos during the yearly gathering of the global elite, explained. Pieth had just returned to Basel after a trip to the Andean inferno. "It is terrifying. It should be banned. But a hundred million families worldwide depend on it."

While financial terror and conspicuous consumption raised the value of gold, a new generation of apocalyptic ideologies rendered it a cult. The longed-for return to the gold standard was a crazed obsession of eccentric goldbugs and, in the occasional remark, of Trump himself, who gained support amongst conservatives from Utah to Bavaria in the years of unstoppable monetary expansion. Like Brazil's neo-Pentecostals preaching the imminent day of judgment, fetishists of the most precious of metals foresaw inflation at every turn. It never materialized. Yet, not even the brief "normalization" of monetary policy in 2017 could curb demand for the yellow metal. Prices oscillated around $1,500 per troy ounce, easily enough to feed the desperate gold rush in the Andean cordilleras and Amazonian watersheds, where 60 percent of the gold sold in the United States was sourced.

The least useful of all metals, gold had always bred fantasy and delirium. Chemically inert, the Au element 79, never oxidized. It has "the kind of longevity we all dream of," writes Bernstein, perhaps with the Silicon Valley billionaire Peter Thiel in mind. Thiel, whose support helped Trump reach the White House, invested in nanotechnology and genetics in a narcissistic quest for immortality while he defended the gold standard with the passion of a medieval king, convinced "it had the virtue of connecting the real with the virtual."

The new El Dorado was irresistible to libertarians like Thiel. Gold, after all, was independent of any state. "It may be a piece of useless, shiny metal, but at least central bankers can't print it," stated Dylan Grice, an investment analyst at Credit Suisse. Even when the Fed slowed its quantitative easing, the goldbugs, like the manic fortune seeker in Edgar Allan Poe's story "The Gold-Bug," could not relax. Gillian Tett, a *Financial Times* columnist, explained the metal's appeal as "an echo of the cargo cults that anthropologists study in the Pacific islands: something that offers pattern and meaning amid terrifying disorder."

The metal was therapeutic too for the goldbugs in the British Conservative Party, who sought a safe haven even while they sang the praises of Brexit. The decision to leave the European club triggered the demise of sterling and the demand for gold soared by 219 percent in a week. The IMF noted drily in October 2019 that gold "is supported by the (possibly irrational) fear of a collapse of major fiat systems."

So too months later when the coronavirus pandemic traumatized the five continents and central banks opened the monetary sluice gates once more the price of gold smashed its previous records, hitting $2,000 per troy ounce launching shares in gold miners skyward. Such was its lure: gold was seen by hysterical investors not only as a hedge against an unlikely return of inflation or even hyperinflation in the postpandemic but also against depression and deflation. Fear trumped ostentation as the virus spread, and sales of gold bars boomed while Rolex watches slumped and conspicuous consumers in Asia melted down their jewelry to cast ingots. "Our stocks run out as soon as they come in," said a British bullion trader in Birmingham as Europe locked down to contain the virus. "It's a bit like the panic buying of toilet paper." These were troubling times and gold was a tranquilizer. On the streets of cities, rich and poor, side by side with evangelical preachers who announced the coming of Armageddon, men with humiliated countenances bore placards that read WE BUY GOLD. The metal was

perfectly tailored to the "end times" movement and the sur-
vivalist militias of Idaho and Texas advised their disciples to
pack a few gold bars along with the assault rifle in the kit for
the postapocalypse.

Or perhaps it was physical solidity that explained the
conservative's fascination with gold, the densest metal of
all. Freud, after all, attributed the gold fetish to neurosis and
anal fixation. For the Maya, superb goldsmiths whose work
Cortés dispatched to the foundry, gold was the excrement of
the sun god, and was of inestimable aesthetic and symbolic
value while lacking any commercial or monetary worth. But
for the goldbugs of the crisis years, the metal had become
the solid excrement of upright conservative Christians,
intellectually constipated and in search of a safe investment.
Although Trump rejected the Guggenheim's mischievous
gift (and would demand the head of the museum's curator,
Nancy Spector, who made the satirical offer to a president
known for choosing gold for the faucets of his luxury real
estate) the golden toilet-throne of Maurizio Cattelan became
a secret object of desire for millions of bathrooms in Republican America's McMansions.

Of course, the neurosis was transformed alchemically
into fabulous profits for the mining multinationals and their
advisers, including José María Aznar, Spain's neocon former
prime minister who had been headhunted for the board of
the largest gold miner in the world, Canada's Barrick Gold,
to combat social resistance to the latest phase of pillage of
Latin America's most open veins. Now in a global crisis, gold
was being mined in "previously noneconomic or marginal
places, and where more people live," explained the Argentine economist Leonardo Stanley. The fever extended from
Tanzania to Mongolia. But the most dramatic development
was the return to El Dorado and the gold rushes of the Amer-

ican Far West. Colombia, Mexico, Venezuela, Brazil, Central America–all less developed in mining than Chile or Peru in the south–became the new mining frontiers for America. Meanwhile, in the north, Alaska, the Klondike, and Nevada were once again the sites of the delusionary dreams of fortune seekers and goldbugs in the new age of fear.

* * *

The Orlando mine in Amalfi, Colombia, sits on a small tributary of the great Cauca River amidst the verdant mountains of northeastern Antioquia. While two excavators unloaded tons of thick cement-colored mud under a mechanical hose in the hope that the flowing liquid would deposit grains of gold, some two hundred *barequeros* searched for their own nuggets of the precious metal in the piles of waste. They dug with shovels in the gray sludge left by the Caterpillar dump truck and tossed it into the pans. Then, submerged up to the waist in a pool as opaque as chocolate milk, they rinsed the mud in circular movements in search of yellow flecks.

The scene evoked those Dantesque images of desperate *garimpeiros* in the Brazilian photographer Sebastião Salgado's reportage, a graphic document of the miserable of the earth in the 1980s. Yet these Colombian *barequeros* did not lament their destiny but rather smiled proudly and defended the dignity of their work. Like casino gamblers, they chose chance and freedom over the monotony of the wage slaves in the megamines higher up in the cordillera. "Here we are the ones who decide when we go to work," explained Raúl Duque, a *barequero* thirty-five years of age, father of three young children and owner of a humble shack in the town. "There are days you win, and days you lose." He lifted the pan to show a golden fleck that glittered against the gray steel. The other miners gathered around and I took a picture with the nugget sparkling like their smiles.

They would sell the gold that afternoon in the town for 180 pesos, about nine dollars. Not much. The *barequeros* had earned three times that per day harvesting coca before fumigation policies under the Clinton Administration's Plan Colombia—a joint initiative between US and Colombian governments to purportedly combat drug cartels that was ushered through the Senate by Joe Biden—deprived so many of their livelihood that the number of autonomous miners increased by one hundred thousand. The owner of the Orlando mine, in contrast, extracted a pound of gold every day at a time when the troy ounce was above $1,500. Such was the inequality of the illegal gold business. But the *barequeros* were grateful for the unwritten contract by which the owner allowed them to seek their fortune in the gray slick of waste from the mine. "If the mine doesn't work, we don't either," said one worker as he returned to the mud.

The history of artisanal gold mining in the northeast of Antioquia stretches back over millennia. When the Spaniards stumbled north in the 1540s after their fruitless pursuit of El Dorado in the Peruvian Amazon, up to a million people inhabited these fertile valleys in a society equipped with advanced agriculture, extensive mining for gold and copper and salt, and complex, centralized power structures. The Quimbaya panned for gold using techniques similar to those of the *barequeros* in the Amalfi rivers, though, of course, there were no Caterpillars for the first strenuous excavation nor mercury to separate the nuggets from the rock. Neither quantity nor price was of great importance to the Quimbaya. Gold was of only aesthetic and spiritual value, though it served, then as now, as a symbol of the privileged elite.

Months earlier in Madrid's charming Museum of the Americas, I had entered a darkened room where the world's largest collection of Quimbaya gold sculptures, dating from 500 to 1000 A.D., glowed in their glass display cases like messengers from another cosmos. Discovered in Filandia, Colombia, in an underground tomb safe from Spanish looting, they included pendants and necklaces in the form of snails, lizards, pectorals, nose and ear rings, bells, and pumpkin-shaped containers for coca leaves and the lime used to enhance the effects of the drug. Minisculptures of the Quimbaya *caciques* (native chiefs)–minute models of both men and women with squinting eyes and tiny bodies–were breathtaking examples of their craft. Sculpted in beeswax molds, "the golden artifacts were not manufactured nor traded according to the simple demands of a 'fashion,'" Ana María Falchetti, a specialist at the Gold Museum in Bogotá, explained to me. (I chose not to inquire why the treasures of the Quimbaya were housed in the little-known museum in the university district of the Spanish capital and not in the internationally famed Gold Museum in the Colombian capital.)

Back in Amalfi, the gold miners of the twenty-first century traveled the one-hundred-mile journey to Medellín through the Antioquian cordillera on hand-painted multicolored *chiva* buses to join thousands of others in demonstrations that filled the square in front of the government offices. The *barequeros* were protesting the hated proposal for a new mining code that would regulate the sector and prosecute artisanal miners without a license. The police and the army that patrolled Amalfi toting US-manufactured M16 machine guns had already closed thousands of illegal mines and confiscated excavators, gasoline, and even the golden nuggets. The future of 1.5 million people was at stake, 5 million if their families were included.

The government claimed the measures were necessary to bring order to the sector, combat organized crime, and protect the environment. In Amalfi the miners pleaded innocence, denying they used mercury when panning in the rivers. But some undoubtedly chose to use the liquid metal, which reacts chemically when in contact with gold and helps identify the nuggets. In Antioquia, the gold was separated from the rock by mixing it in a thick paste of sugarcane molasses, lemon juice, and mercury. In the areas around these mines the concentration of mercury–a highly toxic metal that never degrades–was so high that during one trial the Jerome 431 testing device exploded.

For the *barequeros*, however, there were other explanations for the decision to clamp down on informal mining taken by ultraconservative Colombian president Álvaro Uribe and his more liberal successor Juan Manuel Santos. "The government wants the multinationals to come here," said Alisandro Guzmán, a forty-five-year-old native of Remedios, another mining town in the Antioquian cordillera. Uribe had chosen mining–especially coal–and oil as strategic sectors for his IMF-approved economic plans and chose to open Colombia's sierras and rain forests to the multinationals under conditions more generous than any of his predecessors. Before leaving the presidential palace in Bogotá in 2010 he had approved no fewer than a thousand new concessions. Santos, while more conscious of the scars left by the open veins, pursed the same goals. As the peace process liberated vast areas of Colombia previously controlled by the FARC guerilla, the multinational mining enterprises glimpsed excellent opportunities. At the forefront were the Canadians whose complicity with corrupt governments such as Uribe's and with organized crime, belied Canada's reputation as the most socially and environmentally sensitive society in the Americas. A pioneer was the former investment banker and founder of Goldcorp, Frank Giustra—introduced to Uribe by Bill Clinton in Bogotá in 2005 in return for a $160 million donation to the ex-US president's philanthropic foundation—who became one of the first Canadian magnates to win access to the new Colombian mining frontier

The stock market in Toronto was by now the main source of capital for multinational mining outfits, whose geologists and engineers, disguised as protectors of the environment, scoured Latin America's subsoil in search of precious metals. The new conquest required audacious acts of greenwashing. After opening several mines in Colombia, some in the fragile ecosystem of the Paramo, the Vancouver-based company Graystar was rebranded as Eco Oro. Giustra spent billions on philanthropy and formed, along with Clinton, the so-called Clinton Giustra Sustainable Growth Initiative to boost the Canadian mining billionaire's green credentials. Some Canadian mining executives even seemed sincere in their concern. "Mercury is causing terrible damage to people's health; regularizing the situation in Colombia is urgent," said Jean Martineau, CEO at Dynacor, a small mining multinational headquartered in Montreal that was already established in Peru and had designs on the Colombian cordilleras newly liberated from the guerrilla. Martineau was undoubtedly a sincere Quebecois. A painting of poor Latin American farmers in the style of Diego Rivera decorated his office. But he soon got back to business. "In Canada we have to dig to depths of three hundred and twenty feet below the surface. In the Andes the minerals are there for all to see, right on the surface!"

The question was not just environmental. With the approval of the Uribe government, another Canadian multinational, Gran Colombia Gold, had acquired the cooperative

Frontin in the Antioquian town of Segovia, previously wholly owned by its workers. After firing five hundred members of the workforce and observing at a safe distance how paramilitaries murdered those who protested, Gran Colombia began to buy gold nuggets from the very same miners, now self-employed *barequeros,* for prices well below the market price paid to the miners at Amalfi. For these new *barequeros,* who were free agents yet tied like slaves to the multinational corporation as if they were in one of Galeano's chronicles, the choice was simple: accept the price offered by the Canadian-run mine or face imprisonment for working illegally. Two board members of Gran Colombia Gold were ex-ministers in the Uribe government.

Yet no degree of violence could crush opposition to the new open veins. Soon after the Toronto-based multinational forced the closure of a cluster of small illegal mines in Segovia still operating within its concession, a general strike was called in the whole region, the first mass mobilization of a new protest movement in Colombia that would transform the political landscape. AngloGold Ashanti, a South African mining giant, had been granted generous concessions to the north of Cali for La Colosa, which would be the largest open-cast gold mine in South America. It soon faced popular resistance too. In a referendum held in nearby Cajamarca, whose water supply was threatened directly by the concession, more than 80 percent voted against the mine. Ashanti shelved the project. It was a momentous victory for the campaign against megamines in Colombia, and the protests spread.

Hundreds of municipalities followed Cajamarca's lead and held referenda in an explosion of direct democracy. The Colombian constitutional court ruled that Gran Colombia should also be forced to put its projects to a people's vote.

The Abu Dhabi-based mining concern Mubadala would soon spark another mass protest with a plan to excavate what they hoped would become South America's most productive open-cast gold mine in the environmentally fragile Páramo de Santurbán, watershed for 70 percent of Colombia's rivers, in another area of eastern Colombia where the demobilization of the FARC guerrilla had cleared more terrain for international agribusiness, mining, and still-marauding paramilitary groups.

The new movement against the open veins helped the former guerrilla and mayor of Bogotá, Gustavo Petro, consolidate his leadership of a new progressive coalition, from small farmers in El Cauca to young professionals in Bogotá. It would be the first challenge to the hitherto uncontested power of the Colombian oligarchy. Petro redefined the left as "the movement of life" against "the forces of death" represented by the fossil fuel industry and multinational mining interests from gold to coal. Remarkably, he turned climate change into the central plank of his 2018 presidential bid that was narrowly defeated by Uribe's hand-picked successor Iván Duque. These were ideas, too, that would inspire some of the citizens' mobilizations that filled the streets of Bogotá in the fall of 2019.

Other forces, darker even than the insidiously greenwashed Canadian mining groups, threatened the small mine owners in Antioquia and their *barequeros*. At a makeshift café in the center of Amalfi, I spoke to a handful of informal mine owners over a "*tinto*" coffee. They explained the workings of the *vacuna* system, by which paramilitaries, narcos, and some still-active guerilla cells extorted money and gold from the informal miners. "They killed two of my brothers and kidnapped another," said Octavio, an ex-*barequero*. "They shot three of my workers dead because they hadn't paid the *vacuna*," he added, lowering his voice and shifting his eyes in search of unknown listeners. Other small mining outfits had opted to pay the *vacuna*. "I paid four million pesos per machine," said another.

Organized crime's interest went beyond extortion rackets. Both mines and the gold extracted from them could be bought and sold to launder money. As the writer Alfredo Molano Bravo remarked with the blackest of Colombian humor, the paramilitaries and the narcos were now acutely aware that the prospecting pans used by the *barequeros*, were useful "not just to wash the gold but to wash the dollars too." Research done for the Santos presidency had uncovered that the gold business had now eclipsed narcotics as the main driver of violence and money laundering in Colombia. After all, what could be more appropriate to alchemically purify the blood money of the paramilitary mafias than a thousand gold bars? While the Revolutionary Armed Forces of Colombia (FARC) bravely handed over some nine thousand arms soon to be melted down and sculpted into a steel monument to peace in Bogotá by artist Doris Salcedo, paramilitaries and remnants of the guerrilla continued to wreak terror in the mountains of Antioquia, the epicenter of the violence that had displaced no fewer than forty-seven thousand small farmers from their land.

The attempt to regularize the mining sector coincided with the trials of gold exporters such as Goldex or the audaciously named firm Escobar, headquartered in Medellín, which was accused of money laundering and illegally exporting gold to the United States and Europe. They had bought gold from mines reportedly owned by the FARC guerrilla groups and by paramilitary groups such as Los Urbanos who had enjoyed warm relations with Uribe when, as governor of Antioquia, the future president turned a blind eye to paramilitary extortion and violence from his two-thousand-hectare hacienda, La Guacharacas, on the outskirts of Medellín.

The paramilitaries were what Donald Trump might have for once reasonably called "bad hombres." "What they like is to decapitate people and then play football with their heads," said Lucy, a former FARC guerillera whom I met on the Colombia-Venezuela border. Colombia would soon break its own records for the murder of environmental activists—and quite a few journalists too—many for denouncing mining activities, paramilitary extortion, or the slave-like conditions of the *barequeros*. Hundreds of demobilized FARC guerrillas charged with running sustainable development projects, often in areas of interest for mining, were gunned down. Despite the carnage, the Swiss refinery Metalor, based in the village of Neuchâtel, on the shores of the alpine lake of the same name, bought gold from the Medellín-based exporters and guaranteed excellent returns for the mafias. There was even evidence that organized crime had infiltrated top management at some of the mining companies, specifically Continental Gold, which acknowledged that its vice chairman had worked for the Oficina de Envigado, formerly Pablo Escobar's Medellín cartel.

Yet while the Santos and Duque governments celebrated their clampdown on illegal mining as a blow against organized crime, the miners in Amalfi mistrusted their intentions. From the most insignificant *barequeros* to the owners of five or six Caterpillars, all agreed that both the state offensive and the paramilitary harassment was a strategy agreed upon by multinationals and the government with one sole objective: to drive them out of existence.

* * *

Two of the most striking pendants in the Quimbaya collection at the Museum of the Americas in Madrid share the
delicate beauty of pre-Columbian art found in the Central
American regions that now make up Panama and Costa Rica.
They are the Darién pendants made from *tumbaga*, an alloy
of gold and copper, that in all known examples represent a
human figure with a flattened face, a nose formed by spirals,
schematically rendered arms and hands, and two sticks or
wands reminiscent of those still used by the indigenous shamans in their cosmological explorations. New research sug-
gests the paper-thin semicircles of fine gold attached to the
Darién pendants represent the hallucinogenic mushrooms
smoked by the pre-Columbian shamans. One of the pendants in the collection was found under the great pyramids
in the Mayan city of Chichén Itzá in the Mexican state of
Yucatán one thousand miles north of Antioquia, conclusive
proof of the technological and cultural exchange between
the pre-Hispanic societies in the Andes and the Maya in the
south of Mexico. It seemed logical, therefore, for my own
twenty-first-century gold route to head north from Antioquia and across the Darién strait between Colombia and
Panama to the new mines in Central America.

In Coclesito, a village of some three hundred peasant
families in the Panamanian northwest jungle, Carmelo
Yangüez, fifty-six, whose angular face evoked those *caciques* depicted in the Quimbaya pendants, had been fighting
for six years against the mine of the Canadian multinational Petaquilla Gold, a red crater in the mountain about
ten miles from their town. Morale was beginning to wane.
"People are giving up, looking for work in the mine; the local
politicians have sold out to the company," he said, seated on

the terrace of his pastel-green painted wooden cabin with a jungle of coffee and banana plants in the garden.

Two years earlier hundreds of townsfolk from Coclesito and the indigenous villages downriver had blocked the unsurfaced access road to the mine for sixteen consecutive days. The protest focused not just on the plan to open a mile-wide hole in the landscape but also the use of cyanide in a region of exuberant yet fragile biodiversity. Then, the anti-riot police arrived. Petaquilla began gold production without even the most cursory environmental study and soon produced a thousand ounces of gold, worth more than $8 million, per month. As the fait accompli became apparent, many locals accepted the company's relocation proposal without even consulting a lawyer, said Yangüez. "The company produces a lot of propaganda and many people believe what they say."

The Vancouver-based Petaquilla had certainly designed an imaginative public relations campaign. Descending the dirt road from the mine toward Coclesito, the 4x4 passed signs featuring cartoon drawings of El Niño Petaquilla, a smiling child, shouting: "*no boten basura!*" (Don't litter!). Such environmental sensitivity was surprising for a company that had removed half the mountain. Further down, signs announced organic vegetable plots sponsored by Petaquilla. "They produce nothing," said Yangüez. Having laid waste to five thousand hectares of rain forest to excavate the mine, Petaquilla claimed to have reforested an area close to the river, which, as residents of Coclesito explained to me, already had an abundance of trees and plants. In another PR offensive, the company built a new primary school where "the teachers were strictly warned not to make any criticisms of the mine," said another resident I spoke to in the town.

The greenwashed propaganda of Petaquilla's department of corporate special responsibility could not camouflage the crude reality of an open-cast mine excavated at the headwaters of three rivers in a zone of copious rainfall. Vast quantities of water mixed with cyanide were employed in the gold separation process, the waste stored in tailing ponds that would frequently overflow.

"Before, when we paddled in the river we could feel tiny fish nibbling at our feet," explained the community leader Maria Muñoz as she showed me a series of photos of dead fish floating like plastic bottles on the surface of the river. "We hunted for deer, turkey, and parrots," she added. "God knows how to make things. Now we eat chicken that comes from outside." We walked to the outskirts of Coclesito, where orchids poked out like snowdrops in the dense green foliage, and chanced upon Dario Saavedra, a young cattle driver with an angular face and elongated eyes. He had driven his skeletal herd from their village of Toabré sixty miles to the south, accessible only by river or on foot. "I would rather a road than a mine," he said wearily.

The most creative aspect of Petaquilla's marketing was undoubtedly the tourist development program devised by the Castilla de Oro Foundation, the work of Richard Fifer, former governor of the state of Coclé and chief executive officer of Petaquilla Gold in Panama. Fifer was a close associate of the then Panamanian president, Ricardo Martinelli, who would end up behind bars for fraud. The foundation aimed to encourage the construction of "hotels, convention centers, and theme parks," in order to "put this region back on the international tourist map . . . an earthly paradise where visitors can retread the steps of the adventurers of the sixteenth century," said the investor brochures.

Coclesito's history would certainly make excellent material for a theme park, perhaps registered under the brand name Goldilandia. Columbus had arrived on the Panamanian coast on his fourth voyage in January 1503 and built the first Spanish settlement of the New World nearby, where he announced euphorically that he had seen more gold than on his three previous trips. Soon Núñez de Balboa would cross the fifty-mile isthmus to the Pacific coast and discover that he had no reason whatsoever to continue calling those people from whom he demanded gold "Indians" while dogs snapped at their feet. The new Castilla de Oro jurisdiction was soon decreed by the Catholic kings, spanning what are now the states of Panama, Costa Rica, and Nicaragua.

Hence the name of the innovative leisure project with a theme park inspired by the discovery of the first El Dorado. A hypothetical stewardess from Goldilandia would never admit it, but the catastrophic error of the Indians–the Aztec, the Maya, the Inca, and Coclesito's own Ngöbe was to believe that the Spaniards, so obsessively focused in their search for the sacred metal and excrement of the sun, must therefore have been gods. Perhaps it was the fault of those hallucinogenic mushrooms. By projecting divine powers on to the white, bearded strangers whose horses appeared to be prosthetic extensions of their metallic bodies (clad in suits of armor), the natives unleashed a vicious cycle that would end with their own destruction, writes the infallible Nobel laureate J. M. G. Le Clézio in *The Mexican Dream: Or, the Interrupted Thought of Amerindian Civilizations.* "These are the true symbols of the Conquest: the chain and gold ingots."

The precious artifacts of the indigenous goldsmiths, in homage to the gods of nature, were of no interest at all to Columbus and the conquistadores who would follow. This contrast in aesthetic appreciation is summarized by Oscar Guardiola-Rivera, a young Colombian philosopher, in his refreshing book *What If Latin America Ruled the World?*: "The ornaments of the princes–the golden discs for healing that shamans contemplated for hours, the dazzling earrings and pectorals . . . the excrement of the sun (gold) and the tears of the moon (silver)–when melted down and turned into bars, then sent to Seville, Antwerp, Genoa, Venice and London, became collateral to finance further expeditions to Africa and the New World."

Guardiola-Rivera was a source of inspiration when I read about his own epic journey from Central America, Colombia, and Ecuador to Lima: a reconstruction of Pizarro's odyssey, except that Oscar traveled by car listening to Iggy Pop throughout the trip, and stopped in the Ecuadorian Andes to recite out loud to himself Pablo Neruda's epic poem *Canto General*. We had lunch one day at a restaurant in Covent Garden, near his office at Birkbeck College, where he explained the logic of the massive extraction of gold and silver from the New World: "It made possible the creation of the first global currency which allowed, in turn, the first planetary relations of trade and investment."

Recycled from Spain to the financial centers in London and Amsterdam, gold and silver laid the foundation for the first debt and equity markets in history. "Gold acted as a translator that homologated two worlds," explained Guardiola-Rivera. Gold as translator seemed a perfect metaphor, especially if we understood the language in question as the Orwellian business-speak of the global CEOs at Barrick Gold and Newmont Mining and their equity analysts on Wall Street. So, to summarize: without El Dorado and the lingua franca of gold, the innovative system of capitalism would not have appeared so promptly on planet Earth, where it would proceed to destroy everything in its path. The young Galeano explained the process with his ironic and baroque prose: "In the Middle Ages a small bag of pepper was worth more than a man's life, but gold and silver were the keys used by the Renaissance to open the doors of paradise in heaven and the doors of capitalist mercantilism on earth."

That said, the primitive accumulation of capital by means of the extraction of gold and the meltdown of so many gorgeous works of art met fierce resistance. The indigenous residents of the new viceroyalty of Castilla de Oro soon realized that the decision to deify the Spaniards because of their voracious appetite for the sacred metal had been a catastrophic error of judgement. Quibian, the leader of the Ngöbe who was presumed drowned after being thrown into the river Belén by Columbus's men, swam to safety, mobilized the local communities, and briefly drove out the Spaniards. It was the first indigenous rebellion against the gold seekers and a precedent for five centuries of battles against the insatiable extractivists from the north. From the rebellions of the Huichol in the Mexican Sierra Madre in the seventeenth century and Túpac Amaru's uprising in the Peruvian altiplano a century later, to the twentieth-century insurrections of the Zapatista National Liberation Army (EZLN) in Chiapas or the Aymara and Quechua in Ecuador and Bolivia.

In some senses, the very myth of El Dorado was an astute strategy of indigenous resistance designed to send the European gold seekers off to other, more distant lands. The Europeans were generally seduced by the idea—perhaps history's most effective piece of fake news—of a magical place of material riches somewhere beyond the horizon where the king bathed in liquid gold. A few years after the creation of

Castilla del Oro, Francisco Pizarro and his conquistadores set off from the Pacific coast and headed south. "Follow the coast until there are no trees," were the enigmatic instructions from the native Central Americans. So it would be with later expeditions. "Go further! Go further!" insists the indigenous guide in the Spanish director Carlos Saura's film *El Dorado*, a gripping account of the ill-fated and bloodthirsty expedition led by the psychopathic conquistador Lope de Aguirre as they descend one of the Amazon tributaries. The crew, desperate to return to Cuzco or, even better, to Seville, gaze mournfully at the guide as if pleading him to stop.

The resistance of the Ngöbe proved a brief obstacle to the pillage of Central America, despite the deaths of thousands of indigenous people as contagious diseases like measles spread through a population with few defenses. "Panama is where gold was first discovered in the Americas and where the first indigenous rebellion took place," said the Panamanian historian Julio Yao as we drank coffee in Panama City. Yao said he had survived two attempts on his life when suspected hit men linked to Petaquilla Gold tried to force his car off the winding access road that climbs up to the mine. "And a rebellion is what we need right now," he added.

* * *

Following the Pan-American Highway north through the traumatized Central American isthmus, leaving behind the volcanoes of Nicaragua, the blighted coffee plantations of Honduras, and the sadistic tattooed gangs of the Salvadorean Mara Salvatrucha, the mountains of the Sierra de San Marcos in Guatemala rise forbiddingly toward the

Mexican border. The stage of countless massacres during Ronald Reagan's counterinsurgent wars, San Marcos was now a destination for adventure and exotic tourism. There, like the two oblivious American backpackers in John Sayles's disturbing film *Men with Guns*, tourists climbed to the lost cities of the ancient Maya, ignorant of the fact that the neighboring towns scarred by past atrocities and hidden by rain clouds from the tourist gaze had emptied, depopulated except perhaps for the children, the old, and a US-educated evangelical pastor. The mass exodus to the United States had decimated the population and those that were left depended on remittances sent from the migrants. Eight out of ten families in San Marcos lived in conditions of extreme poverty. And here, stretched across the undulating landscape, was another frontier of the new El Dorado: La Marlin, an immense open-pit mine, owned by Frank Giustra's Goldcorp, which covered an area of two square miles in the high jungle close to the most vulnerable indigenous villages in San Marcos.

The arrival of Goldcorp marked the first time that the search for El Dorado reached the Guatemalan highlands. "Our history is not clear, we don't know how much time we have had," explained Raimunda López, one of the Mam (a branch of the Maya native to the area), "but we do know something: that gold has never been extracted here." Fourteen representatives of the community of San Miguel Ixtahuacán, almost all Mam, had descended from the cordillera to San Marcos, the capital of the department, to attend the presentation of a new report on the economic impact of the mine, authored by economists at Tufts University in the United States.

As in Colombia and Panama (and El Salvador, where all mining investments would soon be banned), there were protests in every village. "The mine is a virus; it is dividing the community and polluting the water," said Fredy Gonzalez, another Mam leader. Science was on his side. The report had verified the existence of dangerous levels of arsenic, cyanide, and mercury in the waters of the Tzalá River and Quivichil streams, both near the mine. This was of urgent concern because there was no running water in many municipalities of San Marcos and, according to the new report, 47 percent of the population of San Miguel Ixtahuacán drank directly from underground wells.

Marlin was the lowest-cost project of the twenty gold mines that Goldcorp managed worldwide. It extracted gold and silver worth almost $1 billion a year—one of 395 mining concessions granted in the previous year. But the mine contributed little to the development of Guatemala, and less to San Marcos. Incredibly, while other governments, in Venezuela, Ecuador, Chile, and Bolivia, had championed a new "resource nationalism," raising the royalties that mining companies paid to the state, Guatemala had lowered them from 6 percent to 1 percent. In any case, for the descendants of the Maya, no exploitation rights would compensate for the impact of the mine on the *madre tierra* or Mother Earth, nor for the plundering of the sun's excrement for purposes as vulgar as a Rolex watch. "I just want the mine to be closed," said Bonifacio Mejía, another resident of San Miguel Ixtahuacán, who, instead of the typical straw hat of the Mam, wore a Barça football cap. Soon the Mam would see their wish fulfilled. Goldcorp announced the closure of the Marlin mine in 2018, after exhausting the last of its veins. But the damage was already done and, despite the promises and a sign hung from the fence at the entrance to the mine in which Goldcorp detailed the taxes it had paid to the Guatemalan state, the communities were no better off than before.

* * *

Just across the border, in the Mexican state of Chiapas, I spoke to a campesino from the Chol people–another Mayan society related to the Mam and reputed to be one of the most combative of the Mesoamerican nations. We were both in a minivan packed with locals driving along the potholed road from Palenque to Ocosingo, the latter one of the towns occupied by the Zapatistas in the 1994 insurrection. I had taken a detour to visit the spectacular ruins of Palenque, the magnificent Mayan metropolis hidden for centuries in the midst of the southern Mexican rain forest and now inundated with tourists. A cacophony of whistles mimicked the roar of jaguars, the sacred animal of the Maya, during my stroll around the ruins. Sold in the souvenir stalls that dotted the site, they were the perfect holiday gift for children bored by the visit, though, in my case, the unrelenting background noise of a faux jungle had brought me closer to an understanding of the ancient Mayan ritual in which children were offered to the gods at the top of the great temple of the jaguar.

My traveling companion as we left Palenque came from the Guatemalan border area, where he had visited his family: members of a group of Central American migrants trapped at the frontier. He explained how the economic crisis had further undermined the Chiapanec subsistence economy and how the coyotes (middle men) bought corn and coffee from them at ever-lower prices with no opportunity to negotiate a better deal.

Many Chol and Tzotzil in Chiapas were forced to work cutting coffee for 180 pesos (nine dollars) a day in the plantations below, close to Tapachula. Evidence of their existential crisis were the countless topes or speed-barriers made of tarmac or dried mud and laid across the road every five or six hundred yards to force the vehicles to stop and so create an opportunity to sell passengers a bottle of Coca-Cola or a tamale. It was an essential source of income in one of the poorest regions of Mexico. Sometimes, if there was no barrier, the children held a rope with colored flags across the road. Anything to interrupt the tourists who would otherwise drive on to Ocosingo or San Cristóbal de las Casas without realizing that the Maya were still alive and present in Chiapas and not just sculpted in stone, although they no longer built pyramids with inner sanctums filled with gold.

We had made painfully slow progress along the dirt road and after an hour of silence, the Chol passenger asked me an unexpected question: "Are there many museums in Spain?" "Well, yes . . . there is the Prado, it has paintings by Velázquez, Goya, you know," I replied. But I realized immediately that this was not what he meant. So, I took out the booklet from the aforementioned Museum of the Americas in Madrid, which I was carrying in my backpack and showed him a photograph of one of the figures of the Quimbaya collection, a seated cacique cast in a delicate silver-colored gold. We leafed through to a page illustrated with a ceramic sculpture of a woman and a child, from the Totonac culture of Veracruz, and then to the reproduction of the *aconchado* painting *La conquista de México*, in which Cortés, in his steel suit of armor, rides a white horse while in the background the "idols" of the infidel Indians are burned on a huge bonfire (except, of course, those made of gold, which would be melted down later into gold bars and shipped to Seville). My Chol friend studied the book with interest as the minivan passed an EZLN sign adorned with Emiliano Zapata's famous slogan: THE LAND FOR THOSE WHO WORK IT. Then he asked me another surprising question: "Who works in the fields in Spain?" After thinking for a moment, I told him mainly immigrants: Moroccans, sub-Saharan Africans, or day laborers from Eastern Europe, Bulgaria, Romania . . . "Aaaah! So, the Spaniards' pillage paid off, then!" he mused, and a broad smile spread across his hitherto melancholy features.

* * *

Unlike Oscar Guardiola-Rivera, who had gone south in the footsteps of Pizarro to the beat of "The Passenger," I sought out the new El Dorado in the north. Specifically in the desert of Utah. The desperate extraction of the gold *bare-queros* in Antioquia and the struggle of indigenous peasants against the megamines in Panama and Guatemala seemed light-years away from Roof, an anodyne restaurant on the top floor of the iconic tower of the Mormon prophet Joseph Smith of Salt Lake City. It boasted spectacular views of the Church of Latter-day Saints, a temple clad in marble with a statue of the angel Moroni on top, finished in the best Latin American gold. Beards were expressly forbidden, rum too. Yet those Mormons, in their own way, were just as obsessive gold seekers as Hernán Cortés or Long John Silver.

I had been invited to the dinner by the economist Larry Hilton, author of a new law passed in the Congress of Utah a few months earlier that instated gold and silver as an alternative currency to the dollar in the Mormon state. The Republican congressman Brad Galvez and David Garrett, a fund manager for Salt Lake City, attended the Angus steak dinner, organized with not a drop of alcohol to lubricate the soft flesh of industrial slaughterhouses, to celebrate the decision to anchor the value of money in that golden excrement. All were staunch defenders of the return to the gold standard and of "solid money" to counter the "inflationary" monetary expansion carried out by the Federal Reserve. "We are already seeing the first signs of inflation that will destroy the economy," said Hilton, while the other Mormons, now aware of my origins in Liverpool, engaged in a long conversation about their family trees on the Isle of Man. Five years later, inflation was still conspicuous by its absence. But the fear of uncertainty, monetized debt, and devalued assets was deeply implanted in the Mormon DNA.

These Republican Mormons were part of a new conservative movement in the United States, one which accused Treasury Secretary Janet Yellen, then president of the Federal Reserve, of being a disciple of the demonic John Maynard Keynes (which indeed she was). The conservative goldbugs defended restricting the supply of money by restoring that irrevocable link with gold reserves that, until it was abandoned in the 1930s, had sunk the world in depression and deflation. But for the Mormon Republicans in the Roof restaurant, only a new gold standard could stop the immoral expansion of money and save virtuous US savers from hyperinflation and ruin. The libertarian Ron Paul, neocon Michele Bachmann, and other self-appointed leaders of the Tea Party movement also backed the readoption of the gold standard. The campaign Gold Standard 2012, sponsored by the American Principles Project, lobbied too for the return to those solid times when paper money was convertible into gold. Glenn Beck, a born-again Mormon whose TV show at its height broke viewership records at Fox News thanks to crazed monologues and conspiracy theories about the United Nations, never missed an opportunity to recommend the purchase of a few bars or urge the government to return to the security of the gold standard.

The goldbugs were in right at the beginning of the conservative renaissance that would help Trump reach the

White House in 2016, despite the president's total lack of concern for Freudian solidity or monetary discipline. The situation evoked the epic battle at the beginning of the twentieth century between conservative defenders of the gold standard and progressives who called for the broader silver standard, a clash which inspired the allegoric message of the eternally retransmitted movie *The Wizard of Oz*. "Follow the yellow brick road," sings Dorothy (Judy Garland), personifying the brave American nation that then demanded the widening of the monetary base to escape from permanent wage cuts. In a hypothetical remake, Trump–who called the gold standard "fantastic" in his election campaign only to later lambast the Fed for being too restrictive and hurting the stock markets–might play the hapless scarecrow singing "If I only had a brain."

Gold had played a key role in the real or mythical birth of Mormonism, the fastest-growing and most lucrative Christian global franchise. The golden glow of the sculptures of the angel Moroni, the favorite angel of Latter-day Saints, was proof of the power of El Dorado even to the good Christians of Utah. Joseph Smith, the founder of Mormonism in the early nineteenth century, was a die-hard goldbug. According to the sacred texts of Smith, resident of the village of Palmyra in the state of New York, the angel Moroni appeared in 1823 and ordered him to consult a series of gold tablets hidden in a cave that would relate the history of the lost tribes of Israel in the New World. Thanks to this advice, Smith extrapolated that the Garden of Eden was in fact located in the Utah desert, on the outskirts of what is now Salt Lake City. "Joseph had the poor man's awe of gold, and it crept into his concept of heaven," explains his biographer Fawn Brodie in *No Man Knows My History*.

But it was no longer just the poor and ignorant in Utah who fetishized the yellow metal. My fellow diners at the Roof restaurant were all professionals, equipped with master's degrees from eminent business schools and homes on the opulent outskirts of the city. Yet they believed in the yellow metal with the same Christian fervor as Joseph Smith or Christopher Columbus. "When I was defending the new gold law in Congress, I really felt that the Lord was guiding me," Congressman Galvez confessed excitedly during dinner.

* * *

Mormons were the goldbugs of the Christian God. But six hours from Salt Lake City, where the route of the new El Dorado ends in the desert of the western United States, no less God-fearing towns were now victims of the twenty-first-century gold rush, just as they were in Latin America. A century and a half after its bonanza, Virginia City in Nevada had become a themed tourist destination dedicated to the 1850 and '60s, when the discovery of huge deposits of silver and gold unleashed a gold rush in the area. Herds of tourists roamed the main street between posters saying WELCOME TO SILVER CITY or THERE'S GOLD IN THEM THAR HILLS and bought souvenirs at the Gold Strike store. The casino's slot machines were arranged around the so-called Suicide Table where nineteenth-century miners lost their winnings in poker games and then shot themselves in the head. Further up in Millionaire's Row, two or three of the mansions that had housed the millionaires of the silver fever remained, the so-called kings of the bonanza, such as John Mackay and James Flood. But in the wake of the 2008 financial crisis and with gold and silver prices soaring to records, the past had returned to Virginia City as a joke in very bad taste.

With deposits of up to nine hundred thousand ounces of gold (worth more than $1 billion, at market prices), Comstock Mining Inc., owned by California financier John Winfield, intended to start a mining operation in Gold Hill, less than a mile from the hotels, museums, and lounge bar on the main avenue. The old Lucerne and Billy the Kid mines had been reopened, creating an imminent danger, just as in Coclesito in Panama or San Miguel Ixtahuacán in Guatemala, of mercury contamination. Although in the case of Virginia City the fear was that the new mine would unearth mercury used in the first silver and gold rush that had been safely buried underground for 150 years. This was not the only example of a gold rush in the western desert. The Canadian multinational Barrick Gold had opened two new mines near its operations in Cortez Hill, in the desert halfway between Reno and Salt Lake City. The mine would be excavated at Mount Tenabo, a sacred mountain of the Shoshone who had already been victims of atomic tests conducted in the Nevada desert in the 1940s and '50s.

Could it be that the open veins of center-periphery dependence were hemorrhaging wealth too from the desert state of Nevada straight into the pockets of an L.A.-based billionaire? That indeed would be a revolutionary idea. Like the people of Colombia, Panama, and Guatemala, the Shoshone and the townsfolk of Virginia City were preparing a battle with the mining companies. "Mining belongs to the past, so we are not going to sit idly by," said Tammy Davis, a member of the Comstock Residents Association who worked at a small themed hotel in town. Tammy was a sort of Erin Brockovich, an unlikely anti-mine activist but now a key figure in the protest. No one in the desert of the American

West–just as in the cordilleras of Latin America–wished to witness so closely the reenactment of those scenes of gold and silver frenzy that Mark Twain, star reporter for the Virginia City daily *Territorial Enterprise* in the 1850s, had called "a factory of slaughter, mutilation and general destruction."

CHAPTER FIVE

Diamonds and Emeralds (Diamantina, Brazil) The Other Side of Paradise

Brazil must surely have left behind those miserable times when desperate men panned in Amazonian rivers in search of gold. So it seemed, at least, during that decade of bonanza in the international commodity markets as Lula and the Workers' Party hauled thirty million people out of poverty. But the past had returned with a vengeance as the deepest recession in history skewered the Lulaist project after a decade of unchallenged power. Unemployment had doubled in a year and fifteen million Brazilians slid back into extreme poverty with income of less than fifty dollars a month. Perhaps that could explain why the *garimpeiro* had returned to the national narrative, reincarnated as the tragic hero who sought fortune in the wilds of the Brazilian interior, or as a violator of nature and indigenous rights.

The Other Side of Paradise, a soap series (*novela* for the Brazilians) with more than sixty million viewers, told a story of *garimpeiros* that was right for the times. Like all Latin American telenovelas, it became compulsory viewing every night at nine o'clock across the huge country, from Rio's favelas to remote villages in the Amazon. Even soccer games between Flamengo and Vasco da Gama at the Maracanã Stadium, now revamped for the 2014 World Cup, had to wait. Of course, each baroque script was written by hipster-styled urban dwellers in Jardim Botânico, a plush district of Rio's South Zone, where the all-powerful media group Rede Globo produced the world's most addictive soap.

Here is a telegraphic summary of the 172 episodes of *The Other Side of Paradise*. Its setting is Tocantins, in the distant north of Brazil, a landscape of dense tropical forests, magnificent rocky plateaus, cascades of sparkling water, and dazzlingly white sand dunes, populated by jaguars and toucans. A gang of *garimpeiros* dig for their fortune in a *latifundio* near a town called Paradise, which God has blessed with valuable emerald deposits. Unaware of their fate, they are being used by an unscrupulous businesswoman and dealer in precious stones. Her accomplice is an even less scrupulous judge who operates in the murky world of international jewel smuggling.

Clara, a beautiful but naive local who has inherited land from her father, incomprehensibly decides to marry the son of the sinister trafficker of precious stones. Soon she will suffer an ordeal of abuse, jealousy, and psychological torture at the hands of husband and mother-in-law alike, both set on seizing her emeralds. As we approach episode 96, Clara is certified insane and interned in a psychiatric institution on the outskirts of Rio. There she meets a kind elderly woman with only mild dementia who teaches her the high society manners of Rio's *zona sur* and even to speak French. After her friend sadly passes, Clara manages to escape from the asylum by hiding inside her coffin.

There is a happy ending. Clara's mother-in-law faces a rebellion by the *garimpeiros* and Clara, after separating from her husband, manages to regain control over the emeralds while falling in love with the doctor who has helped her escape from the asylum.

The reader will have gathered by now that *The Other Side of Paradise* is not exactly a work of Brazilian social realism. Yet in many ways, Rede Globo's melodramatic soap operas were actually more reliable windows onto reality than the Jornal Nacional news bulletin broadcast straight after the *novela*, which had engineered the downfall of Lula in a blitz of questionable accusations and partially fabricated misdemeanors. The *novela*'s *garimpeiros* did at least bear some resemblance to real life.

So I was not surprised to encounter late in 2018, just as the soap opera reached episode 104 or 105, a hundred or so *garimpeiros* immersed up to their waists in the thick mud of an illegal mine on the Jequitinhonha River, an hour from Diamantina, the capital of the eighteenth-century diamond rush in Minas Gerais. Not far from there, the slave Madi Magassa discovered in 1853 the mythical Estrela do Sul–the Star of the South, one of the largest diamonds in the world–and was rewarded with her freedom. It was a fleeting moment of justice for an Afro-Brazilian. After all, as José de Resende Costa describes in his *Historic Memoir of the Diamond*, a notorious decree of 1732 in Minas Gerais determined that all "black men, black women, and brown people be expelled from the region [of Diamantina] since it was the only way to prevent the theft of diamonds." Of course, the problem for the Portuguese then, as it would be for the Brazilian elites for centuries to come, was that without those "black men, black women, and brown people" there would be no *garimpeiros* to unearth the diamonds that would make the rich richer.

The twenty-first-century *garimpeiros* used electric pumps to separate the water from the crushed rock, but in their own way they were slaves too: slaves of fortune. "The *garimpeiro* is an adventurer. There are months you make and months you don't, but finding a job is very difficult in Diamantina," explained Jeremías Martins, forty-six, with a melancholy stare, after removing a tiny crystal from the pan. Just like those gold *barequeros* in the Colombian Antioquia, he would sell it in Diamantina for about ten reais (three dollars and thirty cents), not enough even for the five-hour bus ride to go see his son in Belo Horizonte.

The *garimpeiros*, who lived in a camp next to the mine and returned home once every fortnight, earned between one thousand and two thousand reais ($66 to $330) per month. "If you discount food and fuel, there are many here who end up with nothing," explained João Espiritu Santo, a retired *garimpeiro* with a soft Afro-Brazilian chuckle that suggested nothing in Diamantina made sense. "Everything here is legal and everything is illegal," he added. Another *garimpeiro*, wiry with a three-day beard and a blank gaze, was sitting in front of a shack on top of a mound of rubble. "*Muito*, much, very *mucho* diamond!" he babbled in a cocktail of languages. "Twenty-five million, gold and *diamante*, powerful big *maquinas*. Gutierrez will control tons of diamonds, *muito robo* in Brasil!" he continued, now on the brow of the mud hill, pointing to a meander in the sullied river where the Belo Horizonte–based construction corporation, Andrade Gutierrez, a big player in Brazil's World Cup and Olympic projects, had installed its Caterpillar excavators. There the *garimpeiros* could not wade.

The strange irony of volunteering as a slave to chance while the powerful lined their pockets brought to mind the great Brazilian journalist Euclides da Cunha and his engrossing accounts of *seringueiro* rubber-tappers who migrated to the Amazon from the impoverished northeast of Brazil in the late nineteenth century. The rubber barons had made fabulous fortunes and built pseudo–Belle Époque palaces in

Belém on the Amazon delta and the Manaus opera house nine hundred miles upriver, still standing in the midst of the anarchic jungle metropolis. But the *seringueiro* rubber-tappers trudged through the forest in circles in a daily nightmare "that not even the Siberian tales of Dostoevsky could match," writes da Cunha. They were "men tied to the same route in the jungle, leaving each day from the same place during their entire life." This even though their travel expenses and the cost of their tools exceeded any income they could ever conceivably earn. "They are men who work to enslave themselves," he concludes in "Entre os seringais," his inspired essay on the colonization of Amazonia by poor migrants from the east. History's losers, heroes only in da Cunha's eyes.

For the twenty-first-century *garimpeiros* whom I met in in Diamantina, it was as if delivering themselves into slavery in the hope, no matter how remote, of finding the coveted gem was less painful than a conventional labor relationship. It was better than selling their labor in the new era of wage misery and worker submission at the twilight of the Lula years. Only chance could emancipate Brazil's excluded masses now that the Workers' Party's state-driven redistribution had given way to the militarized neoliberalism of Jair Bolsonaro.

Yet the *garimpeiro* had also become the idealized subject of the new Bolsonarista right: the little guy, *homem do povo*, who risked all to feed his family defying the environmental restrictions of the federal state with its "fines industry," as Bolsonaro called it, and its foreign NGOs concerned only with rivers, trees, and Indians. After all, Bolsonaro boasted that as a child he had learned the art of panning for gold and diamonds in the rivers of rural São Paulo where he was brought up. His father, Percy Bolsonaro, had been a *garimpeiro* in the anarchic gold rush at Serra Pelada in

Amazonia in the 1980s, immortalized in Sebastião Salgado's breathtaking black-and-white photos.

History was repeated in the Amazonian state of Rondônia, where the territory of the Cinta Larga in the Roosevelt Indigenous Reserve was said to contain the largest diamond deposit in the world. Hordes of *garimpeiros* armed to the teeth had sown terror in the indigenous community since the first contact twenty years earlier, followed by in a bloodbath in which 3,500 Cinta Larga were murdered. The massacre would not go unanswered. In 2003, twenty-nine *garimpeiros* were killed by indigenous warriors. When Bolsonaro became president, the mass of *garimpeiros* returned to the Amazon as the new president actively encouraged the miners to enter the indigenous territories he considered obstacles to development. A few months after the inauguration of the new government, police in Rondônia seized five hundred diamonds that had been illegally extracted from the Cinta Larga reserve.

The extraction of these diamonds–highly valued for their form, size, purity, and color–was illegal. But the buyers, mainly European and American, landed in monoplanes at clandestine jungle airstrips to clinch the deal and transport them to global luxury markets. At the other extreme of the international diamond business were the big global traders who sold the stones for thousands of dollars in Antwerp or elsewhere on the black market. Many diamonds would be cut and polished in Surat, India, where cheap labor was the next link in the global chain of hyper-exploitation. To get some idea of a diamond's market value in the age of conspicuous consumption and the new global plutocracy, a twin-stone ring–with two blue-toned diamonds–designed by Graff and auctioned by Christie's in December 2017 was sold for $12.5 million.

For the Brazilian kleptocracy, however, the primary use of diamonds was to launder money, both for personal enrichment and for the financing of Brazil's numerous political parties, where ideology was always second to bribery. According to the judges of the Lava Jato anti-corruption probe investigating a network of kickbacks centered on the state oil company Petrobras, a group of politicians had laundered money in jewelry purchases for at least thirteen million reais (more than $3 million). While the economy of the Olympic city collapsed after the closing ceremony in 2016, the former governor of Rio de Janeiro, Sérgio Cabral, and his wife bought 221 jewels–diamonds, rubies, emeralds, and tourmaline from Paraíba–at the multinational jewelry store H.Stern in Rio's upmarket *zona sul*. All without receipts. They were used to launder million-dollar bribes from construction companies such as Odebrecht (the prime culprit in the Lava Jato scandal), OAS, and that very same Andrade Gutierrez whose Caterpillers I had seen excavating the bed of the Jequitinhonha River. All were granted lucrative public contracts to build infrastructure for megasporting events. Between 2007 and 2011, Andrade Gutierrez paid Cabral between 350,000 and 700,000 reais in monthly bribes. In his bank account in Switzerland, Cabral kept gold and diamond bars worth more than $3 million.

Cabral was already behind bars when I visited Diamantina. The issue in Minas Gerais was now whether those precious stones unearthed by the *garimpeiros* had also been used to launder money from million-dollar bribes that, according to prosecutors at the attorney general's office, had been paid to the former governor of Minas Gerais and presidential candidate, Senator Aécio Neves. In return for public works contracts and other favors, the conservative Neves had also allegedly received money from major construction companies such as Odebrecht, and, once again, Andrade Gutierrez, as well as JBS, the Brazilian meatpacking giant, now the biggest beef exporter in the world.

Reality began to imitate art as the story of Brazil's new blood diamonds surpassed for sheer intrigue and melodrama the unlikely plot of *The Other Side of Paradise*. A bribe from JBS to Aécio Neves for $2 million had apparently been laundered by the Lebanese jewel dealer Gaby Toufic, who was involved in a diamond export network worth over $1 billion, according to federal prosecutors. Neves denied the charge and argued that payment he received from JBS was in fact a loan to pay for his defense in the Lava Jato scandal. But a garbled recording in which Neves was heard arranging the delivery by the meatpacking multinational of a briefcase containing five thousand hundred-real bills seemed proof of guilt. Some episodes in the Neves diamond story would likely have been dismissed as too far-fetched even for the Rede Globo *novelas*. For example, a helicopter intercepted by the federal police hours after landing to refuel at the Neves ranch in Minas Gerais was found to be carrying 990 pounds of cocaine. The case—known as *helicoca*—was never resolved.

Neves's personal wealth doubled in three years, but the main laundering business was to finance his party, the now openly neoliberal Brazilian Social Democracy Party (PSDB), which was furiously railing against the PT for its role in the corruption scandals. Neves had allegedly laundered money with other precious stones, works of art, and real estate. But diamonds were the best laundromats. That, at least, was what I gleaned from an exchange of emails with Vivienne Santos, a Belo Horizonte–based diamond exporter who had been accused of fraud by the Minas Gerais state prosecutors.

I drove to Vivienne Santos's ranch an hour from Belo Horizonte on the road to São Paulo. "Only those who have good relations with Aécio Neves have access to the *garimpo*," she explained as we ate a homemade feijoada loaded with meat from three different species of animal, black beans, and *couve* greens. With a dark mane of hair softening a face lined by five years of legal accusations, Santos explained her conviction that Neves was the head of a vast network selling diamonds to launder drug money. The judicial authorities had just announced an inspection of Neves's bank accounts, but Santos was skeptical: "They will not find anything; Aécio has everything stored in diamonds."

Of course, she had personal reasons to accuse the former presidential candidate. She had lost most of her estate (although not the farm and horses) in a raid against illegal trafficking of diamonds two years earlier, and accused the senator of being behind the police operation. "The legal system is totally corrupt. Aécio has bought the judges," she said with a look of resigned indignation that recalled those of Clara in *The Other Side of Paradise*.

On the other side of the *fazenda*, white and brown stallions galloped across the green pastures of Minas Gerais dotted with the intense lilac of *quaresmeira* trees. It was an image of bucolic peace, but my enjoyment of it was brief. "One thing I must tell you," said Santos. "It is crucial that you consult me before publishing anything. Because Neves could kill us. He doesn't mind having people murdered."

Was this Brazilian melodrama crisscrossing from Rede Globo to real life and back again? Maybe. But there was reason to be nervous. In the crackly recording of the conversation with the JBS meatpacking executive obtained by the police, which I listened to on Santos's laptop, Neves seemed to be encouraging his interlocutors, amidst what sounded like bursts of laughter, to murder his own cousin if he did not deliver the money as arranged. Some suggested that

Neves had simply stressed the reliability of Cousin Freddy, who would "have to be murdered before he squeals." But Santos didn't agree.

All of this was more than just a real-life *novela*. After all, Neves–grandson of the former president Tancredo Neves–and his colleagues in the leadership of the supposedly respectable and conservative PSDB had supported the impeachment of Dilma Rousseff and the prosecution of Lula for allegedly participating in the network of bribes, money laundering, and illegal political financing investigated by the Lava Jato prosecutors. When Neves lost the 2014 presidential elections in a second-round contest with Dilma, he and his party publicly accused the new president and Lula of leading "a criminal organization" responsible for "endemic corruption."

Rede Globo joined in with a full-throttled multimedia campaign denouncing a Workers' Party-run mafia that had supposedly bankrupted Brazil. Dilma was impeached in 2016 by a Congress in which the PSDB and other opposition senators declared sanctimoniously that they had voted for honesty, transparency, and freedom without specifying what crime Rousseff had committed. Months later, after a controversial trial that Lula's international lawyer Geoffrey Robertson likened to the sixteenth-century Portuguese Inquisition, the former president was handed a twelve-year prison sentence for passive corruption and money laundering. But the specific charge against Lula would have produced a yawn in the telenovela studios. He was accused of receiving a bribe in the form of a renovation to a beach resort apartment, which nobody could prove he owned. Corruption was indeed rife in Brazil and had been for decades. Yet while the Workers' Party was tried en masse, few others were prosecuted and Aécio Neves seemed impervious to all judicial investigations.

Elected as member of Congress in the 2018 elections, Neves was protected from trial by any tribunal except the Supreme Court, thanks to Brazil's system of parliamentary privilege. Many thought the PSDB had been spared by the Lava Jato judges for political reasons. A photo in which Neves was seen laughing as the judge Sergio Moro, a closet PSDB supporter, whispered in his ear, added to the suspicion that lawfare had been declared on the Brazilian left while others escaped unscathed. The Neves bribery case would be referred to the Supreme Court, and some pushed to have him tried at a lower level. But as the new Bolsonaro government took over, with Moro conveniently installed as justice minister, the diamonds kept their secret and Aécio Neves continued to walk free.

PART TWO: CONQUEST

CHAPTER SIX

Bananas (Honduras)
Banana Republic, Twenty-First Century

Iris Munguía, a union organizer at the Chiquita plantation in San Pedro Sula, recalled the day with a whiff of
nostalgia: "There was euphoria, especially on the locally
owned farms." That moment of fleeting joy in Honduras,
one of the poorest and most violent countries in the world,
occurred in late 2007 when President Manuel "Mel" Zelaya
announced a 60 percent increase in the national minimum
wage. On the Honduran-run plantations, workers earned
the state minimum of thirty-four thousand lempiras per
month (about $170) for picking bananas twelve hours a
day in temperatures of 86 degrees Fahrenheit and clouds
of toxic pesticide. The wage hike up to $270 a month was
reasonable compensation. The news was also welcomed on
the plantations run by Chiquita–better known to scholars
of the Latin American coup d'état as the United Fruit Company–although workers there had already won collective
bargaining rights and earned more than the legal minimum
thanks to the banana workers' union, COSIBAH, and years
of struggle led by union organizers like Munguía.

But at the headquarters in Tegucigalpa of the Honduran Council of Private Enterprise (COHEP), which represented both national and multinational employers, Zelaya's
announcement was met with pallid stares and knitted

brows. "Nobody should be surprised if companies leave for El Salvador or Nicaragua," warned the council president, Amílcar Bulnes. Anger had simmered in the boardrooms of the Honduran oligarchy since Zelaya decided to join Hugo Chávez's regional Bolivarian Alliance (ALBA) in support of Venezuela's audacious bid to dispute US hegemony in Central America, Washington's historic backyard.

The Tegucigalpa daily newspaper, *El Heraldo*, reported that Chiquita and Dole–the latter formerly Standard Fruit–had communicated to COHEP their displeasure at the increase in the minimum wage. "We are present in several countries of the world. If wages rise we'll go to other countries to produce. It's a question of cost, as simple as that," warned Dole's spokesman in the Honduran capital. The large fruit conglomerates had had enough problems in Honduras when the hurricanes hit the Caribbean coast at the turn of the century, most dramatically the great Hurricane Mitch, which destroyed 50 percent of the banana crop in 1998. Aware of the perils of climate change, Chiquita and Dole adapted their business model to outsource risk, abandoning their own plantations to buy directly from small producers who were not covered by collective bargaining. But, of course, no reversion to the past could entirely erase the conquests achieved since the years of the infamous banana enclaves in San Pedro Sula at the beginning of the twentieth century when Honduras became the world prototype of the "banana republic." From then on the US fruit giants would assume direct political control of regions where their plantations were located and rely on private armies backed by the US miiltary and navy to enforce their rule.

The model was established in 1910 when the Alabama fruit magnate and rival of United Fruit, Samuel Zemurray, traveled to Tegucigalpa with two American gangsters–Lee

Christmas and Guy "Machine Gun" Molony—and overthrew the Honduran president, Miguel Dávila, who had denied him concessions to banana production. The government fell without a shot being fired. "I can buy the Honduran Congress for less than a donkey," boasted Zemurray. William Sydney Porter (known more widely by his pen name, O. Henry), had already coined the term "banana republic" in his sarcastic filibuster novel *Cabbages and Kings*, which showed an intuitive understanding of the power relations of the early twentieth-century Caribbean: "The little *opera-bouffe* nations play at government and intrigue," he wrote. "Until some day a big, silent gunboat glides into the offing and warns them not to break any toys."

Once the Honduran banana republic was consolidated, the enclave economies of United and Standard Fruit "took over [the] railroads and built others, to carry the products of their own plantations exclusively, while monopolizing electric light, the mails, telegraph and telephone, and—a no less important public service—politics." So writes Galeano in the chapter "King Sugar and Other Agricultural Monarchs," his caustic account of the plantation system in *Open Veins of Latin America*, noting that United Fruit paid only one cent in taxes per bunch of bananas exported from Honduras. The enclaves of the fruit conglomerates were devolved entirely from the Honduran state and became quasi-independent jurisdictions that catered almost exclusively to the interests of the two US fruit giants.

"The banana enclaves were military police units where no one could compete with United and Standard," Beth Geglia, an anthropologist specializing in Central America at American University, explained to me when we met in a Washington bar during an International Monetary Fund annual meeting held as the commodity slump burst the Latin American bubble.

The enclave model spread throughout the region, and any government that dared to speak of sovereignty or labor rights had its days numbered. In Guatemala in 1954, the CIA organized a coup against President Jacobo Árbenz, whose only crime had been to "expropriate, with full compensation, uncultivated United Fruit Company land," notes Greg Grandin in *Empire's Workshop*. Readers of Gabriel García Márquez's *One Hundred Years of Solitude* will remember the murder of seventy-five United Fruit workers in Magdalena, Colombia, in 1928, though Márquez ratcheted up the death toll in his imaginary boomtown, Macondo.

Given this historical background, few were surprised when in the early hours of June 28, 2009, an elite squad of Honduran military broke into Zelaya's home in Tegucigalpa, abducted the president in his pajamas, and flew him to Costa Rica. Nor was the communiqué released by COHEP at odds with regional history. The toppling of Zelaya was "proof that the institutions of our democratic order work in accordance with the law," agreed the members of the council of private business.

This original reading of events would soon be accepted by US Secretary of State Hillary Clinton, who, after some hesitation and reported discrepancies with Obama's (and Biden's) White House, welcomed the new president, Roberto Micheletti, who had been chairman of the eminently privatizable state telecommunications company. For supporters of the Honduran regime change in Tegucigalpa and Washington, Zelaya had delegitimized his presidency by proposing to create a Venezuelan-style constituent assembly and modify the constitution to allow his reelection. The eight rifles aimed at Zelaya's chest had restored constitutional order. Iris Munguía and the banana plantation workers, however, preferred another term to describe events: coup d'état.

The coup against Zelaya passed into history with little controversy or ethical dilemmas raised in US or European media, where Zelaya, like Chávez, had been branded as a dictator despite being elected in 2006 with no suspicion of electoral fraud. But a fierce civil resistance to the coup soon emerged in Honduras, where a majority understood that Zelaya, despite his own ties to powerful landowners, was the best option available after a century of puppet governments beholden to the local oligarchy and the US Department of State.

Zelaya had reached an agreement with Hugo Chávez in 2008 in which Honduras would receive twenty thousand barrels of Venezuelan crude oil per day at no immediate cost as well as $30 million worth of development credits from BNDES, the Venezuelan public bank. It was the first time in history that Honduras–number two in the Latin American poverty ranking after Haiti, and the country with the highest level of inequality in Central America– had a shoulder to cry on other than that of bony Uncle Sam. "The American-led project in the region boils down to giving access to private multinationals. We have a different vision of sovereignty," said the ex-president of the ALBA bank and Venezuelan ambassador in Washington, Bernardo Álvarez, when I spoke to him during ALBA's heyday. Who could doubt that Honduras's new relationship with Venezuela was more attractive to the 60 percent of the population that toiled below the poverty line (daily income of less than three dollars and forty cents a day) than the country's historic ties to Washington, the United Fruit Company, and Guy "Machine Gun" Molony?

When I arrived in Honduras in September 2009, three months after the coup, huge protest marches flowed down the avenues in downtown San Pedro Sula. The Chiquita workers–mostly women, some smoking Fidel Castro–style cigars–joined the protest with banners that read: DOWN WITH THE GORILLAS; WE WANT MEL!–a reference to the newly installed president's gangs of armed thugs (*gorilas*). But the protests were soon repressed and order restored. Hundreds of deaths and disappearances stirred memories of past terror and sent many back to their homes in resignation.

Days after the anti-coup protests peaked in Tegucigalpa, the streets had been cleared and a barrage of armored cars stretched out in front of my hotel, the InterContinental. Only one focus of resistance remained. The National Agrarian Institute (INA) in Colonia La Alameda had been occupied by rural farmers' organizations since the day of the coup. Dozens kept guard inside, armed only with *chilinchates*, slingshots loaded with marbles. This was the weapon that the Honduran Maya had used in self-defense for centuries. "We make it from hardwood, orange, or guava. It is the weapon we use to hunt birds or to protect ourselves in the forest," said Santos Ventura Colindre, a fifty-eight-year-old campesino who wore a machete on his belt, while he stretched the rubber of the *chilinchate* to demonstrate its strength. The farmers invited me to share the *sancocho* soup they had prepared in the courtyard of the building. But outside on the streets, armored cars and soldiers armed with machine guns, many trained by US personnel, waited impatiently. That last bulwark of resistance would not last more than two weeks.

I wrote a story on the *chilinchate*, contrasting the Numantine resistance at the INA with the complacent business as usual of Tegucigalpa's Americanized middle class in a McDonald's on the other side of town. But I soon felt reservations similar perhaps to those voiced by Joan Didion from that shopping mall in San Salvador during the Dirty

Wars of the 1980s. "The dead and pieces of the dead turn up in El Salvador everywhere, every day," she wrote in her disturbing chronicle of darkness, *Salvador*. "This was a shopping center that embodied the future for which El Salvador was presumably being saved, and I wrote it down dutifully, this being the kind of 'color' I knew how to interpret; the kind of inductive irony, the detail supposed to illuminate the story . . . As I wrote it down I realized that . . . this was a story that would not be illuminated by such details, that this was a story that would perhaps not be illuminated at all, that this was perhaps even less a 'story' than a true *noche oscura*."

Once Zelaya was removed from the scene and Galeano's "monopoly of politics" was restored to power, the first blueprints of a new configuration for the twenty-first-century banana republic emerged from the ministry of economy of the new government. They had been drawn up in libertarian laboratories somewhere in the United States, adapting the old enclave economy to the requirements of twenty-first-century globalized capitalism. As the list of political prisoners lengthened and corpses piled up in the Tegucigalpa morgue, and as the persecution of environmental activists such as Berta Cáceres entered a new lethal phase, the new Honduran president, Porfirio "Pepe" Lobo, announced the creation of so-called employment and economic development zones, known simply as ZEDEs. It was the beginning of one of the most radical experiments in the transfer of national sovereignty to private foreign entities since the enclave economies of United Fruit.

The idea of creating new jurisdictions governed by committees of mostly foreign businessmen and technocrats outside the control of national governments had been incubating for years in the laboratory of the American economist and Nobel Prize laureate Paul Romer, then chief economist at the World Bank. Romer saw distinct advantages in the enclave economy. He argued that Honduras, a failed state plagued by endemic violence whose public institutions were infiltrated by organized crime, would be the right place to carry out his experiment with "model cities."

Violent crime was certainly entrenched in Honduras and other parts of Central America. The number of homicides in Honduras had reached forty-three per hundred thousand inhabitants in 2018 (for comparison, in the United States it is five per hundred thousand), while San Pedro Sula was now one of the most violent cities in the world, the hunting ground for the Mara Salvatrucha, or MS-13, gang, and several groups of narcos. Such levels of violence meant economic development was imposible, said Romer. Creating self-governed territories within the state could allow Honduras to start again from scratch. The ZEDEs could be a cordon sanitaire that would exclude criminals and violence, small oases of legitimacy in the Central American tropics made in the United States.

He proposed selecting sparsely populated parts of the country and removing them from the existing system of legislation and regulation. They would be islands of good governance, free of corruption and violence, providing an attractive environment for foreign investors. The ZEDEs would allow for the creation of development poles independent of the ten or twelve oligarchic families that had run Honduras for centuries. "The key is to give people the option of participating in the project or not. It should be an area without many inhabitants at the beginning. And at the same time, while it's important to have strong executive power, it is essential that the authorities can be democratically elected," Romer explained passionately in an interview we held in the headquarters of the World Bank in Washington, shortly before he was fired after staff rebelled against his obsessive micromanagement (he had complained about the overuse of the word "and" in their reports). In the course of our conversation, it became clear that Romer was a dreamer capable of creating the worst nightmares.

Porfirio "Pepe" Lobo's government developed a plan to create ZEDE units in dozens of areas of the country. The idea was to attract capital to projects such as the modernization of the ports of Amapala in the Pacific and Puerto Cortés, half an hour from San Pedro Sula, in the Caribbean, connected by a fast highway. "We are going to get 5 percent of the merchandise that goes through the Panama Canal," said Juan Orlando Hernández, an ally of Lobo who led the majority in Congress and did not conceal his presidential ambitions.

Other ZEDEs would be created for projects in mining, agribusiness, and tourism. Defenders of the ZEDEs saw the plan as an alternative to mass emigration from the country. "At first, I thought: Yes! Why not offer Hondurans the opportunity to stay in their country instead of emigrating, by creating a territory with rules and regulations similar to those of the United States but inside Honduras?" explained Julio Raudales, Lobo's former minister of planning, when we met in Tegucigalpa some years later. Raudales, a former student of Romer, had been a key figure in getting the ZEDE project off the ground. But soon both he and the World Bank guru would realize that building the world from scratch is never an easy proposition.

Advised by Ronald Reagan's former speechwriter Mark Klugmann, Lobo implemented a plan that was much less transparent than Romer's proposal. The managing council of the ZEDE project was made up of twenty-one people— nine of them right-wing libertarians from the United States, and only four Hondurans. The American members included Klugmann; Michael Reagan, the son of the former president; Grover Norquist, another Reaganite who had been investigated for his role in financing the Contra death squads in Nicaragua; and Newt Gingrich, Trump's ally in Congress. One of the three Europeans was Barbara Kolm, the Hayekian economist linked to the far-right Austrian Freedom Party. The California Seasteading Institute, whose libertarian fantasies included building floating islands in the Pacific where businesses could avoid paying taxes or respecting environmental and labor standards, also expressed interest in the Honduras project through its director, the son of Milton Friedman, the factotum of Pinochetist monetarism.

These would be the makers and shakers in dozens of new municipalities, some already quite heavily populated, where the Honduran Constitution, with its standard guarantees of rights of free association, free expression, and freedom of movement, would have no validity. An added attraction for the libertarian fantasists of laissez-faire cities atop floating islands and enclaves free of paperwork and corruption was, of course, that there would be no unions like COSIBAH nor workers' leaders like Munguía. Nor, of course, would there be a minimum wage in the ZEDEs.

When the Honduran Supreme Court ruled that the plan was in violation of their constitution, Hernández arranged a vote in Congress in which the four dissident judges were dismissed. He would soon succeed Lobo as president and capitalize upon the now-obedient Supreme Court not just to steamroll the ZEDE program over civil opposition but to oversee a constitutional amendment that would enable his own reelection. (Few in the international media noted the irony that the Obama administration's support for the 2009 coup had been justified by the argument that Zelaya's bid for reelection violated the Honduran constitution.)

It soon became clear that democracy was in shreds in the small Central American state and Romer, now aware that he had helped engender a Frankenstein, disowned the ZEDE project. "The Hondurans have created special zones under the control of an entity that will never be accountable to democratic control," he told me. The utopia of charter cities had turned into "something like an aristocratic club," he concluded.

In Trujillo, on the Caribbean coast, many feared that the ZEDEs would be a pretext for expelling thousands of fishermen and small farmers from the Afro-Honduran community of Garifuna who had no property titles. "Expulsions are already a reality," Félix Omar Valentín, a peasant activist, told me in 2017.

Miguel Facussé, the biofuel magnate (now deceased), had already seized the opportunity to plant palm oil–producing oil palms in the Garifuna region. Palm was the most fashionable plantation crop in the new century, which offered far greater returns than the banana and destroyed far more rain forest along on the Caribbean coast of Honduras. Throughout Honduras, environmental activists and farmers' leaders were persecuted, and others, as in the case of Berta Cáceres, who had dared to oppose a hydroproject, murdered.

The expulsions compounded an existential crisis in rural Honduras caused by climate change. It had been five years since the spring rains had arrived on time, wreaking havoc on the sowing season crucial for the survival of two million campesino farmers in Honduras, Guatemala, and El Salvador. Rising temperatures had also affected coffee growers already squeezed by falling prices in an international market rigged against producer countries. Leaf-eating

parasites had wiped out entire crops of coffee as temperatures rose and the rains failed. The poorest peasants, who
migrated during the coffee and banana harvest season to
work as day laborers on the large plantations, were left
destitute. Thousands left the land for the cities or, in many
cases, headed north across Mexico to the US border and
Trump's ever more militarized wall. This was the "border
in the Anthropocene era: young unarmed farmers with
failing harvests encountering explanding and highly privatized border regimes of surveillance, guns, and prisons,"
wrote Todd Miller in his book *Storming the Wall*, one of the
first analyses of climate change as the key driver of mass
migration from Honduras and the rest of Central America.

Miller's thesis was confirmed in the interviews that
I held with Honduran immigrants who had crossed from
Guatemala to Mexico. The immediate cause of the mass
exodus were threats of violence from of the dreaded MS-13
gangs who ran a regime of terror in Tegucigalpa and San
Pedro Sula, exacting payments even from those who earned
only a minimum wage of fifty dollars a week. But probing
deeper, it became clear that the underlying factor was the
climate crisis that had forced many of them to migrate from
less violent rural areas to the cities. "Many of us here are
farmers. There is no way to live off the land anymore," said
Jorge Ramírez, one of the five thousand immigrants, the
majority Hondurans, who had joined the migrant caravan
that set off from San Pedro Sula in the fall of 2018. He was
speaking in a makeshift refuge set up in a soccer stadium in
Mexico City, where the immigrants had stopped to rest for
forty-eight hours before continuing north to Tijuana.

The Honduran refugees fled from the Mara Salvatrucha
in the cities and from a disrupted climate in the countryside,
but most were escaping too from Hernández's increasingly

authoritarian regime. The president's election victory in March of 2017 against Zelaya's candidate, Salvador Nasralla, showed unmistakeable signs of electoral fraud. When the computer system collapsed halfway through the electoral count, Nasralla was in the lead. But when the technicians finally fixed the problem, Hernández had emerged as the winner. Neither the US administration nor Luis Almagro's Organization of American States considered the accusations of fraud serious enough to call into question Hernández's victory. For most Hondurans, it was another US-supported coup, this time courtesy of the Trump administration.

Again people took to the streets and again the riot police beat and tear-gassed them into submission. Sometimes shots were fired. As the Hernández government privatized public services, the social crisis worsened, real wages plummeted, and gang violence intensified. Denied their democratic rights, the Hondurans voted with their feet. Thousands more left to head north, less in search of the American dream than to escape the Honduran nightmare.

"After the elections, and the election fraud, many people died," said José Reyes, who was sheltering from the desert sun under a small tent with a group of friends and family in a makeshift Tijuana refugee camp. "People were treated like animals. You cannot hold a peaceful protest in Honduras because the president orders the police to fire. They don't come with batons, but with live bullets. We have a dictatorship and the Americans support it."

Reyes ran a tortilla store in San Pedro Sula, and three months earlier the Mara had killed his sixty-two-year-old father. "They would have killed me too, and my brother. We had to leave the country." As he spoke, a Mexican volunteer sang "Amor eterno" by Rocío Dúrcal–"*la misma soledad que tu sepulcro*" (the same solitude as your grave)–and the

Hondurans yelped like mariachis within the fenced shelter. They had been traveling mostly on foot for a month across the most violent terrain in Latin America, where nearly thirty thousand Central Americans had disappeared in their bid to reach the United States border. Organizations excavating unmarked graves had begun to unearth the scale of the tragedy. Reyes retold his story from the beginning: "They removed Zelaya from power because he was a friend of Hugo Chávez, because Chávez helped us, he gave us tractors for planting and harvesting, and fuel too. But then they organized the coup d'état and sold the tractors."

Under Hernández's Honduras, ties to the United States had never been so close. US border security had been outsourced to the Central American migrants' countries of orgin. The Honduran armed police wore the star-and-wing crest of the US Border Police on their uniforms and specialized in arresting immigrants before they started their odyssey to the United States.

At the same time, the degree of cooperation between the Pentagon and elite Honduran troops, trained by US experts for the war against narco drug traffickers, was unprecedented. "I am more proud of Honduras than of any other country," announced General John Kelly, former commander of Southern Command, the center of US military operations in Latin America, in March 2017 who was then serving as secretary of Homeland Security in the Trump administration. That summer at a summit held at the headquarters of the Southern Command in Miami, Hernández and Kelly agreed to provide the country with more US military support. Honduras was a new enclave economy with its military police units and 21st century versions of O. Henry's "silent gunboats" protecting the ZEDEs.

Romero was right about one thing. An "aristocracy"

had taken control of the ZEDEs. While the banana multinationals had now transferred most of their production
to other countries, the local oligarchies that controlled
the Hernández government were the very same ones that
ruled in the days of O. Henry and the Honduran banana
republic. The development zones had been designed to be
islands of good governance, but Romer and Raudales were
now acutely aware that this was not the case. The activities
that were being lined up for the new ZEDEs were precisely
those run by the old ologarchies: agribusiness, mining, or
new luxury tourism.

"The ZEDEs are now perceived by local investors as an
easy way to get capital. They are the same companies that
have captured the government," said Raudales . Nevertheless
the 21st century enclave economy looked set to proliferate.
"Honduras is the pilot case, the most radical experiment of
all, and the model is expected to spread across multiple poles
of investment in a new race to the bottom in Latin America,"
explained Geglia, who had completed her doctoral thesis on
the reappearance of the enclave economy in Honduras.

Romer's dream had become a dystopia. And as was often
the case in Latin America, the best ideas of the smartest
economists from Chicago or Washington came up against
even smarter, less scrupulous minds in the headquarters
of organized crime. According to Geglia, many now feared
that the most lucrative of all raw materials, cocaine, would
be the ideal business for the decoupled territories. There
were indications that the ZEDEs, far from being sanctu-
aries from crime and violence, were becoming "liberated
territories" for use by the narco gangs. Lending credence
to the idea, in the spring of 2020 Hernández himself was
accused by attorneys in New York of belonging to a criminal
network of drug dealers.

CHAPTER SEVEN

Potatoes (Puno, Peru)
From *Chuño* to the Potato Chip

There were few unpleasant surprises for contemporary
visitors to Machu Picchu, the lost city of the Inca. The tourists rolled in from Cuzco on a retro-themed train run by
the luxury vacation provider, Belmond, complete with an
onboard fashion show staged by waiters and ticket collectors who donned the latest baby-alpaca garments from the
Lima-based Michell Group and paraded reluctantly up and
down the carriages. The views were breathtaking (even the
carriage roof is made of glass) and tourists could admire the
"arid landscape" from a "sanctuary aesthetically inspired by
Peru." Or so said the promotional brochure locally adapted
for the multinational's Peruvian subsidiary, Belmond Hiram
Bingham, named after the American archeologist who
rediscovered the Inca ruins in 1911. Passengers could also
observe from a safe distance the picturesque Aymara street
vendors in their authentic dress and surroundings, freed of
the moral pressure to buy their corn *choclos* or empanadas.

During one stop, I crossed glances with an Aymara
through the cleansed Belmond glass, her red-cheeked face
crowned by a tiny pressed-alpaca hat so small that it covered
only the top of her head above an oily braided ponytail. She
gestured to me as if to say *"Cómpreme"* ("Buy from me" or,
"Buy me," is the ambiguous translation of the street vendor's

standard proposal), and, for a moment, recalling journeys in the distant past on slow, grime-caked state-owned railway wagons, I felt the urge to get off the train right there and order a dish of *caldo de gallina*, a hen broth with one of those tiny gray dehydrated potatoes, the *chuño*, floating in the soup. Or, at least, to have the Aymara come aboard as they once did freely and perhaps sell me a meat-stuffed potato croquette, the emblematic *papa rellena*, mouthwatering even when handled with dirt-ingrained fingers and nails.

But that was the unhygienic past of Andean tourism, before the arrival of new travel experiences that gave contactless views onto extreme poverty. Like the Olympic-era cable cars that climbed silently above the Complexo do Alemão favela in Rio de Janeiro, offering aerial views of the black kids playing *futebol* on the slum roofs. "No one can board the train at the stations for passenger security," explained the Belmond hostess while she served me a cheese sandwich with pesto sauce. "But I can assure you that all products served on the train are handmade by indigenous people."

Hermetically sealed in the glass train, the tourists could enjoy "a unique South American gastronomic experience," assured the English-language Belmond brochure. "Indulgence will be the order of the day while the train snakes through the mountains. Choose between a long brunch or a decadent dinner washed down with delicious regional wines, a perfected Peruvian cuisine." This was the à la carte Machu Picchu experience offered by Belmond, now a subsidiary of the global luxury brand LVMH Moët Hennessy Louis Vuitton, which provided gourmet experiences for the planet's most privileged travelers, including the six-star Copacabana Palace hotel in Rio. This was an extraction from the veins of Latin America that not even Eduardo Galeano could have imagined.

The visit to the ruins, the fifth wonder of the world according to an online survey of global public opinion–above the Taj Mahal and Rio's redemptive Christ–was generally by guided tour. Despite the queues, there was ample time for selfies with the Temple of the Sun as backdrop and the sheer mountain slopes carpeted to the peak with lush cloud forest beyond. These were prized images on Facebook. As I admired the ruins, I wondered if the young tourists ahead of me in the line might disconnect for a moment from their smartphone cameras and stop to reflect on the reasons for the collapse of the pre-Columbian civilizations. Overpopulation perhaps. Shortage of water. Climate change . . . But the guide would interrupt any unsuspected moment of introspection. "OK, guys, let's move on. No time to think!" The group had to be at Aguascalientes station in the chaotic hostel-crammed valley below in time for the return to Cuzco and the onboard Incan dance routine by a train guard dressed as a jaguar. Not to forget the "four-dish South American banquet" provided by Belmond: a pisco sour cocktail, the Pumahuanca trout baked in rock salt, maize from the sacred valley, kiwicha caviar, and a seafood-stuffed potato *causa*.

Belmond described itself to investors as an expert connoisseur for the creation of unforgettable worldwide experiences. But, with record temperatures on the altiplano that October, the Machu Picchu experience would soon come close to turning into a nightmare. Tourists gathered at one of the viewpoints built by the Inca to scrutinize the stars and calculate the exact day of the always imminent apocalypse noticed a dense cloud of gray smoke rising from the rain forest. The fire spread across the mountainside toward the sacred city of the Inca and a shower of gray ash fell upon the group of nervous sightseers. An evacuation was prepared. Thankfully, it was no more than a momentary scare, a striking image of smoke advancing toward the sacrificial altar of the condor. But the following day, the deputy director for environmental management and regulation for the province of Cuzco, Edwin Mansilla, warned in an interview with *La Republica* that "due to the drought, rising temperatures, and the high volume of dry brushwood" the number of hectares burnt would rise dramatically that year. During the following weeks, there were twenty fires in the province of Cuzco alone, which included Machu Picchu. The underlying causes, said Mansilla, were "climate change and El Niño."

The Tyndall Centre, a UK-based meteorological institute, ranks Peru as the third-most vulnerable country to climate change, although other Andean societies such as Ecuador and Bolivia face similar peril as temperatures rise in the altiplano. Historically, melting ice and snow from the eighteen tropical glaciers in the Peruvian Cordillera Blanca, along with the Cotacachi glacier in Ecuador and the Bolivian Chacaltaya, had provided a reliable water supply for the two million inhabitants of the Andean region. But no longer. The Cotacachi and the Chacaltaya have disappeared. The Peruvian glaciers that remain are shrinking at an alarming melt rate. Since 1975, they have lost 30 percent of their ice mass. Scientists reckon that those below sixteen thousand feet will melt by 2035. The cause is obvious. Data from the two meteorological stations in Puno on the shores of Lake Titicaca showed that temperatures in the region had risen 0.6 degrees Celsius in the five years prior to my visit, with further increases of between 1.3 and 1.8 degrees expected by 2030. This would prove a devastating existential blow for the inhabitants of the altiplano.

"For the moment, water from glacier melt has filled the lakes that supply most Andean communities," said Suyana

Huamaní from the NGO Rights, Environment, and Natural Resources in Lima "In twenty years they will be dry."

While the Hiram Bingham train meandered through the Andes, its passengers, protected in their glass capsule, enjoying the "arid landscape," the farming communities on the altiplano faced the new normal of climate change. Stretched water resources had forced them to descend from the Andean highlands, a painful decision for small farmers whose ancestors had lived for millennia amidst the Andean peaks. The potato, their staple food for time immemorial, could be more easily cultivated in the colder climes of the highlands, where there was less risk of plagues. But the dreaded "late blight"–*phytophthora infestans*–which had killed a million Irish farmers in the mid-nineteenth century was now present in the lower stretches of the Andes for the first time. Rising temperatures threatened food security, guaranteed for millennia by thousands of varieties of potatoes developed in the region as well as that dehydrated *chuño* floating in the hen broth that I had yearned for. "The *chuño* must be harvested immediately after the first frost; this enables conservation during months, even years, when other food is scarce," said Zenón Choquehuanca, coordinator for the Association of Rural Education in Puno. "If there is no frost, there is no *chuño*."

* * *

On occasion, trapped in solitary tropical hotel rooms with humming ventilators and cockroaches scuttling under the minibar, I have empathized self-indulgently with the tragic heroes of English literature in Latin America, and, especially, Mexico. But, unlike Malcolm Lowry's consul or Graham Greene's whisky priest, my vice was neither mezcal nor cognac but rather the cheese-and-onion or spicy-chili potato chip. Or the plain salt Pringles hidden in that very same minibar. Like so many others in my country of origin, I am a potato-chip addict. The British consume some six billion packets a year, more than one hundred per inhabitant. And although the United Kingdom, together with the United States, is a world leader in the per-capita chip league, the rest of the planet, and specifically Latin America, is fast closing the gap.

It all began, as is always the case, in infancy. I became hooked at ten or eleven years of age. Salt and vinegar were my heroin and roast chicken my cocaine. By twenty, I had reached a critical state in which I derived pleasure from extracting the powdered flavor from the chip in long licking motions and leaving the rest for later. Salvation came, or so I thought, when I moved to Spain at twenty-five years of age. There I learned that the potato chip made by the traditional churro donut fryers, served with white *boquerón* anchovies in olive oil, parsley, and chopped garlic and accompanied by a glass of vermouth at the outdoor cafés in Retiro Park, could in fact be a delicious *aperitivo*, a precursor to a *cocido madrileño* stew or an oven-baked sea bream. This was enjoyment of a dangerous substance that involved no compulsive licking. But the Retiro bars were later refranchised, and the locally-made La Zamarona chips replaced by those of the multinational brand Frito-Lay, subsidiary of the global giant PepsiCo, which sought to conquer the global chip market in the foamy wake of its high fructose corn syrup–laden fizzy drinks.

Frito-Lay's arrival in Retiro Park was a symbolic event. The US multinational had no interest in preserving or even profiting from Madrid's traditional *aperitivo*. The plan was to hasten Spain's tardy adaptation to a neurotic habit that had transformed food consumption in the United Kingdom and the United States: snacking.

"Snacking means eating anywhere at any time; eating mechanically, without thinking, without enjoyment," explained Michael Moss, the Pulitzer Prize–winning food columnist from *The New York Times* whose bestseller *Salt Sugar Fat: How the Food Giants Hooked Us* had just been published in Spanish. The book was a damning exposé of the role of junk-food multinationals in the epidemic of obesity that was spreading like a virus across the world. "Snacking has replaced meals in the United States, and the Big Food multinationals are now in the process of exporting the model worldwide. Warn your readers in Spain."

For megacorporations like PepsiCo, driven by its share-holders to a ceaseless expansion of sales and profits, the key to snacking was to create addiction. Frito-Lay's catchy advertising slogan said it all: "Betcha can't eat just one." The corporate goal was to get the world hooked ASAP. Addiction, a guarantee of permanently rising sales, was of great interest to Wall Street. "Stock markets want products that seduce consumers and those are the ones that contain fat, salt, and sugar," said Moss. Having lost market share to Coca Cola and seen its share price stagnate, PepsiCo depended increasingly on the introduction of Frito-Lay potato chips in every country in the world.

How could a simple potato chip meet Wall Street's requirements for hyperaddiction? The answer could be found in the Frito-Lay laboratory in Dallas, where a hundred or so chemical engineers, psychologists, and marketing experts with an annual budget of around $30 million experimented with diverse blends of salt and fat in search of the most pleasure-inducing formula to mix with the natural sugar contained in the potato's starch. The lab's scientific jargon labeled every sensation. The mouthwatering moment in which the salt-laden chip triggered the salivary glands was known as the saliva burst. The exquisite sensation of fat melting onto the tongue was the mouth effect. While the potato starch was not sweet to the taste, the glucose high set off a second wave of hunger attacks, the perfect guarantee of "Betcha can't eat just one." In neuralgic experiments, a glucose high lit up the brain's encephalogram as brightly as a line of cocaine.

At the Dallas laboratories the range of addictive flavors would widen and diversify like a Pablo Escobar business plan. Mesquite BBQ, dill pickle, cheddar cheese and cream, jalapeño chili. In a patriotic response to the new America of Donald Trump, Frito-Lay launched its "ten flavors for America" range, which included spicy crab (Washington and Chesapeake Bay), chili with cheese (Southern California) and fried pickles (Midwest). In the United Kingdom, the latest flavors included barbecue spare ribs, steak and onion, and stuffed turkey. Latin America's more innocent taste buds were tempted by fried chicken, barbecue, chile and lime, and, in Brazil, by the *peito de peru* (turkey breast), which at least was a native species. Meanwhile, the chemical structure of the salt used in the manufacture of the potato chip was modified into a fine powder so that it could be more rapidly absorbed onto the tongue. This would optimize addiction and, at the same time, unleash an insatiable thirst, the perfect business complement for the PepsiCo fizzy drinks range. It was a world-beating synergy to be emphasized in video conferences with investors.

The global potato chip, in truth, was a mere platform, a tool for injecting the Dallas flavors into the open veins of new markets. Soon after my first trip to the Peruvian altiplano, I visited a ranch on the other side of the border from Dallas in the Mexican state of Nuevo Leon, surrounded by the mountains of the Sierra Madre, which supplied potatoes for Frito-Lay's operations in Mexico. There, PepsiCo controlled to the last detail the precise shape of the potatoes with which it would launch its assault on the Mexican tongue.

Being selected as Frito-Lay supplier was considered a privilege, explained the ranch owner Paco Chapa Góngora while he drove me around the Hacienda La Soledad, recently sown with the PepsiCo's patented seed. The multinational guaranteed steady demand and a stable price over the long term. "Working with PepsiCo gives us stability but we have to use a class of potato which allows no irregularity. Inspectors control everything we do," said Góngora while we ate with a group of farmworkers who had chosen to stay in Nuevo León rather than cross the militarized border three hours north to work on the Texan ranches.

Unlike commodity cereals like corn or soy, US-produced potatoes could not be exported to Mexico, nor Paco's to the United States, due to sanitary controls. But the obsessive supervision that PepsiCo exercised over the Nuevo León farm guaranteed a uniform and borderless wafer necessary to transport that intense fried-chicken flavor onto the tongues of the expanding Mexican market. Not to mention the texture. Paco was required to cultivate a potato which, once fried, would meet PepsiCo's global corporate goal to be the crunchiest of all chips. "Research has shown that the louder the sound of the crunch the more potato chips will be consumed," Moss had told me.

Indeed, I had noticed during the years I lived in Spain how the word *crujiente* (crunchy), rarely used when I arrived in Barcelona in 1984, was now ubiquitous in restaurant menus. Now in Latin America, too, menus were liberally sprinkled with the addictive epithet *crocante*.

Moss considered the potato chip the "most iconic product" in the bid by Big Food to create mass addiction, ever-expanding profits, and soaring stock prices. The strategy went global just as obesity levels exploded in the United States to around 40 percent of the population. Having undermined public health in the United States, the potato chip set out to conquer the planet with snacking as the military outpost, the Jesuit mission, or the evangelical macrotemple. And Latin America, whose vibrant Castilian provided the Spanish diminutives useful even in the United States, where young Latinos were the key demographic for junk food, became the new frontier market for crispy, salty snacks called Doritos, Fritos, and Tostitos, all made by Frito-Lay.

They advanced across a continent where obesity, diabetes, and heart disease were now endemic and would soon become the underlying conditions that would turn COVID-19 into a mass killer in Latin America. Mexico and Central America, with the highest obesity rates in the world, were the worst hit by the cross-border invasion of crispy snacks, and Mexican president Andrés Manuel López Obrador would soon announce a national emergency program to combat the effects of junk food. Across the southern border things were worse. "We only have socks for diabetics. I'm sure they'll be OK for you," said the assistant in a clothing store in Guatemala City when I lost my suitcase and had to buy essential items in the capital.

Eleven-year-olds in Mexico, Central America, Brazil, Chile, and Peru would soon be as addicted to the Frito-Lay flavors as I was. There was now no need for Spanish blunderbusses nor US marines, measles, or alcohol to persuade the natives of the need to modernize their lives. A packet of barbecue Ruffles or Cheetos would soon win over young

Peruvians once millions of advertising dollars had shown them how uninteresting a *papa relleno* or a plate of *frijoles* really was.

Frito-Lay was an expert at the marketing of corporate social responsibility. The India-born CEO Indra Nooyi, hired at the start of the global expansion to preempt the accusations that would inevitably follow, became a master of greenwashing and socially aware cosmetics. Her successor, the Catalan Ramon Laguarta, maintained PepsiCo's difficult synergy. While creating a global dependency on sugar, salt, and fat, the multinational earnestly committed to playing its part in the fight against obesity, diabetes, cancer, high blood pressure, and heart disease. PepsiCo sponsored hundreds of projects in support of public health in Latin America. It even announced a campaign in partnership with the Inter-American Development Bank (IDB) called *Proyecto Cuchara* (Project Spoon) to combat child obesity in Guatemala, Mexico, Colombia, and Peru.

"At PepsiCo, we believe we have a key role to play in forming public-private partnerships designed to improve the health and nutrition of communities," said Nooyi after a meeting with the president of the IDB, the Colombian Luis Alberto Moreno.

But, according to a study undertaken by Harvard University in 2011 with the participation of twenty thousand volunteers over a twenty-year period, the potato chip was responsible for a greater increase in weight than any other kind of junk food. The consumption of fifteen potato chips per day produced a weight increase of 1.6 pounds, far more than sweet snacks. "The potato chip is the product that makes people most fat," confirmed Michael Moss in our interview. Perhaps the dramatic increase in snacking and chip consumption would explain that in 2017 in Latin

America, a region where forty-two million people still went hungry, 56 percent of the population was overweight and 23 percent obese.

Meanwhile, the 180 milligrams of sodium in one small bag of Frito-Lay chips exceeded the maximum recommended by food experts, a second health threat in a region afflicted by chronic heart disease. While the governments of countries like Mexico and Brazil passed legislation that banned salt shakers on restaurant tables, the Sabritos and Tostitos mounted up in hypermarkets like Carrefour and Walmart in strategically placed stacks where tired children could see them and tug at their mothers' skirts. The daily intake of salt in Latin America was now twice the recommended level.

Not only the health of Homo sapiens was at stake but that of the entire planet. As a core business of global Big Food, the potato chip was also one of the principal factors that explained those carbon emissions that were liquefying glaciers in the Andes. Research sponsored by the British chip-maker Walker (soon to be acquired by Frito-Lay) came to the embarrassing conclusion that one bag of British crisps weighing thirty-three and a half grams generated no less than seventy-five grams of CO_2.

That a product so unnecessary and damaging as a packet of potato chips could generate a carbon footprint twice its own size was the result of the supply chain that led from the potato to the chip. First, the pesticides and fertilizers employed to grow the potato. Then the fossil fuels used to make the chips and the nitrogen to conserve them. Next, the emissions from transport, usually trucks, that distributed the chips across their local markets. And finally billions of plastic and aluminum bags partly responsible for the catastrophic pollution of the oceans and that island of plastic in the Pacific that is bigger than Mexico.

As a victim and accomplice to the crime, I decided to delve further into the roots of my addiction and explore the distant origins of that plasticized packet of chips whose flavor exploded on the tongue. I'd seek the answer to a literally existential question: How could such a miraculous product of nature and pre-Columbian agriculture as the potato, vital for food security first on the Andean altiplano and then beyond, have been turned into an overfried wafer bursting with saturated fats and consumed obsessively across the planet?

The potato, the staple foodstuff of the Inca, was one of the four basic sources of nutrition that had supported the rise of civilizations and it seemed the most horribly abused by twentieth-century Big Food. Of course, the other foundational crops had also suffered humilation. Wheat, the essential nutrient for the ancient Egyptians, could never recover from the blow delivered by Kellogg's Shredded Wheat and Weetabix, insipid platforms for the consumption of sugar in breakfast cereal. Maize, the all-protecting god and principal source of nutrition for the original inhabitants of Mesoamerica, had sunk to depths unimaginable to even the most apocalyptic Mayan shaman when Frito-Lay began to market those crunchy Doritos and Fritos. Rice, the sine qua non of those great mandarin civilizations, lost all its greatness when Quaker invented the popped rice snack. But the most terrifying transformation of millenary culture into mass addiction, chronic illness, and fabulous multinational profits was the conversion of the potato into the chip.

I decided to visit Puno in the southern Peruvian altiplano, and meet Edilesa Olvea, an Aymara community leader who worked closely with the region's potato farmers. Olvea had organized visits to Lima that year in an attempt to connect the Aymara potato farmers with a new generation of celebrity chefs surfing the wave of the globally fashionable new Peruvian cuisine. She accompanied me on a tour of the farming communities both Quechua and Aymara. It was the week of the Candelaria festival and the potato plants were in flower. Patches of brilliant lilac, luminous under the dazzling altiplano sunlight, unfolded before the dark silhouette of the Andean peaks while the Aymara women, bent double in the collectively owned *chacra* land plots, were uprooting the first potato harvest of the year.

* * *

In the Aymara and Quechua villages around Lake Titicaca, 12,500 feet above sea level, the potato had been the key source of nutrition for tens of thousands of years. Packed with protein, carbohydrates, sugar, fiber, and vitamins, "the potato is the only one of the four foodstuffs which sustained the great civilizations that has everything necessary for life," explained Alberto Salas, director of the International Potato Center in Lima, (CIP) an agency of the United Nations Food and Agriculture Organization (FAO), during a visit to the center.

The potato had another exceptional quality. It was the only one of the big four that could survive at high altitudes amidst the clouds of Machu Picchu in the fifteenth century. Over millennia of trade and exchange, the potato had spread from the northern Andes across the Amazon to the Caribbean coast where Columbus chanced upon several varieties during one of his journeys. It was not the gold the admiral sought, but he took sacks of the tuber back with him to Spain as a second-best trophy or at least a source of sustenance for his crew during the return journey. On the way, he left dozens of species in Tenerife, laying the foundation for the delicious Canarian *patatas arrugadas* (wrinkly potatoes), a dish of tiny potatoes served in a tangy *mojo* sauce.

According to sixteenth-century documents archived in Seville, a local hospital in the Andalusian capital ordered several sacks of potatoes for patients, citing its nutritive properties. Indeed, the potato was a far more valuable gift to humanity than the gold pillaged from these very same Andean plateaus. But the inhabitants of the altiplano not only had the raw material but the science too. They had developed no fewer than four thousand varieties of potato through crop selection and a basic form of genetic engineering. They also innovated methods of conservation that guaranteed food supply in times of scarcity by dehydrating the potatoes and so creating the condensed *chuño* and another dried version of the tuber, the *tunta*. Concentrating the extraordinary properties of the potato, from the vitamin C to the protein and carbohydrates, the dehydration process became a key element in the food security of the altiplano by solving the potato's greatest weakness as a staple food: it could not be stored from one season to another.

"The potato is the Andes' gift to the world, and the *chuño* dehydration process is the invention that the Andes has given to humanity. It multiplies by ten the nutritive properties of a potato in relation with its weight," explained Salas on the campus of the CIP, where experts in nutrition from the five continents trundled back and forth from the potato fields behind the center to the laboratories. "People often talk about the silver boom of Potosí, but it would not have been possible without the *chuño* easily transported up the mountain thanks to its low weight-nutrition ratio to feed the miners."

In the street market in Juliaca farther along the lake shore from Puno, the Quechua and Aymara saleswomen laid out multicolored cloths displaying hundreds of dehydrated potatoes the size of golf balls, the *chuño* a grayish black, the *tunta* white like the vanishing Andean snowpack. Just as they had thousands of years before.

Apart from disrupting harvests and forcing the potato growers onto lower, more blight-prone areas, climate change had two permanent effects on the process of dehydration and conservation in the Andes. First, it was increasingly difficult to make *chuño* at lower altitudes. "Now you have to go up to fourteen thousand feet to get enough frost for the *chuño* and the *tunta*," explained Salas, a short man with the air of a detective. Second, higher temperatures had increased the incidence of plagues and parasites. "There is a moth that can completely wipe out the *chuño* when it is in storage. My parents kept *chuño* at ten thousand five hundred feet in Ayacucho, but in just thirty days the shed was full of moths."

In Puno, Edgar Ramírez, an Aymara community leader, explained the problem at first hand. "We harvest from May to July but if we try to keep the potatoes without treating them they rot. We use the frost to turn the potato into *chuño* or *tunta*, which last for years. But it's impossible now to be sure when the frost will come even if we use cell phones to call the meteorological service," he explained while we sat on a grassy slope surrounded by a tapestry of pink and lilac potato flowers. While he spoke, a volley of short explosions resonated through the rarefied mountain air. They were fireworks the Aymara used in an attempt to protect the potatoes from hailstorms. "The hail crushes the potato plant before the harvest. If we get prior notice of hail in the area we set off fireworks to dissolve the cloud," said Ramírez. But nothing was foreseeable anymore for the *chuño* makers. Hail fell without warning. Frost arrived too late to seal the *chuño* before dehydration. "It's much hotter here now. Sometimes it rains a lot, sometimes it doesn't rain at all. Frost comes in January or February after sowing the potato seeds, which is bad for us, but when we need to freeze the *chuño*, there's no frost," said Nélida Peralta Escobar, an Aymara mother wearing an intricately woven shawl and a wide-brimmed hat, who arrived from her daily round of the different Quechua communities on a motorbike.

The dehydration process is complex and ingenious. After the harvest, the farmers select those potatoes which are to be processed into *chuño* and *tunta*. They are left out during the night as the first frost descends, then placed in baskets and submerged in the fast-flowing rivers of the altiplano: the *chuño* for a few hours, the *tunta* for up to three weeks. In some cases, they are refrozen during a second night of frost. Finally, the skins are removed. "In the past we took the skins off by stamping on the *chuño* with our sandals; now we have the latest technology: peeling machines," said Edgar Ramírez with an ironic smile. Stored in jute sacks, the *chuño* and *tuntas* can last up to twenty years without losing their nutritive properties.

That afternoon, a dozen Aymara families enjoyed a collective lunch of boiled hen accompanied by *chuño* and *tunta*, served on a grass meadow in front of their adobe-clay homes. This was no compulsive snacking binge but rather a drawn-out social encounter, on this occasion to celebrate the first potato harvest. As well as the dehydrated *chuño* and *tunta* there were several varieties of fresh potatoes grown on the altiplano, some brightly colored—scarlet, lemon yellow, even turquoise blue. After dinner, the Aymara would take part in an open-air dance further up the mountain, where the women's traditional pollera dresses painted circles like multicolored fans that opened and closed to the cadenced rhythm of the Andean *huaiño* vigorously interpreted by a small orchestra of local Aymara musicians.

Peruvian cuisine, with ceviche leading the way, was by then de rigueur for a global class of sybarites and chefs, mostly men, such as Gastón Acurio, chef and owner of the Lima restaurant chain Astrid y Gastón. The *papa huncaina* from the Andean town of Huancayo, boiled and slathered with a sauce made of yellow chilis and cheese, and the *causa limeña*, a potato and seafood mousse, were other star dishes of Latin America's most coveted gastronomy. But the fashion had ignored the *chuño* and the *tunta*. Ceviche is generally served with *camote*, a sweet potato grown on the tropical lowlands of Peru. In Puno the tastiest dishes had not descended from the solitary peaks of the Andes. The chefs were not male celebrities but anonymous Aymara women. "We administer the family, work on the *chacra* and at home too. And we are the cooks," said Nélida, making clear that the sexual division of labor was not as egalitarian as might be expected in the Aymara and Quechua societies where private property and social class do not exist.

The dehydrated potatoes were also served in soups, sometimes after adding a green *uchi* chili sauce and the Andean herb *huacatay*, or with a sprinkling of coriander (the gift from Asia to Latin American cuisine). Sometimes the *chuños* were boiled and served au gratin with cheese. (Hernán Cornejo Velásquez recommends in his book *La cocina Aimara* (Aymara Cuisine) adding a leaf of *muña*, an Andean mint, and half a spoonful of anise.) *Tunta* was even a useful fast food for hard-pressed Aymara women short of time during a working day that started at three in the morning and ended at dusk. "We can prepare *tunta* in no time.

Chuño needs soaking for a day or more but *tunta* only needs a few minutes soaked in water," said Loyola Escobar, another family head, during the collective lunch. "When we get back from the *chacra* feeling tired we make a few small dishes of *tunta*." Each variety of potato in the Quechua collective meal, fresh or dehydrated, had a unique taste and texture.

While we spoke seated on the grass I decided to try out a question which might have interested the taste engineers at Frito-Lay's Dallas laboratories and the creative marketers of Belmond's Andean-themed train. "You are bilingual. Do you have words in Aymara to describe tastes that do not exist in Spanish?" The Aymara women exchanged glances and then spontaneously unleashed a string of adjectives impossible to translate perhaps because these tastes were unknowable to the palate of the Spanish conquistadores, the Belmond tourists, and of course, for those like myself, whose taste buds had been violated by the flavors of the flame-grilled Frito-Lay chip. "Yes. We have *quiispiña, aco, quiia, mamora* . . . They are different tastes; the taste of quinoa, of *chuño* flour."

We continued the meal of potatoes, *chuño* and *tunta* whose flavors, from bitter to sweet, would have been dismissed by PepsiCo testers and excluded from the permitted range of salty to spicy. Nor would their texture, sometimes pasty, sometimes tough, have been easily assimilated into the world of the crunchy "Betcha can't eat just one." The linguistic teams at Frito-Lay, however, would have taken note when the women described in an excited stream of Spanish diminutives how their grandfathers used to prepare wheat and quinoa dough, mixing it in sheepskin bags and roasting it into bread. Did they still bake? "Not now, we're modern," said Nélida.

So many potatoes devoured at once left our mouths dry and I imagined that a glass of *chicha morada*, the pre-Columbian maize-based beverage, would soon be served. But the Aymara no longer made chicha. To my horror, they washed the meal down with liters of fizzy drink. It was not even the old developmentalist yellow Inca Kola created in 1935, which, in any case, had been taken over by Coke. The Quechua had chosen Pepsi cola for their collective lunch. "We don't have it every day," said Loyola Escobar. "But today is a fiesta; the Pepsi cola is a *cariño* (an affectionate treat) from our authorities."

* * *

After discussing the potato's uncertain future with Nélida Peralta Escobar, Edilesa Olvea, Loyola Escobar, and Edgar Ramírez, I discovered that the formerly state-run Cuzco-to-Puno train had also been privatized and was now called the Andean Explorer and owned by LVMH, just like the Hiram Bingham service to Machu Picchu. Among other VIP fantasies and privileged nostalgia the branded train provided while it snaked through the parched altiplano was "a fiesta of the senses, the traditional Andean gastronomy creatively reimagined," per the brochure. Passengers were invited to the restaurant wagon of the vintage trains painstakingly restored to evoke times of silent Indians and European gold-and-silver seekers. There, the chef Diego Muñoz offered a "gourmet lunch, his signature version of the classic dishes of the region made with the abundant products of the Andes," which included a creative version of the *papa huancaiana*. "You can only pay for the ticket in dollars, so we can't go on that train," noted Olvea.

But not all was lost on the Peruvian altiplano. There was still reason to believe the potato might withstand the impact of climate change and perhaps even the impact of Belmond's luxury loving pillagers. The weapons of resistance would be precisely those four thousand–plus varieties of the millenarian tuber that still existed thanks to the sophisticated agricultural engineering of the pre-Columbian societies. "There are so many varieties of potato here that it's very likely we'll be able to develop seeds resistant to climate change and blights," said Alberto Salas, with the satisfied expression of a detective about to close the case. The CIP had already stored germ plasm for more than four thousand types of potato in strategically located secret seed banks. Another seventeen hundred varieties were conserved in the so-called Potato Park near Cuzco.

Disasters had already been prevented in some parts of the Andes threatened by climate change. "We went to support a community that was reluctant to use chemical pesticides and fertilizers. They had avoided the potato 'late blight' for centuries, but in 2003 it destroyed the entire crop," explained Manuel Castelo, an agricultural engineer at the CIP, as we walked through the plots behind the center. "We had a population of potatoes derived from a number of ancient strains that were resistent to the 'late blight.' So we were able not just to eliminate the blight but also quadruple the yield without pesticides or fertilizers," he said. "Climate change is a disaster but thanks to the diversity of potatoes left to us by the Andean peoples, at least it will not be a catastrophe," chimed in Salas. Other specialists at the center had developed potato varieties with added iron to combat the anemia endemic in some of the Andean communities.

I imagined a happy ending for the story of the potato. But then came a sinister twist. In addition to helping the Aymara and Quechua in the Andean altiplano to combat climate change and anemia, the center was using its expertise and the multiple varieties of potato inherited from the Inca to support the big brands of potato chips. Climate change, it turned out, had not only set nerves on edge on the indigenous councils of the altiplano but also on the boards of executives of the global snack multinationals. The Frito-Lay potato chip was in danger too. Higher temperatures would raise the sugar content of the starch in the potatoes and, at the same time, darken the color of the tuber threatening those strict requisites pertaining to size, color, and texture of the industrial potato chip.

"We are developing varieties of potato that meet the conditions of the industry," said Castelo. When I asked why a public institution should help multinational companies to combat the climate change for which they were responsible, the answer was concise: "Because they pay more to the potato growers." It turned out that Frito-Lay, which bought twenty-three thousand tons yearly from Peruvian potato farmers, was the biggest source of demand in the country and was a highly appreciated buyer for the mid-sized producers in the Andes who would otherwise have gone out of business. The multinational guaranteed reasonable prices and stable demand, just as it did for Paco Chapa Góngora's ranch in the north of Mexico.

The managing director of PepsiCo in Lima, Mirko Astudillo, explained the relationship at a conference in the Peruvian capital: "Our partners, the farmers, work the land with dedication, and in return we not only pay a fair price, we also build their technological capacity." In its never-ending mission to disguise itself as the NGO of the junk food industry, Frito-Lay had even launched a new line of chips made from some of those four thousand varieties of traditional potato, which included *illa pilpintu, puma chaqui, paq'ari-yt'ika, inkatipana,* and *kusisonq'o.*

So only PepsiCo and the barbecue-flavored undulated crispy Ruffle could save the millenary culture of the Andean potato. It was logical but perverse. Even more so when Salas added a terrifying coda for an addict like me: "The potato is an extraordinary food. The Inca knew that perfectly well. But you must include in your book something extremely important. The industry will never admit to it, but we now know with absolute certainty that the potato chip is carcinogenic."

CHAPTER EIGHT

Copper (Apurímac, Peru; Atacama Desert, Chile)
Two Press Conferences and a Revolution

It was one of those questions that journalists ask when the editor-in-chief has already told them what the headline is. "Regarding the 25% [growth] estimate that is being offered for copper which is our main commodity . . . Do you think that will be a reason for growth in our GDP and a reduction in poverty which is what we have been trying to do over these last years?" The young journalist from the Peruvian news agency Andina had been one of the first to raise his hand at the opening press conference of the International Monetary Fund (IMF) and World Bank meeting held in Lima in 2015.

This was an annual meeting with a powerful ideo-logical message. Peru, after all, was one of the IMF's best alumni. Lima had joined Santiago de Chile in the league of Andean capitals most receptive to the new Washington consensus showcased by the fund's managing director Christine Lagarde, a glamorous French lawyer who went to great lengths in Lima to assure the Latin American people that the IMF was no longer the monster that it had been in the past.

Unlike neighboring heads of state–Rafael Correa across the border in Ecuador, Evo Morales in Bolivia, the recently impeached Brazilian president Dilma Rousseff, and, of course, the late Hugo Chávez in Venezuela–successive Peruvian presidents had enthusiastically implemented Washington's liberalizing recipes. Moreover, the president of the moment, Ollanta Humala, was a useful example for the IMF of a chastened prodigal son who had returned home. Humala, a former army officer whose father, inspired by the Inca's egalitarian social structures, had founded the Marxist indigenist movement known as *etnocacerismo*, had won the 2011 presidential elections with a program of radical transformation, surfing a wave of indigenous protest that had led to pitched battles between small farmers and the police in the Peruvian Amazon. He was supported by Chávez and Morales, making Peru the next likely scenario for the ongoing Andean revolution that had already toppled Washington's allies in Ecuador and Bolivia. In his manifesto, Humala promised to embark upon a "great transformation" and take back resources such as water, land, gas, and minerals for the campesino communities. But, once settled into the presidential palace (not accidentally known as the Casa de Pizarro), he backtracked and implemented broadly the same policies as his predecessors.

At the Lima meeting, Humala was warmly received at every act and presentation, where the IMF's globetrotting technocrats were keen to try the latest gourmet ceviches and delighted to be in Peru. Lagarde had even compared the IMF's new socially sensitive adjustment programs, more subtle and less spicy than those of the first Washington consensus, to the latest dishes served at Astrid y Gastón.

"As the ministers and the governors are arriving in Peru, they are going to be totally seduced by Peruvian cuisine, as many have been. I would like to use the Peruvian cuisine analogy for what our policy recommendations are to the policymakers who are coming to Peru . . . [M]y key message

to global policymakers is that they need to apply those recipes of Peruvian cuisine, look at the best practices around,
and upgrade their policies in order to reinvigorate growth,"
Lagarde announced. Of course, by the time the IMF arrived
in Lima, Humala was suspected of involvement in shady
affairs related to that network of bribes paid by Brazilian
construction companies in return for contracted public
works that were investigated by the intrepid Brazilian Lava
Jato prosecutors under the crusading judge Sergio Moro.
Humala would soon be indicted like his predecessors. But,
to paraphrase that well-worn leitmotif of US policy in the
region, the IMF was aware that Humala might be a corrupt
Peruvian with an unpronounceable name, but at least he
was their corrupt Peruvian with an unpronounceable name.

With all this in mind, Peru's relative economic success was praised effusively at the annual meeting in successive pisco sour toasts and highlighted as an example
of the virtuous Latin America as opposed to the "populist"
Latin America under the control of left-wing governments.
Nobody in the IMF could forget that countries like Brazil
and presidents like Lula had committed the unforgivable
heresy years before of paying off all their debts to the Washington institution.

Once a technical failure was resolved in the simultaneous translation from Spanish to English, Adrienne Cheasty,
United States deputy director of the IMF team responsible
for Latin America, professor at Harvard and Johns Hopkins
Universities and a resident of Washington, DC, answered
the young reporter's question: "Oh no, absolutely . . . The
role of copper is very important." The orange metal, after
all, had been a highly valued mineral for the old economy
and so it would be for the new economy of zero emissions
of greenhouse gases.

A standard car with an internal combustion engine, like those that began to clog the streets of Lima after the arrival of the 178 ministers and central bankers, contained fifteen hundred copper cables, forty-eight pounds of a metal that filled the veins of Peruvian and Chilean Andes. An electric car, equipped to meet the challenge of climate change, would use more than sixty-six pounds of copper. So, too, a photovoltaic electricity plant would use forty times more copper than its gas-powered equivalent to generate the same amount of energy. Many now expected another global copper boom as the transition to renewables gathered pace. The IMF enthusiastically applauded Humala's latest plans to open the doors even wider to multinational mining companies (ninety-two of them Canadian). Copper was "the key input to explaining the recovery of growth to long-term potential" in Peru, Cheasty wrapped up. The other IMF experts on the panel nodded and we all jotted the answer down. Mission accomplished for the Andina news agency.

Days later I attended another much more improvised press conference, surrounded by the towering peaks of Apurímac. This was the southern Peruvian altiplano eight hours in a 4x4 from Cuzco, the legendary capital of the Inca Empire, which was, incidentally, the "must-see" destination after the meeting for many IMF participants on their way to Machu Picchu on one of those privatized LVMH luxury trains. The briefing in Apurímac with the international press–that's to say, myself–was also focused on the impact of copper production and, specifically, the enormous open-pit Las Bambas mine–a huge gray crater in the mountains, watched over by stern-faced armed guards.

The largest copper mine in Latin America would start production in early 2016, and initial excavation was well underway, to the profound concern of the local Quechua farming communities. About twenty *comunero* farmers from the Allahuan community, one of the thirty Quechua villages directly impacted by the mine, stopped the day's work building a small school next to their adobe-brick homes. Seated on the ocher-green earth, against a backdrop of sixteen-thousand-foot mountains whose lower slopes were blackened by the fires of the new era of climate change, they explained their predicament. The dress code at this press conference was not the obligatory dark-gray suit of the IMF male technocrat or the Hermès or Prada outfits in Lagarde's wardrobe. In Apurímac the panelists combined the traditional pressed alpaca-wool hat known as an *oveja* with orange construction jackets and, in one case, a Barça soccer shirt.

The briefing had more of a "micro" focus than that of the IMF. There was no mention of inputs or potential GDP growth but rather of growing fears that sulfuric acid in the mine's tailing ponds might end up in the village's underground freshwater aquifer, which was already half empty because of the drought. The questions were not as skillfully worded as that of the young reporter from the Andina agency, nor were the answers predetermined. No one would have the luxury of resorting to simultaneous translation like Adrienne Cheasty. The language was Spanish, just like the consultations with the mining company executives, despite the fact that two out of every three of the residents of Allahua spoke only Quechua. Whatever the language used by the company PR team, few could imagine what was going on behind the hermetically sealed security fence on the other side of the mountain. Only five or six years before, Apurímac had been a region with no experience of mining. Rural, indigenous, and silent, it was also Peru's most backward region according to human development indicators. Now with 61.75 percent of its territory farmed out under concession to the multinationals, it had become the new copper frontier overnight.

After the bonanza when copper prices quadrupled during the first decade of the new century came the crash. The price collapsed to half its former value in four years, as demand from China declined. It was the end of the great cycle of raw materials that had unleashed an avalanche of resource extraction in Latin America and Africa. After its New Deal-style response to the 2008 crisis and recession—an enormous public works program—China was no longer investing billions in infrastructure megaprojects linked up by millions of feet of copper cables, nor was it building new cities with five million homes, all of them with their corresponding copper piping. Despite this, Peru was placing a bigger bet than ever on mining. The Humala government planned to approve forty-two mine-expansion projects in the following decade, with nine of those projects in Apurímac. Total investment would exceed fifty billion euros, explained the hostess at the Peruvian government promotion stand at the Banco de la Nación Convention Center, where the IMF assembly was held.

In 1970, the year before Galeano published *Open Veins of Latin America*, the Peruvian state had granted mining concessions to over two million hectares of the country's interior. By the time the IMF arrived in 2015, the concessions, mainly to multinationals from China, the United States, and Canada, covered twenty-five million hectares. So, it was not such a surprise that the IMF backed Peru's unfailing commitment to open its own veins. After all, as Galeano caustically wrote, even before the neoliberalization of the Washington institutions the Fund had always specialized in prescribing solutions to the problems caused by its own recommendations.

The first issue to be addressed at the Andean press conference on the parched altiplano of Allahua was that of the copper separation plant, which, following the Chinese multinational MMG's blueprint, had been built at the watershed of the Challhuahuacho and Ferrobamba Rivers. Both rivers, already diminished by the disappearance of the Andean glaciers, were the life source for these communities. The Quechua farmers had resignedly accepted the mine, but on condition that the separation plant should be located in Espinar, a mining center over one hundred miles to the north.

"We have already had to come down from the mountains because the water supply has declined so much up there," lamented Félix Agüero, one of the community's youth who at twenty-nine led the resistance. "Now the mine is diverting the course of the river, and when mining begins there will be contamination," he explained in Spanish, with reassuring Quechua vowel sounds. While mining-multinational CEOs stressed the importance of copper for the low-carbon economy when they visited Apurímac, indigenous leaders responded with less encouraging data for a sustainable future. Twice as much water was needed to produce a pound of copper at the beginning of the twenty-first century than at the beginning of the twentieth. And water was increasingly scarce in the Andean highlands.

Pollution in the rivers was already a fact even before the start of mining operations. The population of Challhuahuacho, the closest town to the mine, had quadrupled to eighteen thousand inhabitants in two years, but the town still lacked effective sewage treatment. "We used to make soup out of frogs but they have disappeared, and there are far fewer trout in the river," explained another community member from Allahua. The air, already rarefied at fourteen thousand feet of altitude, with oxygen levels 40 percent lower than on the coast, had also been polluted. Dozens of trucks that brought construction material daily to the area "raise clouds of dust and we can no longer grow anything in some parts," explained a Quechua farmer from another nearby community. Once the mine was opened, 250 trucks would carry five hundred tons of copper and molybdenum concentrate daily by road to the port of Matarani in the Pacific, four hundred miles away.

Even though there was no tradition of mining in Apurímac, the Quechua knew, from the experience of other communities in southern Peru and the Central Sierra, what the legacy of Las Bambas would be. News had come from the region surrounding the La Conga open-cast gold mine near to Cajamarca, which had removed the top of an Andean peak. Only one indigenous family remained in the area. Pitched battles had been waged with the Peruvian riot police and a handful of Quechua were killed. The same occurred in the freezing central Andes.

"The *comuneros* of Cerro de Pasco have told us about the contamination there. They cried; they were totally trauma-tized that year. Now the same thing will happen here," said Daniel Quispe, the forty-nine-year-old community leader who did most of the talking during the press briefing on the mountain. In the older mines in the central Peruvian Andes, such as La Oroya, lead levels in children's blood were found to be ten times higher than the Ministry of Health's advised limit. "All the water comes down from the mine into our communities."

Private ownership of land was unheard of in these Quechua *comunero* communities. For that reason perhaps, the mining company had persuaded the Quechua leaders to sell part of their communities' millennial territory for twenty cents a hectare. Not a lot. The previous year, an MMG-led Chinese consortium had bought Las Bambas for more than $6 billion from the Swiss mining giant and notorious corporate-tax evader Glencore Xstrata.

"There is an asymmetry between power and knowledge and people feel cheated," explained Henry Vásquez, organizer of the NGO Cooperacción in the town of Tambobamba, six miles from the mine. When the concession was granted in 2004, Glencore Xstrata, based in the tax haven of Zug in the Swiss Alps, paid around ten million euros into a regional development fund. But "most of the employment and business generated to date has benefited outsiders," Vásquez explained to me.

The second issue to be addressed at the impromptu press conference thirteen thousand feet above sea level was the fate of the twenty-four-year-old Berto Chahuallo, one of the four Las Bambas *comuneros* who had been shot dead by the police three weeks earlier during a protest against the Las Bambas mine.

"I was with my nephew. The bullet that killed him flew past me and I felt it like a burning nail," said Daniel Quispe without a hint of melodrama, showing me a small red scar on his chest. The death of the four protesters had shaken the foundations of the Quechua community whose consciousness was more collective than individual. "They have murdered us," said Beatriz, who sold fruit juices in the Tambobamba market. Perhaps the disproportionate violence of the police was not such a surprise. On leaving Allahua, we overtook a convoy of six or seven buses full of riot police that were heading down the highway in the direction of Cuzco. "Those buses are paid for by the mining company," Vásquez remarked.

It would be the beginning of five years of conflict over the gargantuan Las Bambas crater, a mine that would soon produce 2 percent of the world's copper and generate foreign exchange worth $2.8 billion thanks to exports, mainly to China. Out of that amount, only $85 million would be paid in royalties to the Peruvian state and a tiny amount would reach the Apurímac region to compensate the Quechua for the destruction of their mountains and rivers. But, as I could verify at the Andean press conference, the Quechua *comuneros* were tenacious protectors of their lands and the planet. They would not give up and they would not sell out. Over the subsequent years, protests were held with increasing frequency. The roads down to the Pacific were blocked and high-ranking officials and mining managers kidnapped. Many more Quechua peasants would die defending their communities against the Las Bambas mine.

Who would investigate those deaths? Had they occurred in Lima, the international media might perhaps have ventured out of the cavernous press room in the convention center with its rows of laptops and TV screens broadcasting the minister's addresses to the IMF assembly. The murder of Berto Chahuallo might have served as material for one of those fearless investigations by heroic reporters committed to defending the most vulnerable and improving the world, now all the rage on CNN. But in these distant mining regions, stalked by heavily armed semiprivate police forces, only the local reporters would have time to do the follow-up work necessary to uncover the facts behind the murders. And tenacious local reporting by anonymous journalists prepared to investigate the truth behind a Latin American mine involved significant risks.

According to the Green Blood campaign, thirteen reporters, most of them Latin Americans, had been killed since 2009 while investigating the environmental damage and violence caused by mining and other extractive activities. All of them worked for local radio, local newspapers, or barely funded online outlets unknown to the thousands of journalists in the international media circus that descended upon Lima to cover the IMF–World Bank meeting for those five days.

That April, as the men in dark suits filled the ceviche restaurants and Lagarde posed with a group of Quechua women after a quick trip to Machu Picchu on the luxury glass train from Cuzco, the Peruvian elite's tolerance was waning. When an alternative forum in Lima, organized by the Latin American indigenous movement, defended a "postextraction" model and the closure of the Las Bambas mine, Carlos Gálvez Pinillos, president of the National Society of Mining, Petroleum, and Energy, exclaimed: "Don't waste my time! Nobody in their right mind wants to put such a large investment in danger." The protesters "want an economy of self-consumption to ensure the highest level of poverty, because where there is no poverty there will be no leftists," he continued, forgetting that the Latin American pink tide had made massive strides toward eliminating poverty in the previous decade.

The media echoed these positions–even the Peruvian TV networks who sent teams to Allahua. "The newspapers do not come to find out what is happening, they just repeat what the mining companies tell them," said Rodolfo Abaco Quispe, leader of one of the rural communities of Apurímac. Of course, the support for the mines by Washington's financial institutions, not just the moral support offered in the press conferences, was enormously helpful to the Peruvian oligarchs. The World Bank, through its subsidiary, the International Financial Corporation, had invested $20 million in the Yanacocha gold mine in Cajamarca.

At the alternative Lima forum, Elmer Campos, a Quechua farmer who had participated in the protests against the La Conga mine, turned up in a wheelchair to tell his story: "The police shot me and my kidneys and lungs got infected. I will never walk again. But fighting is my destiny." Máxima Acuña, who had refused to abandon her house in the mining area, remaining alone as the Caterpillar excavators ripped the mountain away, sobbed as she denounced police intimidation the threats to her life and that of her family. "Anything can happen; they ride over our rights every day," she told me. "There are no police to protect the campesino, only the company."

The IMF economists defended the concessions with arguments from the neoliberal handbook. The eternal defense of GDP growth, now conditioned by the commitment of the new Lagarde-Washington consensus to protect the most vulnerable. But other economists doubted whether mining was the appropriate response to the social problems of Peru and Latin America. "This strategy of extracting everything possible in the shortest possible time is not sustainable. It causes socioenvironmental conflicts and is very vulnerable to changes in the price cycle," explained José Echave, former deputy minister of environmental management in the first government of Humala when we met during the alternative forum. In conflicts like Las Bambas, "the people are not against the mine per se; they just want to be consulted. We need state institutions independent of mining companies." The truth was that, despite rapid GDP growth in Peru, few presidents were ever reelected (Alan García was an exception, and he ended up shooting himself). The reason was simple: the benefits of mineral-driven growth had not reached most of the population.

The biggest irony, perhaps, was that the impatient Gálvez Pinillos was wrong even in his caricature of the Andean left only appearing to be opposed to mining in order to guarantee the votes of the poor. In fact, mining had driven the pink tide. Rafael Correa's Ecuador, after a valiant attempt to leave oil underground, had handed out drilling concessions in the Yasuní environmental reserve in the Ecuadorian jungle. Even his counterpart Evo Morales, who had changed the Bolivarian Constitution in the name of Mother Earth, had chosen natural-gas extractions, zinc, nickel, and silver mining, and, as we shall see in the following chapter, lithium, to drive GDP growth. Both faced rebellions from parts of the indigenous bases that led them to power. The difference between leftist governments and disciples of the IMF like Peru was a question of redistribution of the profits from the extraction. "In Latin America we have two classes of government, the neoliberals and the more progressive post-neoliberals. But extractivism is a common factor," said Echave, as the two summits came to an end and the riot police were deployed in the streets of Lima, just as in Apurímac a few days before.

* * *

Only four years after that triumphal IMF meeting held in Lima, Christine Lagarde's new Washington consensus had been blown into smithereens in the country most closely identified with its philosophy: Chile.

As concern grew over possible acts of sabotage, the state-run copper mining company Codelco had cancelled all visits to the gigantic Chuquicamata mine four miles from Calama, a troubled town set in the lunar landscape of the Atacama Desert. After the first explosion of protests in

Santiago triggered by an increase in the metro fare, demonstrations against Sebastián Piñera's government had cascaded throughout a country that stretched for twenty-five hundred miles within a narrow two-hundred-mile corridor between the Andes and the Pacific.

In Calama, a forlorn mining town of brothels and casinos, gangs of hoodied teenagers fought every evening with the carabinero riot police. After one pitched battle, a group of street fighters had retired to an incongruous replica of a New York diner on the main drag, where they were devouring hamburgers with ten varieties of sauce and watching heavy-metal videos. One of them was wearing a Che Guevara T-shirt, which was entirely appropriate since Che made a life-changing stop-off here in early 1952 during his Latin American odyssey on a Norton motorbike. The journey would end in the Sierra Maestra of Cuba, shoulder to shoulder with Fidel Castro.

At twenty-four, Guevara had his epiphany at a refuge near the Chuquicamata mine, then property of the US multinationals Anaconda and Kennecott. He spent a freezing desert night there in the company of two unemployed workers who were both members of the Communist party that had just been released from jail. For the young Che, a child of the then comfortable Argentine middle class, halfway through his degree in medicine, this "strange human species" metamorphosed as the night progressed into "a living symbol of the proletariat the world over," to end up by morning as a "red blaze dazzling the world." All this according to his *Motorcycle Diaries*, which was later adapted for the big screen by Walter Salles with a particularly realistic scene in Chuquicamata, maybe because, as was mentioned back in chapter 2, Salles was himself part owner of the biggest niobium mine in the world in Minas Gerais, Brazil.

Some seventy years later, the tragic coup d'état against Allende now a distant memory, along with Pinochet's neoliberal massacre, the Chileans had risen in a spectacular collective demand for change. It was as if someone, maybe the ghost of young Ernesto "Che" Guevara, had lifted the veil from the country's eyes after decades of democracy closely watched by the military. And the most subversive thing was how much Chile actually resembled Europe or the United States. After five decades of structural reforms from the neoliberal textbooks, the results had been relatively positive in terms of GDP growth and Chile had narrowed the income gap with developed countries more successfully than the rest of the region. Chile was now the Latin American country that most closely resembled peripheral Europe (in GDP per capita it was now richer than most of Eastern Europe). It was an extremely unequal society, but in the twenty-first century the chasm between the plutocratic class and a mass of poorly paid workers was no longer a peculiarity of Latin America. In conversations I held with Chileans in the streets of Santiago, the outrage at entrenched elites, monopolies, and oligopolies disguised as free competition and privatized public services echoed that of Europe. There was one difference, however. Unlike the Chileans, the Europeans had been unable to identify with clarity the true culprits of the monumental fraud that liberal democracy had become.

Here, in the toxic mining desert, another set of demands were added to those of the protesters in Santiago. "In mining areas we have what neoliberals call with their damned euphemisms 'externalities.' An externality would be, for example, that the water runs out and the little that remains is laced with arsenic," remarked Esteban Velásquez, a deputy from the Antofagasta region, while sitting in his modest apartment in the center of Calama. A strange bird in Chilean politics, who some likened to the Uruguayan José "Pepe" Mujica for his personal austerity and strong convictions, Velásquez well understood the roots of the protests in Atacama. "The philosophy of the elites in Santiago, when it comes to this region, has always been: The desert can take anything."

The smelters in Calama that produced the copper concentrate ready for export had been the most polluting in the world. The eye-stinging atmosphere in Atacama already contained dangerous levels of arsenic due to volcanic activity, but until well after Pinochet's fall there were hardly any controls over what poured out of the smelter chimneys. All of northern Chile and much of the country suffered severe water shortages. Further south, the city of Copiapó had literally run out of fresh water and the government was forced to finance the construction of a desalination plant on the coast to pump water from the sea into the arid interior.

From a viewing point on the twisting road above the ghastly open-pit mine, Calama's environmental crisis was plainly visible. Gigantic Caterpillar trucks descended the gray mounds loaded with copper ore, swaying on massive wheels that seemed larger than the miners' living quarters, with tires as hard as rock. The ore had 0.5 percent copper content, so for every hundred tons of rock extracted from the immense hole in the desert, eleven hundred pounds of copper would be recovered. The rocks were crushed using millions of gallons of water and then transported to the plants below to be transformed into a concentrate with 30 percent copper content and then exported to China. Beyond the mine, orange flames flickered in the distance and thick smoke rose in black curls from a landfill.

With climate change well advanced in the 6,500-foot-high desert, the Calama protesters understood better than most the importance of the central demand of the 2019 protests: a constituent assembly that could design a new constitution. This was because the existing Chilean Constitution, drawn up in 1980 under the cold stare of dictator Augusto Pinochet, defended the private ownership of water as a constitutional right, a generous gift from the dictatorship to mining and agribusiness both multinational and national. Furthermore, the constitution protected the inalienable right of foreign companies to obtain fat profits without paying any royalties. With those incentives it was no surprise that multinational corporations had opened twenty new mines in Chile, which now represented 70 percent of the extraction of national copper. That the Chuquicamata mine belonged to the state was not an oversight but the result of Pinochet's insistence on diverting 10 percent of its income for the benefit of the armed forces.

The mine was a good example of how nationalization, as Galeano had warned, "is not enough" if production is limited to raw minerals and only the speeches are refined. Despite those "refined" IMF reports that applauded the Chilean model, its dependence on the export of copper and other raw materials with barely any industrial transformation closed the doors to a new phase of development in Chile that could be less dependent on low wages, extreme inequality, environmental destruction, and gifts to the multinationals.

While the barricades went up on the outskirts of Calama, in the Park Hotel four hundred yards from the airport the unease of the mining executives and engineers was palpable. Thanks to twelve daily flights to Santiago, most run by the Piñera-owned air carrier Latam, they could avoid having to live in Calama. On arrival at Santiago Airport, a toll motorway run by European multinationals would take them through the San Cristóbal tunnel directly to Vitacura and other well-heeled districts in the mountains to the east of the city where they could continue to evade the unsavory reality of the failed Chilean experiment. They had avoided labor disputes because the miners' union, after decades of struggle supported by socialist leaders like Chuquicamata-born Carmen Lazo, was co-opted by the state and reluctant to join the popular rebellion against Piñera. But the mining executives understood the dangers of the uprising.

When the leaderless protest movement, coordinated through social networks, called for a national general strike, barricades of burning trash appeared on all the exit roads from Calama, and the buses that transported workers to the mines could not proceed. Only a week before, workers at the port of Antofagasta on the Pacific coast had joined the first strike. Hundreds of tons of copper were left in the rail wagons waiting to be unloaded on to huge bulk carriers that would ship them to China. The prospect of another stoppage sent blood pressures rising in the Santiago-bound flights. "There's a good reason or them to be worried," said Velásquez. "This is their moment of reckoning."

* * *

After witnessing those depressing anti-Dilma protests where half a million Neymar jersey-clad Brazilians marched down the Avenida Paulista in São Paulo, convinced that privatization and deregulation would erase the evils of the Lula years, my visit to Santiago de Chile in November 2019 was a breath of fresh air.

Tens of thousands of Chileans, most of them in their twenties but with the obvious support of their parents, rallied every evening in the Plaza de Italia in the center of the Chilean capital to express their rejection of the oligarchically monopolized free-market economy and call for a political U-turn or even Piñera's resignation.

In Chile, people understood how it felt to be the guinea pig in Latin America's most celebrated neoliberal laboratory. The economy had had its praises sung so many times in *The Wall Street Journal* that there was no need even to pay for the advertorial. At investor roundtables, the admirers of Chile who were least troubled by the nightmarish past located the origins of the Chilean miracle precisely in Pinochet's September 1973 coup. From that ominous date on, the infamous Chicago Boys, inspired by the Nobel Prize–winning economist Milton Friedman, had applied their economic shock therapy while Pinochet's infamous DINA intelligence agency discharged its own less metaphorical shocks in the torture chambers.

Friedman's address before the military junta in March 1975 would lay out the basis for years, decades, of economic torture in Latin America and beyond at the hands of the IMF, whose latest example was peripheral Europe, especially Greece. Delivered under the name "Gradualism versus Shock Treatment," the speech included the unforgettable line "there is no sense in cutting a dog's tail off by inches," a metaphor that must have pleased the gathered generals. (Forty-six years later I attended an IMF event in Riga during the euro crisis at which the Latvian finance minister repeated verbatim Friedman's advice to hack the tail from the dog, while Lagarde described the Baltic country's implementation of the fund's shock therapy as a "tour de force" with Latvia "showing the way"; wages had fallen by 30 percent, poverty had risen to 40 percent, and 10 percent of the population had migrated.)

Chile was the forerunner of the Friedman approach. It would later inspire Margaret Thatcher, Ronald Reagan, and

Boris Yeltsin, but Pinochet had premiered the new neoliberal model of shock therapy, deregulation, privatization, dismantlement of state pensions, health, and education, and generally a shrinking state (with the exception of the bloated military budget), which would soon become fashionable worldwide.

I had the opportunity of interviewing Friedman in 2002, four years before his death, when he was vacationing at his summer home in a gated community for the leisurely retired in Florida. "They did very well!" he said, in reference to Sergio de Castro and the other Chilean Chicago Boys who had studied under his tutelage at the University of Chicago. "But they didn't need a dictatorship to do it." A convenient lapse of memory, at his ninety years of age, had allowed the founding father of monetarism to ignore the fact that when he visited Santiago that March of 1975, the torture and liquidation of some forty thousand dissidents was well underway. Three thousand of them simply disappeared, often shackled to a length of steel from the old mine railways and thrown into the Pacific from a helicopter.

More politically sensitive emerging-market analysts–those aware of the ideological importance of tying economic success to liberal democracy–located the source of the Chilean miracle to the democracy that emerged in the 1990s after the 1989 referendum and the subsequent fall of Pinochet. Yet even these economists felt secretly obliged to the old dictator, now rebranded, with the help of Margaret Thatcher, as a smiling, avuncular protector of the people. The rules of the game established by the Chicago Boys had been inscribed into the 1980 constitution and handed on to the new democracy with hardly any modifications. This had protected the Chilean model from the danger of "populist" governments, said analysts from Banco Santander and Moody's, which might have undone all of those brave sacrifices made by the Chilean people.

But having Friedmanite policies written into its constitutional bedrock was not such a source of pride for those Chileans who suffered the consequences. For example, the pensions of 80 percent of retirees who earned them were worth less than the minimum wage of $400 a month. The world-famous system of capitalized pensions designed by the president's brother José Piñera during the Pinochet years had been tirelessly promoted in global road shows as the solution to the demographic time bomb. All Chileans had been forced to save 10 percent of their income, which was then invested in capital markets. But as the first generation of contributors reached retiring age, the results were, to say the least, disappointing.

Alejandro Quiroga, a secondary-school teacher with a craggy face, a long white beard, and a long mane of snowy hair, succinctly framed the problem: "My pension is not enough to live on, so I have to carry on working at ninety-two years of age." Santiago was full of aged moonlighting workers with two or three jobs. A handful of pension fund administrators, owned by global insurance companies like MetLife, managed Chilean forced savings worth no less than $250 billion. This massive pool of capital guaranteed low-cost finance for the Chilean oligarchy, from mining companies to food exporters to a business group owned by Bolsonaro's finance minister, Paulo Guedes, whose stock price soared thanks to the investments from Chilean forced savings. (No wonder Guedes campaigned hard to have a similar system adopted in Brazil.)

Banks and investment funds made spectacular profits from the system. But pensioners were impoverished. Education and health were also heavily weighted in favor of the moneyed classes, and student debt had soared and was subject to stratospheric interest rates. These were familiar issues across a world scarred by decades under the neoliberals. The difference was that the Chileans, the first laboratory rats, had sniffed out the guilty parties and now demanded their heads in the Plaza Italia soon to be re-named Plaza de la Dignidad, Dignity Square.

Few questioned that decades of robust GDP growth in Chile had delivered some advances. Copper had driven the economy during the explosion of growth that occurred in the first years of Pinochet and the Friedmanites. Growth slowed in the latter years of the dictatorship, but thanks to burgeoning prices for copper and intelligent policies designed to stabilize the impact of the volatile commodity cycle, Chile reached an average growth of 5 percent between 1990 and 2003, and 3.5 percent subsequently. It wasn't Asia, but such growth was exceptional for Latin America.

Moreover, Chilean democracy had also chalked up excellent results in poverty reduction, particularly under the socialist administrations of Michelle Bachelet. Average monthly wages had risen from $20,000 to $25,000 in a decade. But the statistical average had never told the whole story in the most unequal continent in the world. Half the Chilean workforce earned less than $600 a month. Inequality was not as extreme as in the Pinochet years, but it was the second highest in South America after Colombia. Besides, there were clear signs that income distribution was skewing even further in favor of those who dined on fusion ceviche in Vitacura while in the west of the city protesters faced off with the carabinero riot police. According to the minster for social development, the top 10 percent earned 13.6 times more than the poorest 10 percent in 2018, up from 11.9 times more in 2015 under Michelle Bachelet's center-left government.

Aware that nothing would change unless the house was rebuilt from the foundations up, the young protesters in Plaza Italia demanded a new constitution. At first Piñera flatly rejected the demands. He had announced, in reference to the violence, especially in Santiago, where groups of anarchists had destroyed nineteen metro stations, that "[he was] at war with a powerful and relentless enemy." First Lady Cecilia Morel pointed the finger at outside provocateurs whom she described as participants in an "alien foreign invasion." The presidential couple's conspiracy theories were inspired by Luis Almagro, the Uruguayan secretary general of the Organization of American States (OAS), who had accused "the Bolivarian and Cuban dictatorships . . . [of] financing, supporting, and promoting political and social conflict" at the protests in Quito and Santiago. Galeano's definition of the OAS as "the donkey who never forgets where it is fed" was still painfully relevant, and Almagro was an obedient warrior for Trump's Cold War 2.0.

Of course, the suggestion that all was a foreign-inspired communist plot was met with guffaws in the streets of Santiago, where the protests had broadened to include teachers, health workers, taxi drivers, pensioners, and users of both public transportation and private cars . . . When General Iturriaga, chief commander of the Chilean armed forces, remarked in response to Piñera's declaration of war on the demonstrators, "I am not at war with anybody," the president's error of judgment was clear. Days later, when more than a million people—in a country of nineteen million—poured onto the streets in protest of the pension fraud, it became clear Piñera would never recover his credibility.

With a plan to cut taxes for his friends in the oligarchy, Piñera had attempted to go further in the neoliberal project than any of the previous democratic governments. But it was the worst moment to do so. He furiously backpedaled on all the recently announced measures, from the fare hike in public transportation to cuts in corporate taxes. He also announced a referendum for a new constitution that would finally bury the Pinochet legacy.

But the protests continued in Santiago and the rest of Chile in city landscapes transformed by millions of graffitied slogans. *chile se despierta* (Chile is waking up) was a common slogan daubed on walls and statues. *milicos* (MILITARY) WE WILL RETURN YOUR BULLETS! read another graffiti, after the death of some thirty people and hundreds of eye injuries from close-range rubber bullets, many leaving their victims blind in one eye.

The new street artists could not compete with the avant-garde muralism of Roberto Matta and the *brigadistas* who had painted entire buildings in the Allende years. But hundreds of official statues smeared with three or four layers of multicolored paint, adorned with Mapuche flags and gas masks, looked like tributes to Chilean revolutionary pop art from the 1970s. One of the most revealing graffiti messages read: CHILE, WHERE NEOLIBERALISM WAS BORN AND WHERE IT WILL DIE. If that were true, it was not clear what would replace it. Another graffiti confessed: THERE ARE SO MANY THINGS TO CHANGE THAT FUCK KNOWS WHAT TO DEMAND HERE.

In Plaza Italia a thunderous round of pot-banging was staged every evening by thousands of protesters. But the most deafening clank of all was made by hundreds of young people who bashed a sixteen-foot-high metal barrier protecting the Telefónica tower in front of the plaza using rocks, wooden sticks, and sometimes just their fists. It was the head office of the Spanish company Movistar, which had bought the newly privatized Chilean state telephone monopoly in 1996 at a discounted price. A massive transfer of wealth occurred between the state and the Chilean oligarchy along with international investors as the cell phone boom created profits hitherto unheard of in the industry. It was the perfect example of the neoliberal method and the young Chileans had finally seen through it. They banged against the steel barrier. Some even applied kung fu techniques to amplify the noise. It was a perfect soundtrack for the crisis of what some had described twenty years before as the second Spanish *conquista*.

Other Spanish companies were also the target of the protesters, especially construction companies such as Ferrovial and Abertis, which had managed to win lucrative concessions for private toll roads under a quintessential Friedmanite model in which the bigger the gridlock the more the toll rose. It was an idea clearly inspired by neoclassical economics of supply and demand, and the invisible hand of the market, which would redistribute traffic efficiently and thus avoid traffic jams. The problem was that there were no alternative routes, so drivers in general, after paying the most expensive rush hour toll, had to resign themselves to continue mired in traffic. Whoever did not pay, in a system that offered excellent returns to the Spanish and to other European multinationals in the business of public-private partnerships, would lose their driving license.

Not that the October outbreak was a nationalist rebellion. The Chilean elite was the first target, and the Spanish multinationals followed. The truth was that, as the movement for change understood well, there was not much difference between the Chilean oligarchs and their Spanish friends. At the heart of Chilean neoliberalism was not just Friedman. Jaime Guzmán, the intermediary between the Chicago Boys and Pinochet, was an enthusiastic admirer of the Spanish dictator Francisco Franco.[9] So it was not surprising that the protesters came equipped with Mapuche flags and hawsers to pull down the statues of the conquistadores like Pedro de Valdivia, killed during the Arauco War in 1554, and Francisco de Aguirre. The Chileans were tearing down the landmarks of colonialism and racism six months before Black Lives Matter protests would spread across the United States and statues would fall across the world.

Extractivism was ever present in debates on an alternative economic agenda that emerged from the wave of protests. The broad front of the left that rejected the post-Pinochet consensus policy, managed by the Social Democrats Ricardo Lagos and Michelle Bachelet, defended alternatives to dependence on mining, the contaminated salmon farms, or the lumber industry that were denying the historical rights of the Mapuche. "There is a feeling here that we are being screwed by everyone, from pension funds to banks and large companies connected to the government, including transnational mining companies that do not pay taxes and own our water supply," said Lucio Cuenca, director of the Latin American Observatory of Environmental Conflicts, during a workshop on the rights of nature in Santiago.

Even economists less directly linked to the environmentalist movement saw that copper, which made up 80 percent of Chile's total exports during the supercycle years and generated 30 percent of tax revenues, was the economy's weakest point. "Piñera has two Achilles' heels: he does not know how to correct inequality and he does not know

---

9 Oscar Guardiola-Rivera explains the links between far-right thinkers in Spain and Chile in *Story of a Death Foretold: The Coup Against Salvador Allende, September 11, 1973* (New York: Bloomsbury Press, 2013).

how to advance from a copper-based economy through greater investments in research and development," said Stephany Griffith-Jones, a Chilean economist working with Joseph Stiglitz at Columbia University, when I interviewed her during the great Santiago rebellion.

After raising so many expectations and helping to reduce poverty from 50 percent to 10 percent, the commodity supercycle had ended. The fall in copper prices slowed down the Chilean economy and frustrated expectations that at some point the elite would finally begin to distribute the profits. Chile did not even assemble cars, since the Chicago Boys had dismantled protective tariffs that had forced exporting companies to build plants in Santiago. "Chile is the most successful democracy in Latin America, but it has three problems. A high dependence on copper, high levels of inequality, and a corrupt political system," wrote the Chilean sociologist Patricio Navia at New York University. Anyone who traveled around Chile could see that the three elements were closely interrelated.

The sad desert city of Calama was a microcosm of Chile's disenchantment. "The feeling on the street is that we are the kings of copper, but we export concentrates with no industrialization and little development. Pure extractivism. Nothing more than removing rock. It may be an exaggeration, but that's the perception. The supercycle and Calama are already half-exhausted," explained Iván Valenzuela, a former Codelco engineer who worked for a consulting company in Calama. "We had the opportunity to avoid repeating the mistakes of the past, but nothing was done."

Calama had become a perfect symbol of the new open veins of Latin America. "Here in Calama, you have the largest productive copper district in the world. There are a dozen public and private capital mines. In other words, it is a world-class area of copper mining," said Valenzuela. "But look at Calama. It is a shit of a place. How is it possible that after more than a century of extraction in the world's biggest copper mines and after a decade and a half of soaring prices, we have not been able to create a real city?"

As I drove away from the Park Hotel, a Bolivian immigrant working in the water-stressed gardens around the parking lot provided me with something similar perhaps to that moment of discovery experienced by the young Che in Chuquicamata during his conversation with the two proletarians. Wrapped up in a protective suit, perhaps because of the merciless desert sun, or perhaps because of the arsenic and lead being released as he dug, he described a general feeling that the Chilean miracle was a huge bluff: "My mother in Bolivia is poor but she receives a pension three times higher than she would here! It's incredible!" The comment helped explain not just the revolts against the failed neoliberal model in Chile but also another epic event that I was about to witness across the border. A coup d'état against Bolivian president Evo Morales, with the support of the United States and its regional ally Jair Bolsonaro, was in its initial stages at that very moment on the other side of the Atacama Desert.

CHAPTER NINE

Lithium (Potosí, Bolivia)
Coup on the Salt Flat

Before setting off for the Salar de Uyuni, an enormous salt flat in southern Bolivia, I made a two-day stop-off in Potosí, the legendary capital of the conquistadores' sixteenth-century silver rush. There, panting and breathless at thirteen thousand feet above sea level, as the twenty-something Galeano would surely not have been, I retraced the steps of the author of *Open Veins of Latin America* through a labyrinth of steep cobbled alleyways flanked by baroque churches, metaphorical ruins for the young Uruguayan, now restored with the help of Spanish development aid funds and the occasional European bank. An advertisement announced SILVER MINE TOURS in English, run by former miners guaranteeing total security against armed gangs.

I was after my own raw material: prized testimony for reportage with a quick dose of psychogeography to delve further into Galeano's method. Testimony like that of the "old Potosían lady, enveloped in a mile of alpaca shawl" who describes Potosí in *Open Veins* as "the city which has given most to the world and has the least," a quote for which I would have given an arm and a leg.

I tried to locate the heretic work of Melchor Pérez de Holguín, Latin America's indigenous El Greco in Galeano's eyes, who had painted scenes far too risqué for his Spanish masters, such as the baby Jesus suckling from one breast of his Virgin mother while her husband, José, sucked at the other. How I longed to see these paintings! But nobody in Potosí seemed to know where they were.

Behind the town, rising above the horizon, was the imposing Cerro Rico, the most potent of all Galeano's metaphors, which had changed shape and hue over the centuries as successive assaults on its silver, zinc, or tin reserves transformed the mountain's geology. When I contemplated the Cerro at dusk, its colors alternated as the sun set from iridescent purple to explosive crimson and finally faded into ashen gray as the Andean cold began to funnel through Potosí's narrow streets.

Seven million indigenous miners had died in Potosí's Cerro Rico by the end of the eighteenth century, when the Spanish removed the last trace of silver from the mountain and "even swept out the seams with brooms." After the silver frenzy, the plunder, the destruction, and the extenuation, Potosí was a "still audible 'J'accuse'" of whom the world should beg for forgiveness, says Galeano.

As the new Latin American Left emerged in the 1960s and '70s, the Cerro Rico became a powerful symbol for those theories of dependence and the curse that condemned the peripheral economies to permanent misery despite their abundant resources. But Potosí had not only been pillaged by the conquistadores. "Tourists and parishioners have emptied their churches of whatever they could carry," notes Galeano.

When *Open Veins* was published in 1971, the population of Potosí was still only a third of that of the eighteenth century, when more people lived in the city of silver than in all of Argentina. "The rich left first and then the poor," the old lady in the shawl tells Galeano in another enviable quote. When I visited, though, the outflow had reversed. After the meteoric rise in the price of metals during the twenty-first-century international-commodity supercycle, and as global warming strafed the Bolivian altiplano, the Cerro Rico reverberated once again with the metallic clanking of thousands of informal miners, mostly illegal, hacking away at the rock in search of a remnant of tin or nickel. The rural crisis caused by climate change in the Andes–drought in the southern cordilleras, floods in the north–had driven rural migrants back to the old epicenter of the new world.

"The campesinos have come to work in the mines; mining is still what makes Potosí's wheels spin," said Juan Colque, a Potosíno whose gravelly breathing was a reminder of his days in the zinc mines, as we clambered up the mountain. Suddenly the crackling of fireworks echoed across the Cerro. Two girls and their mother, all dressed in blue pollera skirts and dirty white broad-rimmed Quechua hats, scrambled down the slope to investigate why anybody would choose to visit such an inhospitable place at such a late hour. They were a family of campesinos so poor that even the impoverished miners could afford to hire them to patrol the zone under orders to set off rockets to warn of the presence of strangers like us.

Rereading Galeano during the five-hour bus journey from Potosí to Uyuni was not just a necessary distraction from the Lara Croft movies shown at deafening volume on the TV sets hung from the roof. It was also the perfect preparation for an assessment of Bolivia's Aymara president Evo Morales's plans to exploit, this time responsibly and in accordance with the rights of the *Pachamama* (Mother Earth), the largest deposits of lithium in the world that lay under the salt flat. But, just as in San Luis Potosí, the Mexican twin of the tragic Bolivian capital of silver and pillage, the question of lithium's impact on the Quechua *sumak kawsay* or "good life" would have to be temporarily put aside. A new metaphysical dilemma had burst into the story. Could anybody's "good life" coexist with the arrival each year of seventy thousand global tourists desperate to take the perfect selfie in the Salar de Uyuni to post on Instagram?

* * *

More tourists flocked yearly to the Salar de Uyuni than to Lake Titicaca three hundred miles to the north. Once the salt flat was looped into the globally marketed circuit of Machu Picchu–Cuzco, the number would increase even more. In February, at the beginning of the rainy season, almost all the tourists who arrived by SUV from the tiny airport in Uyuni were Asian. "The Asians like the rainy season and the Europeans like the dry season," said the harassed-looking receptionist at the Hotel De Sal Luna Salada, a luxury boutique hotel ($300 or $400 a night) despite being built out of huge blocks of salt.

This intriguing difference between Orient and Occident was apparently aesthetic. The Europeans chose to visit between May and September, when they could gaze upon the gigantic crust of dazzlingly white salt and lose themselves in the mirages of the sodium desert so disorienting that, on occasion, they caused rival convoys of Jeeps to crash into each other. The Asians, by contrast, preferred the rains of January and April that turned the *salar* into an enormous lake that perfectly reflected the islands of salt rising like icebergs from the shallow water. From one of these salt islands they could capture with a Huawei or an iPhone those symmetrical images of the tourist me-myself-and-I reflected in the water and easily transferred to Facebook. As the advertisements in the small airport announced over a picture of a cotton-wool cloud duplicated in a perfect replica like a psychological Rorschach test: SALAR DE UYUNI: WHERE THE BEAUTY OF THE WORLD IS REFLECTED.

Around ten in the morning, a convoy of 4x4s set off from the hotels and crossed the *salar*. They stopped at an island where the first salt-block hotel, built illegally two decades before, had been closed when the authorities discovered it had discharged fecal waste directly into the *salar*. The tourists then waded into the lake in knee-length wellington boots or Brazilian Havaianas rubber sandals and posed before the cameras. The best reflection required standing on one leg, like the fabled stork, inclining the body forward and pointing to the horizon with outstretched arm and index finger. Another option was the Buddhist tower pose, with hands pressed together over the head in the form of a pointed roof. Two Japanese women had chosen to wear bright scarlet skirts to optimize the mirror effect. Others carried bunches of multicolored balloons fashioning pictures that might have graced a Miu Miu ad in a Shanghai shopping mall. It was obvious that everything had been meticulously planned in Tokyo or Beijing before embarking on the exhausting journey, a twenty-or-so-hour flight to Lima, another two hours to Cuzco, an hour more to La Paz, and the last hour by air to Uyuni. Not forgetting the final hour-long ride on a bone-shaking salt road from the airport to the hotels. "They come in search of the biggest mirror in the world. They love to visit at sunrise or sunset or even at night, which creates the impression of being surrounded by stars, like in space," said José Luis Huayllani, our Quechua-speaking guide who, with inexhaustible patience, suggested I try the easiest posture, with two arms raised and legs apart reflected as a double X. Ten centimeters of water was the optimal depth for the photogenic reflections, whose sharpness required not only the glass-like surface but also the white bed of salt, filtered through the water and only visible at this precise depth. "With climate change it rains less and we're not reaching the ten centimeters," said Huayllani with a look of concern.

On our return to the Hotel Luna Salada ("salty moon"– words that not even Federico García Lorca would have dared to juxtapose) a Chinese couple rehearsed for the desired evening photos, the bride dressed in white and the groom too. At five o'clock they joined the second convoy, which crossed a shallow stretch of the lake to a salt jetty where the tourists waited like fishermen for the trophy of the day. When the sun began to melt into the bleached-sodium horizon, they simultaneously lifted their cameras or cell phones into the air and pressed the button. Some had chosen the "champagne package" and celebrated the moment with a glass of Veuve Clicquot. The most sought-after sunset for the global Instagram community lasted barely eight minutes. Then everybody got back into the jeeps, which, with motorized roars and a whiff of gasoline, crossed the *salar* back to other hotels, water up to the bonnets.

During the return journey, those few who chose to look out of the window rather than at their cell phone picture gallery would have noticed a torn poster on the wall of a ruined building. LITHIUM, MORE INDUSTRIALIZATION TO LIVE WELL! proclaimed the slogan with a Maoist flourish that would have been familiar to some of the older Chinese tourists. On the other side of the *salar* was the new plant, which had turned out the first prototypes for Bolivia's new industry, the production of lithium carbonate.

Set up by the Bolivian state, aided by engineers and capital from China and Germany, this was the Morales's government's most ambitious attempt to place the indigenous socialist revolution at the service of a new low-carbon economy of batteries and electric cars. It would definitively prove that Bolivia and specifically the Potosí department, of which Uyuni was part, could move beyond dependence on raw materials, mainly natural gas sold to Brazil, and metals such as tin and nickel for the international market.

Just as in the rest of Latin America, the end of the commodity supercycle now threatened the excellent economic results achieved during the decade or so Morales had been in power. Thanks to the nationalization of extractive industries, gas and minerals had generated the income necessary for a spectacular reduction of extreme poverty (those living on less than a dollar a day) from 45 percent of the population in 2000 to 15 percent in 2018, thanks to wage increases, subsidies for poor families, and more generous old-age pensions, not to mention improved labor rights. But they had not created much value added for the economy.

Lithium would be different. According to the government plan, the entire production process would be located within Bolivia, from the extraction of the raw material under the *salar* to the manufacture of batteries. A Bolivian electric-vehicle manufacturing industry even seemed possible. But after thirteen years in government, Evo's popularity was waning, especially amongst the urban middle classes and the young. A Christian ultraconservative movement–fundamentalist on one hand, fiercely neoliberal on the other–had emerged in the cities, especially Santa Cruz, whose mission (crusade, said some) was to remove the Aymara from the presidential palace and raise the tricolor national flag in place of the *wiphala*, a multicolor ensign that represented Bolivia's thirty-nine indigenous peoples.

Morales had also lost the support of part of the left due

to his pragmatic alliances with the big commodity exporters. The right-wing opposition movement was encouraged by Washington and Miami to go further. And, to everybody's surprise, it was the city of Potosí, a historical symbol of indigenous struggle against plunderers from without and within, that would deliver the fatal blow to Morales. While the tourists admired their reflections in the mirror of the waterlogged salt flat, the Salar de Uyuni and its vast lithium deposits were to become a critical factor in the latest Latin American coup d'état.

* * *

Covering an area of five thousand square miles, the salt flat was what remained of a sea trapped between mountains forty thousand years ago, after a series of antediluvian seismic movements. An estimated nine million tons of lithium worth some $160 billion at 2019 prices lay under the photogenic layer of salt, and processing this natural treasure for the benefit of Bolivia was Morales's most ambitious plan in his bid to abandon the historic Potosí model of extraction and pillage and replace it with state-directed industrialization. Climate change had exacerbated the rural crisis on the Andean altiplano, but at least the era of the electric car would generate unprecedented demand for lithium batteries made in Bolivia.

Lithium, after all, had progressed from its days as a mood stabilizer sadly mythologized by Nirvana's Kurt Cobain to become the mineral of hope, one of the most sought-after raw materials for the new green economy. In its natural state, it was a silver-white powder dissolved in the underground lakes of the salt flats of Argentina, Chile, and Bolivia. Extraction simply required pumping the brine into large surface pools where it would evaporate, leaving the lithium carbonate.

Uyuni was the largest of the South American *salars*, although extracting lithium and removing impurities in the Bolivian deposit had never been considered feasible. Executives and engineers from dozens of multinational mining companies and representatives from the automobile industry boarded those same flights from La Paz to Uyuni to take their own photos of the *salar*. But Morales, after nationalizing gas, oil, electricity, and water, refused to give free entry to the private sector, at least in an initial phase. "Lithium is the gasoline of the future and Bolivia has the largest reserves in the world," explained Hernando Larrazábal, the Bolivian director of the Inter-American Development Bank and Morales's ex-minister of planning and development, during a lunch in Washington before an annual International Monetary Fund meeting: "We are late to the lithium business. In Chile they have been extracting for thirty years and in Argentina twenty. But in those countries the multinationals are the sole players. They have not moved beyond the phase of simply extracting and exporting the raw material."

In Bolivia, the plan was to develop technology for developing lithium carbonate. The first phase would be reserved for the Bolivian state, as required by the plurinational constitution, redacted after Morales's first historic electoral victory in 2005: "The state will be responsable for all underground mineral wealth (. . .) Non-metallic natural resources in the salt flats, brines, evaporites, sulfurs, and others are of a strategic nature for the country (. . .) the state will control the whole productive mining chain", it stated. Later, foreign private companies would be invited to participate, but only as minority partners of the state-owned company Yacimientos de Litio Bolivianos (YLB). This was not the carte blanche that Chile handed over to private-sector mining corporations (one of them owned by the Pinochet family) to extract lithium from the Atacama Desert, a gift that, among a hundred other injustices, triggered the Chilean popular rebellion in October 2019.

Morales intended to build a battery factory in the department of Potosí that would be the perfect counterpoint to the infamous Cerro Rico. The project seemed increasingly viable thanks to the quadrupling of the price of lithium in the previous ten years, from $4,000 to $18,000 a ton. Moreover, demand for lithium carbonate was also expected to quadruple in the next two decades as automobile lobbies finally accepted that the era of the combustion engine was over.

But if plans for a new Bolivian lithium industry were moving forward, the political situation in La Paz had become toxic. Opposition to Evo's reelection had turned into open rebellion. After losing a referendum in which he proposed to modify the constitution so as to allow him to run for a fourth consecutive term, Morales won the support of the Supreme Court for his candidature under the dubious principle that running for president is a universal human right. A decade before, protest against the newly elected president had been confined to the ultraconservative city of Santa Cruz, where a coup d'état was disguised as a regionalist bid to secede from the new Plurinational State of Bolivia. But in most of the country Evo commanded wide support thanks to anti-poverty programs, minimum-wage hikes, and improvements in pensions and public services.

This time, though, the anti-Evo movement had spread to all cities, although the majority of the rural and indigenous population still backed Morales. It was no easy task to defend Evo's desire to cling to power. But after listening to a group of furious middle-class anti-Evo protesters during a protest, I decided to make the effort. "The campesinos want to trample all over us. They are disobedient and insolent. It was not like this in the past," said Jimena Machicao, a perfume seller who was at the protest march with her two daughters. It was obvious that by "campesinos" Machicao really meant the Aymara or Quechua. Overt racism was acceptable again, as it had been before the indigenous revolts of the early twenty-first century. Other protesters, twenty-year-old students who had been fortunate enough to go to college thanks to the economic success of the Evo years, railed against the president for his poor schooling. The wrath of the middle classes, many of them only recently emerged from poverty thanks to Morales's social policies, was rising.

That same February day in 2018, while the coup held its dress rehearsal in the streets of La Paz, I interviewed Luis Alberto Echazú, the vice minister of technology responsible for the Uyuni lithium project. He made strenuous efforts to justify the president's decision to seek another four years in power. "Evo is very smart, despite his lack of studies. It is very difficult to find others like him and we have very important projects to complete," he told me. Neither the government nor Evo's party, the Movement for Socialism (MAS), wanted to put development projects at risk, let alone their flagship plan: the industrialization of lithium. An electoral defeat would usher opposition politicians into power who would open up the *salar* to multinationals. In the new cold war over natural resources, Donald Trump's empire would exploit any sign of weakness if Evo wasn't in charge, implied Echazú. "Evo is like Lula—unique," he closed his case. Leadership was crucial because Bolivia had a plan that would not go down well in the global power centers: "What we want in the long term is to take advantage of the amount of lithium that we produce in order to control the price in international markets. We will coordinate this with other producing countries." Who could doubt that an OPEC (Organization of the Petroleum Exporting Countries) for lithium in the age of the electric car would make hairs stand on end in Washington? So the Aymara president prepared to fight for a fourth presidency, which would make seventeen years in the presidential palace.

Despite the budgetary problems caused by the collapse in the prices of other raw materials, especially gas and metals, Morales decided to step on the lithium accelerator by means of a presidential decree. The government signed a contract with the small German company ACI Systems, one of the battery suppliers to Tesla, to produce lithium hydroxide from the mineral extracted in the Uyuni *salar* and manufacture lithium-ion batteries for the European market. The Chinese company TBEA would do the same for Asia. Both would be partners of the state company YLB.

In five years Bolivia could be producing 150,000 tons, 20 percent of the world's lithium, estimated the government. It would be a major supplier to China, whose planners forecast that the new electric-car industry could generate demand for 800,000 tons of lithium per year by 2025 in China alone. In times of growing geopolitical tensions between China and the United States over access to dwindling resources of critical minerals, lithium seemed to be the "white gold" of the future as demand for the metal was expected to increase by 20 percent every year. The Potosí region would charge a 3 percent royalty to complete the state-driven national supply chain, and YLB signed a contract with the electric-vehicle manufacturer QuantumScape for a plant in Cochabamba.

It was a national development plan that every Bolivian would surely be proud of. But Morales underestimated the new Bolivian right and its ability to mobilize the urban middle classes against everything he proposed. He also miscalculated the deep historical resentment embedded in the traumatized psychology of Potosí after five hundred years of pillage. As Galeano noted, the depleted Cerro Rico was "the outstanding example" of "descent into the vacuum." In the following weeks, lithium, like all the other minerals mined in Potosí over the centuries, would become a curse to Latin America's only indigenous president.

Evo Morales's nemesis in Potosí was Marco Pumari. He was thirty-eight years old, the son of a miner and as dark-skinned as his Quechua mother. Yet Pumari did not see himself as indigenous, but rather as a true Bolivian and a Potosíno loyal to the Bible and not *Pachamama*. Ambitious and opportunistic, as president of the Potosínista Civic Committee he aimed to emulate the success in Santa Cruz of the ultraconservative Luis Fernando Camacho, the Bolivian Bolsonaro and self-labeled Macho Camacho. Camacho had led a series of citywide *paros* (intimidating road blockades designed to paralyze the city) in Santa Cruz in protest against Morales. In Potosí, which was much poorer than Santa Cruz and much more indigenous, mobilizing the working and middle classes against Evo would be a greater challenge. But three weeks before the start of the October 2019 electoral campaign, Pumari came up with the perfect formula. He would exploit Potosí's historic grievance: the collective fear that the extraction of wealth from the region's subsoil would benefit others and not Potosí.

Perfectly valid questions had been raised about the viability of Evo's plan to build an industrialized supply chain from the lithium salt flat to the QuantumScape electric car. Environmentalists wondered how water would be pumped from under the *salar* for the evaporation process without causing the salt crust to subside and so spoil a million tourists' selfies along with the livelihoods of thousands of quinoa producers in the surrounding area. Across the border in Chile, the mining company Sociedad Química y Minera de Chile (Soquimich), whose majority shareholder was Pinochet's son-in-law, had become one of the targets of the Chilean protests due to contamination and wasteful water consumption at its operations in the Atacama Desert. Nobody wanted the same to happen in Bolivia. Others pointed to the low concentration of lithium in the Uyuni brines, which were seven times less productive than the Chilean *salar*, and a painfully slow evaporation process due to higher humidity levels at thirteen thousand feet of altitude, compared with the arid sea-level Atacama. Meanwhile, fiscal conservatives doubted whether the $10 billion invested in the project to date had been well spent. In general, the idea of making automobiles in the Andes seemed optimistic, if not fanciful. Pablo Solón, Evo's first ambassador to the United Nations, who had broken with the president over projects in agribusiness and mining, wondered why a seventy-year contract had been awarded to a small German company with only twenty employees and little experience in lithium extraction. "They should have made the lithium hydroxide on their own, with state money, without partners," said Solón.

These were all valid criticisms. But it was hard to imagine that Morales could be branded a traitor to the patria for promoting what was undeniably a plan for national industrial development. Pumari, however, understood the revolutionary power of victimism in Potosí. The young Potosíno had become a leader of a new variation of identity politics in Bolivia, which some sociologists and journalists called the *ninguno* or "nobody" rebellion. Those Bolivians who were neither properly indigenous nor properly white felt unrepresented. And as in other countries where racism lay buried in the substratum of the national psyche, these "nobodies" became the cannon fodder of Bolivia's new right. Pumari knew how to channel their resentment perhaps because he was one of them. He attacked the indigenous president for selling the resources of the Uyuni salt flat without benefiting Potosí. "This government persists in handing over the natural resources of the department of Potosí to the transnational companies," he ranted at one meeting. A 3 percent regional royalty was insulting, he protested, considering that Camacho and the Santa Cruz citizen's movement had achieved 11 percent for oil extracted from the eastern territories. His enraged tirades against the government's lithium project won the support of dissatisfied Potosínos on the right and the left. He also won over many of the autonomous miners in Potosí and other regions who opposed Morales's attempts to nationalize and regularize the industry. (In 2016 a group of these conservative-minded self-employed miners beat the vice president, Rodolfo Illanes, to death in a mining region near La Paz.)

Allying the *ningunos* and the autonomous miners with the professional middle classes of Potosí, Pumari forged a regionalist identity and joined Santa Cruz–secessionist whenever the left governed in La Paz–in the lobby for more autonomy from La Paz, where the indigenous left was dominant. The Potosíno civic committee organized sometimes violent blockades and demonstrations citywide. Merging Camacho's anti-indigenous Christian fundamentalism with the sovereign defense of Potosí's natural resources, Pumari forged a powerful anti-government coalition. He even went on a hunger strike to claim a larger piece of the lithium pie for Potosí.

Finally, Morales yielded and rescinded the contract with the Germans at ACI Systems, just as Pumari had demanded. The president promised to invest in a battery factory in the city of Potosí and to move the YLB head offices from La Paz to the chaotic city of Uyuni in the middle of the *salar*. Morales even suggested that the Potosí royalties could be negotiated. But it was too late. The Potosí campaign against the government's lithium project had metamorphosed into a coup against Morales. "We have won the battle [over lithium], but unfortunately our struggle can be of no use if Evo Morales remains in power," Pumari announced in October.

The president had won in the first round of the elections by a narrow margin but enough to avoid a second poll. However, an unexplained pause in the count by the electoral authority raised suspicions. Inspectors from Luis Almagro's Washington-friendly Organization of American States (OAS) predictably denounced electoral fraud, after an audit carried out in record time. Almagro urged Morales to hold a second-round vote, which Morales seemed prepared to do. But Pumari and Camacho now wanted the president's head.

Blockades went up in Potosí and Santa Cruz; public buildings and the homes of ministers and MAS leaders were attacked. A mob forcibly entered the president's house in Cochabamba. Other violent opposition gangs burned down the house of Evo's sister. Morales's supporters responded with attacks on opposition leaders. Pumari was now competing with Camacho for ownership of the new crusade against the "pagan" president. "They must return the word of God to the Governmental Palace! No more heresy!" bellowed the young Potosíno at a rally in Los Yungas.

Hours later, the police mutinied against the president in Santa Cruz and other regions. Camacho and Pumari traveled to La Paz from their respective cities and, escorted by dozens of rebellious policemen and a mass of furious opposition supporters, to the presidential palace, which Morales had already vacated, aware of the fate of another leftist president, Gualberto Villarroel, who in 1946 was stabbed and beaten to death by a mob and then hung from a lamppost. Once inside the presidential palace, Pumari and Camacho knelt down, announced that "God has returned to the palace," and placed a Bible on top of a Bolivian flag before reciting the Lord's Prayer. They then left a presidential resignation letter that they themselves had drafted for Morales to sign. On Sunday, November 10, 2019, Morales resigned under pressure from the military and flew the next day to Mexico City, after being granted political asylum by Mexican president Andrés Manuel López Obrador.

Pumari had "defeated Morales with his [Evo's] own arguments: accusing him of handing over national treasures to foreigners and the transnational corporations and suggesting that the Germans and the Chinese were going to steal from us," explained Gonzalo Chávez, an economist at the Catholic University of La Paz when I interviewed him soon after the coup. "All Bolivians are nationalists, especially Potosínos, and they all believe that natural resources will save us; Pumari exploited this brilliantly." Of course, it was not the first time that fascism had hijacked the discourse of the left.

Morales's resignation seemed to consummate the victory of Marco Pumari's new Potosíno urban rebellion. However, in rural municipalities in the department of Potosí, the regime change did not generate the same euphoria as in the capital. "The countryside is with Evo, but the city is not," said a Quechua woman who had crossed the border to Uyuni from Chile on the same bus as I had two days after the coup. Moreover, despite Pumari's rhetoric, the extreme right now taking power in Bolivia seemed far less interested than Evo Morales in creating a national lithium industry. Morales's supporters began to point out a possible link between the operation against the president and the *salar.*

"This coup d'état is because the United States wants our lithium," said an Aymara protester during a protest rally near Plaza Murillo in La Paz three days after Morales's resignation. That day, while the Aymara anti-coup protesters blocked the access to the city center, chewing coca leaves to heighten their powers of resistance, riot police and the military took up their positions, protected by a new executive order from the new interim president, former senator Jeanine Añez, that exempted them from criminal responsibility in the event of the death of a protester. About twenty people had already been shot dead in less than a week, first during a pro-Evo march by coca growers in Sacaba, then in the Aymara city of El Alto in the Andean peaks, where the anti-coup movement had blocked supplies to La Paz, three thousand feet below. At Senkata, a fuel deposit in El Alto, at least eleven demonstrators and local residents were shot dead. While the Añez ministers denied that the bullets were from the security force's weapons, witnesses in El Alto told me the day after the massacre that they had seen the soldiers fire. Months later, the Harvard International Human Rights Clinic published an exhaustively researched report whose title reproduced the testimony of another witness: "They shot us like animals."

Donald Trump called Morales's departure "a significant moment for democracy in the Western hemisphere." The day after proclaiming herself president while holding a huge leather-bound copy of the Bible, Añez announced that she had established diplomatic relations with Juan Guaidó in Venezuela and that Bolivia would withdraw from the Union of South American Nations (UNASUR) and the Bolivarian Alliance for the Peoples of Our America (ALBA), organizations created by the left-wing governments in Latin America a decade earlier as a regional alternative to the OAS. Washington had managed to impose its geopolitical agenda in La Paz in forty-eight hours, and Morales's team in Mexico warned that Trump would soon impose the business agenda of his corporate backers, especially in a sector so attractive to General Motors and Tesla.

"I have no evidence, but it is highly probable that this coup has to do with the global dispute over lithium," declared Álvaro García Linera, Morales's vice president now exiled in Mexico together with the former president. When asked what he would do with state-owned companies, the interim minister of development, Wilfredo Rojo, replied: "There are many options. They can be rented, capitalized with private capital, sold, or closed." Would this agenda be applied to YLB? It was not clear, but Tesla founder Elon Musk heightened suspicion that lithium was behind the coup when he tweeted months later: "We'll coup whoever we want."

Nothing could be ruled out in the murky story of the anti-Evo coup. But Musk's remark seemed more like another example of the billionaire entrepreneur's woeful sense of humor than an admission that Tesla had backed the ouster of Morales. As in the case of Bolsonaro's niobium in Raposa Serra do Sol, a cruel irony lay behind Bolivia's lithium project. With its low concentration levels, six or seven times weaker than in the Chilean salt flats, and high production costs, all the analysts I spoke to assured me that the Uyuni deposit was not a priority either for Washington or Beijing. Australia, Chile, and the lithium deposits in territory directly controlled by the two superpowers (Lake Zabuye in

Tibet and Clayton Valley in the Nevada desert) were much more important. The US support for the coup in Bolivia, rather than being a grab for lithium, seemed to have more to do with ideology. Specifically, the desire to drive a stake through what was left of twenty-first-century socialism in Latin America, and exploit the damage that Evo's fall from power would entail for Venezuela, where oil was indeed a resource worth organizing a coup for.

Likewise, the regionalist outrage that Pumari and the pro-coup movement in Potosí directed against a supposedly sweetheart deal with the German and Chinese investors had no basis in fact. Most leading multinationals in the lithium sector, after analyzing the viability of the Uyuni *salar,* had not shown much enthusiasm. Nor had electric car makers like Tesla. Evo had no choice but to partner with ACI Systems and the Chinese companies because few others were interested. Both the young leader of the angry Bolivian *ningunos* and Evo Morales had overestimated the mineral value of the Salar de Uyuni. The role of lithium in the coup against Morales appeared much more symbolic than real. It was a means to tap into Potosí's historical resentment regarding the pillage of its mineral wealth. As Marco Pumari intuitively grasped, in the country of the Cerro Rico there would always be opportunities for a politician prepared to exploit the complex psychology of the open veins of Latin America.

* * *

The story of Evo Morales's failed attempt to reconcile GDP growth with *Pachamama* and the *sumak kawsay* vision of the good life seemed over–the latest domino to fall in the cascading demise of the Latin American left. But a year after the coup I returned to Bolivia to cover the presidential elections, finally held after repeated attempts by the increasingly despised Añez government to remain in power with support from Washington until it could ban the MAS opposition and criminalize all of its leaders. On this occasion, however, the strategies of lawfare employed in Brazil and Ecuador to outlaw progressive leaders did not succeed, thanks to MAS's deep roots in Bolivia's indigenous movement and labor unions.

The direct democracy of the Quechua and Aymara on the Bolivian altiplano would prove resilient. Luis Arce, Morales's former economy minister, ran for the presidency on a double ticket with the indigenous leader David Choquehuanca and won the October 2020 elections by a huge margin: 55 percent against 30 percent for the nearest rival, the centrist Carlos Messa. Camacho and Pumari, candidates for president and vice president for the far-right alliance Creemos, were heavily defeated, winning only 14 percent of the vote. Pumari proved a huge disappointment in Potosí, and took only 3 percent of the vote in an MAS landslide in the city of the Cerro Rico. In an ironic preview of the US presidential elections to be held a month later, Camacho and Pumari tried once again to denounce the result as fraudulent. I held a tense interview with a black-shirted leader of the Santa Cruz cryptofascist youth movement who unwittingly further undermined the OAS report on fraud in the October 2019 elections by asking, "If MAS only won 42 percent of the votes when the OAS denounced fraud, how could they get 53 percent when the elections are supposedly clean?" The most likely answer was that there was in fact no systematic fraud in October 2019 or 2020.

Arce, a respected economist trained at the University of Warwick in the United Kingdom and praised even in orthodox circles for his savvy macroeconomic management during the Morales years, pledged to return to growth as the economy reeled from the coronavirus pandemic, and announced a new strategy for lithium. It would be firmly based on the principles of state-led industrialization. But this time partners would be more astutely selected. "There are no barriers to a state-owned enterprise succeeding in the lithium business. In fact, the truth is that the results achieved by the private sector have been very poor," said Andy Leyland, a British lithium expert who had advised the Arce team, when we spoke several days after the historic victory. "Bolivia will need to bring in technical expertise but Arce will not repeat the mistakes of the ACI deal," he said. Arce was also keen to use Bolivian lithium and nickel to drive a national transition to renewable energy sources where power storage was now the crucial challenge for the future. The happy ending was further confirmed by news that the cutting-edge technology of direct lithium extraction involved a chemical process that bypassed the need for evaporation pool, avoiding the need to pump water from below the *salar*. Bolivia could be competitive in the world lithium market with far less ecological impact. "Luis is acutely aware of the importance of protecting ecotourism in the Salar," said Leyland. It was time to celebrate and perhaps post my reflection selfies on Facebook.

CHAPTER TEN

Quinoa (Uyuni, Bolivia)
The Rise and Fall of the Miracle Grain

News of Evo Morales's shocking resignation and escape to Mexico in November 2019 had fallen on the municipality of San Agustín, between Uyuni and the Chilean border, like a lava slide from the spectacular Ollagüe volcano, which dominated the horizon to the west. The councillors feared for the future of their social projects in a region that, like most of rural Bolivia, had been transformed by a wave of state-financed investment in development and anti-poverty transfers from the Morales government.

The number one concern was the future of a new quinoa-processing plant in which the government in La Paz had invested four million bolivianos (over half a million dollars). "We think that the future of the plant is secure because we already have almost all the money, but right now you can't be sure of anything," said Emilio Muraña Huanca, director of economic management at the tiny municipality in one of Bolivia's most important quinoa-growing regions. "Quinoa is our greatest challenge," echoed the mayor, Juan Tomás Catur, in a Castilian refined by sibilant Quechua vowels. "Could you help us find buyers?" The San Agustín quinoa, after all, was not just any old variety of the Quechua cereal. It was *quinoa real* (royal quinoa), the most sought-after variety of the world's most fashionable grain.

That, at least, was what the San Agustín council members and farmers hoped it was.

Quinoa was by then a worldwide craze, a supergrain for health-conscious consumers in the developed world, where a fierce reaction against gluten was transforming the diets of millions raised on chlorine-bleached, industrial sliced bread. Quinoa was being marketed as a superfood thanks to an endless list of wholesome properties. The grain contained twice as much protein as rice or barley and was also an excellent source of calcium, magnesium, phosphorus, potassium, and sodium, as well as vitamins B and E. All this without a trace of gluten.

The Quechua supergrain also had more street cred than its rivals in the epic consumer rebellion against globalized Big Food. A key subsistence grain for Quechua and Aymara societies in the Andean highlands, it was the alimentary foundation, together with the potato, for the sustained demographic expansion of the great pre-Columbian civilizations of the altiplano. As indigenous movements finally came to power in Bolivia and Ecuador in the early twenty-first century, the most resistant of the Quechua grains was seen by many not only as a path to robust physical health, but also to cultural, even political, commitment.

The explosion of global demand for quinoa—coinciding with the euphoria that characterized Evo Morales's early years in power—had sown a seed of hope in the Quechua-speaking rural communities in southern Potosí threatened by climate change, open-cast mining, and economic isolation. Ironically, the extreme climate of the altiplano, with nocturnal temperatures below zero rising to seventy degrees Fahrenheit during the day, was thought to be the crucible of the supergrain. The challenge to survival had reinforced quinoa's genetic makeup in a Darwinian process now highly valued by disenchanted shoppers in Western supermarkets in search of their own route to the Quechua *sumak kawsay* or "good life." The arid heat and intense solar radiation of the altiplano also helped make quinoa truly a superfood. As, of course, did the sophisticated agricultural techniques of a thousand generations of indigenous farmers. The southern altiplano's volcanic soil was a nutritious fertilizer. Some scientists even argued that the proximity of the salt plain at Uyuni had made the *quinoa real* in Potosí an even stronger variety of the grain thanks to a unique process of photosynthesis.

Hugo Bautista, a Quechua agronomist, quinoa grower, and authority on the Salar de Uyuni considered the local quinoa to be qualitatively superior to other varieties. "In the Uyuni *salar* almost nothing grows, but a few miles away the microclimate for the *quinoa real* is exceptional," he explained as he drove an enormous pickup along the unsurfaced road from Uyuni to San Agustín, stopping from time to time to allow herds of llamas time to cross. The high desert valley had flooded during the wet season and hundreds of pink flamingos were feeding on microorganisms somehow able to breed and survive in the salt-laden water of an ephemeral lake.

Here the land was communal property for the Quechua, and the llamas grazed freely. Centuries-old indigenous authorities—parallel administrations that coexisted with the San Antonio council and Potosí department—assigned the dimensions of the quinoa plots according to the perceived needs of the Quechua and Aymara families. "In two months, when the harvest approaches, all this will be painted red, purple, ocher, and pink," said Bautista, sweeping his arm in an arc from the mountains to the valley in reference to the multicolored flowers of the quinoa. "It is a unique niche; nowhere else in the world produces a *quinoa real* like ours."

In the past, like most elements of Andean indigenous culture, quinoa, even the five-star *quinoa real*, had been looked down upon with contempt by a broad swathe of Bolivian society. Even the Quechua and Aymara felt a little ashamed of their staple grain. It was "food for the poor," or worse, "the food of the Indians." But in the new century of indigenous revolutions, the perception of the grain was dramatically transformed. The revolution started in fashionable restaurants in Europe and the United States, then spread to Western health stores and the gourmet shelves of global supermarkets. Only afterward would the urban middle classes of the Andean countries cotton on to the cultural cachet that their campesinos had acquired. In Bolivia, the indigenous communities, especially that of the Aymara in El Alto, which overlooked La Paz from an oxygen-deprived thirteen-thousand-foot peak, began for the first time in five hundred years to enjoy a degree of cultural self-esteem. It was showcased, with mixed fortunes, in the fashion catwalks of luxury versions of the Aymara pollera skirts and baby alpaca shawls, and in postmodern *cholet* architecture (the fusion of chalet and cholo, the nickname for the indigenous-mestizo mix): four-story, brightly colored rococo apartment buildings built in El Alto for the new Aymara commercial bourgeoisie.

Meanwhile the quinoa boom, the grain now as fashionable as a mimosa or Caesar salad on brunch menus in New York and London, began to improve life in the farming communities of San Agustín. The price of quinoa rose from $40 a quintal (unit of 100 pounds) in 2005 to $350 in 2013, an increase of 800 percent. That year demand exploded further as Evo and his then-indigenous counterpart in the Peruvian presidency, Ollanta Humala, organized the International Year of Quinoa with an aggressive campaign of global marketing. It was a spectacular success. World quinoa exports multiplied by seven in five years.

But Evo's thoughtful investment in quinoa was one of the two faces of a schizophrenic agricultural policy in which Morales, like other governments of the progressive Latin American "pink tide," tried to reconcile *Pachamama* with the global commodities market.

While supporting small quinoa producers, the Bolivian president had followed the example of Lula and Dilma on the other side of his northeastern border by allying with the agro-industrial oligarchy, principally cattle ranchers and soy producers in Santa Cruz and the tropical lowlands of the east. The consequences would be catastrophic. In the dry season of 2019, an uncontrollable wave of forest fires devastated nearly six thousand square miles of forest in eastern Bolivia as cattle ranchers used fire to deforest.

"The government implemented the agribusiness program that we had set out to bury," explained Pablo Solón, Evo's former friend and minister whom we met in the last chapter. Solón had designed the first *sumak kawsay* programs based on a new model of alternative development that rejected mining and export-driven corporate agribusiness. Leading a coalition that included indigenous people, coca farmers, urban workers, miners, and students, Morales won the 2006 elections thanks to that revolutionary program. But the bid to build a low-growth, small-scale good life would not last even two years. Nor would Evo's friendship with Pablo Solón.

I met Solón at the run-down offices of his foundation in the center of La Paz, a week after Morales's removal from power, which Solón (such is the bitterness of old comrades) unconvincingly defined not as a coup but as just rewards for Morales's authoritarian abuses. Soldiers patrolled the center of La Paz, and that day riot police had tear-gassed a funeral parade for pro-Morales campesinos shot dead at the Senkata fuel depot in El Alto, their coffins abandoned in the street by as the pallbearers fought for breath. But Solón felt little sympathy for the deposed president or his followers.

"Our original project, embodied in the philosophy of *sumak kawsay*, was the end of extractivism," he explained. "We were heading toward a process of industrialization that would respect Mother Earth. We wanted to escape from the logic of exporting raw materials. That's what we said in our 2006 election program." But soon after Evo and Solón's victory, the first of several attempted coups took place, and like the rest, it was designed in Santa Cruz and the so-called Half Moon region in the wealthy conservative lowlands of the tropical east. The coup plans took the form of a secessionist bid designed by the Santa Cruz agribusiness oligarchy with the support of Macho Camacho, the extreme-right leader. Morales managed to foil the Half Moon plotters and escape a terrorist attempt on his life. But from that moment "a fundamental change occurred in Evo's political stance," said Solón. "He stopped thinking about how to implement the plan for the good life and started to think of how he would keep himself in power . . . and power meant reaching an agreement with Santa Cruz agribusiness oligarchy."

Of course, Solón's utopian critique of Evo's desire to stay in power overlooked the inconvenient fact that without power nothing is possible, least of all the good life. Evo's pragmatism perhaps was necessary to move ahead with the most radical program of income distribution ever implemented in Bolivia and the beginning of the repayment of a historical debt to its indigenous majority who were denied real citizenship until the revolutions of the early twenty-first century. But the modus vivendi with the Santa Cruz oligarchy undeniably required problematic concessions to multinational agribusiness. The commitment to ban genetically modified crops was abandoned. The use of biofuels that the indigenous movement considered a threat to food security was reinstated. And Evo gave the green light to the expansion of monoculture cash crops through the tropical forests toward Brazil. All this, said Solón, "meant that more than five thousand hectares of forest have been burned to clear the way for cattle, soybeans, and sugarcane for ethanol."

The deal with the Santa Cruz oligarchs, along with gas and mineral exports, provided Evo with the political stability and economic dynamism necessary to push the Bolivian GDP annual growth rate up to a spectacular 5 percent, a regional high, and so finance his poverty reduction and development programs. But the Aymara president lost the support of key sections of the indigenous movement and of his allies on the environmentalist left like Solón.

"The income generated in the gas export boom was not used to transform the productive apparatus and diversify the economy. Investments were made in policies that would win votes, such as building soccer stadiums in small towns, paving roads, distributing subsidies to help the poorest people," Solón went on. "And when the crisis struck in 2014 and the price of gas fell Evo tried to compensate for the error of dependency on gas extractivism by giving free rein to other extractivisms, like mining, hydroelectricity, and agro-industrial and livestock production."

It was a damning critique from Evo's former comrade to which Morales might reply that without votes, power is lost, and without the foreign-exchange income from the extractive economy the quinoa-processing plants and the lithium-battery factory would have been mere fantasies.

Quinoa was proof, in any case, that Evo, despite his pragmatic alliance with the Santa Cruz oligarchy, had not forgotten the small farmers of the highlands both in Potosí and in the president's region of birth, Oruro, where quinoa (though not the five-star *quinoa real*) was also a staple crop. The idea was to follow advice from the United Nations's Food and Agricultural Organization (FAO) regarding the export of traditional smallholder-produced food in the international market as a way out of poverty that would not destroy millenary culture or undermine food security. But if any single lesson could be drawn from the old and the new open veins of Latin America, it was that when a product enters the global commodity market, it is extremely difficult to control the consequences.

Before long, tens of countries had been swept along by the quinoa craze. Europe and the United States began planting the Quechua-Aymara grain, while in Bolivia's neighbor, Peru, production tripled in just one year. Worryingly, most of the increase did not occur in the Peruvian highlands, where the indigenous farmers, like their Bolivian counterparts, had cultivated the supergrain since well before Pizarro garroted Atahuallpa.

Big agribusiness interests in the Peruvian coastal strip, especially in the wealthy Arequipa region, planted quinoa across thousands of hectares of land. With a warmer climate and industrial pesticides and fertilizers to combat plagues, the coastal Peruvians harvested two crops a year–a feat inconceivable for the Quechua growers in the colder altiplano. The result was overproduction and a boom-and-bust cycle that Eduardo Galeano would have described with fatalistic irony. After peaking at around $360 per quintal, quinoa prices plummeted to $40. Just as it did when the tourist convoys crossed the Uyuni salt flat, the global quest for authentic experience and a foretaste of the Quechua *sumak kawsay* threatened to destroy the object of its desire.

Quinoa's roundtrip to the stratosphere and back delivered a devastating blow to the small farming communities in San Agustín. "In 2016 the price of the quintal rose to twenty-four hundred bolivianos, it was very good news for us. Then it went down to three hundred bolivianos and then it went back up again; now it is at seven hundred and fifty bolivianos (about a hundred dollars)," said the mayor, with an expression that combined puzzlement and resignation.

Price volatility in the boom-and-bust commodity economy was only part of the problem. The Quechua farmers, whose ancient agricultural techniques had turned quinoa into a superfood, received only seven dollars of the hundred that was paid per quintal in the international market: "Seven hundred and fifty bolivianos means around fifty for producers here." The mayor's tone became increasingly desperate: "Once we finish the plant we'll be able to clean and process the quinoa right here, and we plan to industrialize, to make cookies and other foods. But our concern is that the market is not there."

At a nearby school young Quechua students and entrepreneurs had put on a display of the quinoa-based snacks they had designed, some of them far more attractive than a packet of potato chips. "This is a laboratory. We are creating the first high school course in industrial transformation of the foodstuffs we produce in our region," announced Professor Jorge Quispe as the young quinoa creatives stood by. "We have delights made from red, white, and black quinoa. Biscuits, cakes, and energy bars; no conservants, no chemicals." But they, too, worried how they would scale up production and compete with the new global quinoa snack business. PepsiCo's Frito-Lay's new line of quinoa chips with garlic, for example.

As if that were not a daunting enough task, the Uyuni salt-flat area had not been able to gain exclusive rights as the unique granary of the royal quinoa. From Whole Foods in New York to Barcelona fair-trade cooperatives, shoppers were not aware of where the quinoa they so conscientiously bought was grown, complained Bautista. "People are buying sweet quinoa as if it were *quinoa real*. We have not been able to explain the difference." It had not even been possible to compel exporters to stick a "Product of Bolivia" label on the packets of quinoa.

Bautista had tried on his own to create a certificate of origin. But he explained that "instead of supporting [him], [the government had] put up barriers. They said that they could help with the certificate only if we included Oruro, just because Evo was born there." Since the certification of origin could not be achieved without the recommendation of the Andean Community (CAN) the request had to be handled through the Bolivian Ministry of Foreign Affairs. "Instead of trying to support *quinoa real*, a political decision was made. It always happens; Evo Morales surrounds himself with people who care only about politics and not about expertise, that's why he fell from power," said Bautista, who, like Pablo Solón, accused Morales of using a system of patronage to maintain support.

But Evo's dilemma was easy to understand. Expanding certification for Oruro producers was not just a bid for their vote; it had helped protect smaller producers there to face the competition from Peruvian agribusiness. The truth was that 50 percent of Bolivian quinoa production did not come from the Uyuni region in the south of Potosí. Moreover, scientific opinion was divided between those who believed that the royal quinoa of the Uyuni salt flat was unique (with more protein and more health-giving properties) and other experts who did not differentiate between sweet quinoa and royal quinoa.

Likewise, Morales's commitment to agribusiness in the east, as in the case of Brazil, had delivered spectacular growth during the years of high prices in the supercycle, and Morales had managed the windfall far better than Lula and Dilma. Bolivia was still growing robustly as most of the region stagnated, although the growth was now dependent on a rising budget deficit. Generating foreign exchange by extracting raw materials and then distributing the rents had reduced extreme poverty (income of less than a dollar a day) from 39 percent to 15 percent of the population. As Luis Arce's Movement Toward Socialism prepared for power once again, and Evo returned to Bolivia after his yearlong exile in Mexico and Argentina, the debate continued.

Perhaps the future of the climate would help resolve the dispute between pro-growth extractive developmentalists like Arce and growth-skeptical environmentalists like Pablo Solón. Gazing across the San Agustín valleys, beyond the quinoa plots, the herds of llamas, and the flamingos, the difficult choice between growth or environmental protection seemed academic. Huge volcanos rose in perfectly drawn ash-gray triangles against the azure sky of the *salar*. Some released a plume of white smoke, denoting an active volcano. But none of them showed even the slightest trace of snow. "Ten years ago each peak would have had a layer of snow at this time of year, but not anymore," said Bautista. As in Puno and Apurímac, climate change was turning the epic debate over the development model into an unnecessary luxury.

The quinoa seeds sown in September had grown into small plants poking out of the dry Andean soil. But a closer look revealed small holes bitten into the plants' thick green leaves. "It's the moths. Everything seems fine, but you turn your back for a moment and in a couple of days you've lost the whole crop," lamented Jorge Bautista Huanca, a Quechua farmer who worked his two-hectare plot by hand. Just as they had wiped out those stores of *chuño* potatos in the ever warmer Peruvian altiplano, moths had destroyed several quinoa harvests in southern Bolivia. "It was not like this in the past. Temperatures have risen," said Bautista Huanca.

In addition to the heat and water scarcity, the problem was the randomness of the new altiplano weather patterns. Those unique climatic conditions, the secret of the *quinoa real* described by Hugo Bautista, were no longer reliable. "This week there may be rain and next week it will be winter again, nobody knows. Once we knew when the frosts would come. Not now," he added stoically, as hardened by the passing years as the quinoa he planted. But both now seemed vulnerable. "We need rain in January and in February. We don't want rain in March or April. But the weather has changed and, if it comes late, the frost kills everything."

On my return to La Paz, I decided to try some of the new haute cuisine quinoa dishes at Gustu, a restaurant owned by the Danish chef Claus Meyer in the wealthy southern district of the Bolivian capital. Owner of the two-Michelin-star restaurant Noma in Copenhagen, Meyer believed that gourmet cuisine should support small farmers and was one of the first international promoters of the Uyuni-sourced *quinoa real*. Thanks in part to the culinary cachet of restaurants like Noma, the Andean supergrain took off. Yet that night there was not a single quinoa dish on the Gustu menu. "We don't serve much quinoa these days because it's so widely used in Bolivia and throughout the world; it's turned into a mass-market food," explained Marsia Taha, the Bolivian executive chef at Gustu. "Bolivia is no longer the country with the highest quinoa production. The big producers are in United States and in Europe, so we want to promote other grains in the Bolivian highlands that do not have the same visibility. Everybody talks about quinoa, but there are ten or fifteen more grains in the Andes." It was a brave coun-terattack against globalized monoculture and the fads and crazes of the superfood business. But Gustu was a niche boutique restaurant with only seven tables.

CHAPTER ELEVEN

Silver (San Luis Potosí, Mexico)
"Racers" and the Fourth Transformation

"Good afternoon. My name is Marciano La Cruz. I am from the community of Santa Catarina, municipality of Mezquitic, state of Jalisco. I'm a Wixárica, but, since people do not know how to pronounce 'Wixárica,' we call ourselves Huichol." With such resignation, Marciano introduced himself to my digital recorder. It was the three-day *puente*, a short holiday held for February's Candelaria carnival, and I had finally located his shop, packed with explosively colored textiles, on a narrow street in the center of Real de Catorce, the granite-built colonial capital of the nineteenth century Mexican silver boom. The raw material I hoped to extract here was firsthand testimony for a story already told, perhaps too often, but I hoped still no less attractive. This particular account of pillage and indigenous resistance would focus on the hallucinogenic cactus peyote. "Silver versus Peyote" seemed the perfect headline as the twenty-first-century silver rush descended upon the parched mountains of the Sierra Madre.

Each spring, the Huichol embarked on a marathon pilgrimage across more than three hundred miles of the central Mexican mountain desert from Jalisco to the San Luis Potosí. There on the Cerro Quemado, an arid peak marked by a spiral of boulders, half an hour from Real de Catorce, they ingested the hallucinogenic cactus. In a desperate attempt by Enrique Peña Nieto's "reformist" government to attract foreign investment, and thus raise Mexico's stunted economic growth rate, this sacred site was one of the twenty-two concessions awarded to the Canadian mining company First Majestic Silver across seven thousand hectares of the sierra. First Majestic sought to reopen an old silver mine first opened in the late nineteenth century by the Spanish businessman Gregorio de la Masa a few miles from the Cerro Quemado. But to safeguard Huichol culture, the mountain and most of the rest of the sierra had been protected under San Luis Potosí state law, with the backing of the Mexican Constitution.

It was an example, not uncommon in Mexico, of a federal government that in its desire to comply with US-dictated trade and investment rules had clashed with constitutional guarantees made after the 1917 Mexican Revolution. To the intense annoyance of its executives and shareholders in Toronto, First Majestic had still not been able to commence mining eight years after being granted the concession. In a forlorn attempt at public relations, the company had opened a museum in the old Santa Ana mine in La Luz, three miles down the winding mountain road from Real de Catorce. There, First Majestic offered tours of the claustrophobic tunnels where the miners slaved and died during the first silver boom, and of the spacious ballrooms where actors dressed up as Fernando and Isabel, the Spanish Catholic kings, received the visit of the prerevolutionary dictator Porfirio Díaz. Our guide to the museum, Dalila Aguilera, who lived in La Luz, passionately defended the new mining project. "I can tell you with total confidence that most people in La Luz want this mine to open," she said as we observed the fifty-foot-tall faux-Renaissance bell tower, which had comically proven too small for the bell, that was built by Gregorio de la Masa to alert the miners at the start of each shift. "This town is proud of its mining tradition; the Huichol want to stop our development," insisted Aguilera.

La Cruz, tall and serene, was dressed in the traditional costume of the Huichol: a turquoise-blue tunic and white cotton pants, though he chose a baseball cap instead of the wide-brimmed sombrero with multicolored pendants worn by the Huichol street vendors outside. He spoke a sibilant Castilian cleansed of the conquistador's diphthongs: "We are not opposed to the mine but we don't want it here right in the heart of the Cerro Quemado where we make our offerings and take the peyote; if they contaminate the peyote, we will die." He removed from a plastic bag several specimens of the *Lophophora williamsii* cactus packed with psychotropic *mezcalina*, a legendary plant at least for those who had read the esoteric teachings of Carlos Castaneda's *The Teachings of Don Juan* or *The Peyote Dance* by the wandering surrealist poet Antonin Artaud as adolescents. The smooth bulbous plant resembled those green bagels fashionable in Brooklyn on Saint Patrick's Day. But out of it sprouted a flower whose intense electric-violet petals were unquestionably psychedelic even for those like myself who had balked, for fear of never returning, at a trip to the Huichol underworld. La Cruz, by contrast, spoke of the experience with routine directness, as if describing a visit to the gym for a session of Pilates. "For us, the peyote is a sacred plant. It purifies, it cleanses, we have visions and connect with nature, with the plants, with the animals, and with the stars."

How extraordinary, I thought, that Mexico's revolutionaries Emiliano Zapata and Pancho Villa, even a century after their victories against Díaz and his US backers, were still constitutionally blocking the path to the latest set of invaders from the north intent on destroying the Huichol utopia.

But other threats less tangible than the First Majestic Silver bulldozers had emerged. La Cruz's instructions as to how to collect the peyote seemed neurotically detailed. "Pull it out well above the root, well above, then take off the shell, clean it well, remove the hairs on the top because they are bad for you, and then chew it, but the important thing is to leave the root. It is small but has to be left; many people are pulling out the entire root and the peyote takes fifteen or twenty years to grow." The plea to save the root, I soon realized, was aimed at my readers who, like those European tourists trekking through the Ecuadorian jungle in search of the hallucinogenic vine ayahuasca in Paul Theroux's novel *Blinding Light*, might choose to reserve a peyote tour in Real de Catorce.

As La Cruz spoke, the roar of one-hundred-cylinder engines reverberated outside the store and white beams of light illuminated the images of eagles, turtles, and coiled snakes woven into the rainbow-colored textiles hung from the walls. The "racers" had arrived, a procession of cross-country desert buggies built from motorcycles equipped with a battery of blinding spotlights and finished in flashy chrome and stainless steel. They had crossed the desert from San Luis Potosí piloted by forty-year-old men determined to fend off their midlife crises by donning suits that might have been worn by world motocross champion Fernando Alonso. Mingling with them in the crowded street, tourists from Europe and the United States, clad in Huichol ponchos, were waiting for a shaman to take them to the desert for a transcendental experience. My story of invading barbarians had just found new protagonists.

* * *

The history of the Huichol, originally from Nayarit and Jalisco to the west of San Luis Potosí, was one of a tenacious and fierce resistance to invasion. Even J. M. G. Le Clézio, who catalogues the plethora of indigenous rebellions in Mexico in *The Mexican Dream*, is especially impressed by the "warlike" Huichol whose dexterity with a bow and arrow could rival the muskets and cannons of the conquistadores. But the explanation for this fearless resistance was not just those obsidian-tipped arrows dipped in poison that caused instant and deadly paralysis. Peyote was not just a route to the transcendence of the mind but also to extreme bravery: "Peyote, datura, [and] hallucinogenic mushrooms . . . enhanced the Indians' exaltation and comforted them with an idea of their invulnerability, as hashish did during the Arab wars . . . [They] found strength in an illusion of immortality to wage a hopeless battle."

Who could doubt that the Canadian mining companies had run into a tough adversary? Perhaps thanks to the peyote's emboldening psychotropics, the Huichol were considered the best-organized of the fifty indigenous peoples still present in Mexico even at the beginning of the twenty-first century. Now more accustomed to blandishing the laptop than the bow and arrow, a new generation of Huichol had attended universities in Mexico or even the United States, often to study linguistics and so defend their language, art, and literature. First Majestic was not well equipped to deal with Indians with postgraduate degrees.

But there were many other veins in Mexico's rocky deserts and tropical forests. Thanks to Peña Nieto and his predecessors, mining corporations had been granted concessions valid for up to a hundred years with royalties close to zero. First Majestic's investment was part of a veritable invasion of Canadian mining capital throughout Latin America funded from a deep pool of speculative capital on the Toronto stock market. This even provided venture capital to what the brokers called "juniors," small firms specialized in exploration for the frenetic search for gold, silver, copper, platinum zinc, and other hidden treasures in the Latin American subsoil. Canadian multinationals had invested some $20 billion in Mexico, which made up no less than 70 percent of total foreign direct investment. Peña Nieto's predecessor Felipe Calderón, who had declared war on the narcos and lost, generously awarded lucrative concessions to a handful of multinationals, mainly Canadian, that stretched over twenty million hectares of Mexico. During his six-year term (2012–2018), Peña Nieto had granted licenses for another sixty-five new mining projects, most of them open cast. Twenty-five percent of the country's surface area was now tendered out in mining concessions. Not even in the classic era of the open veins, when Porfirio Díaz dutifully handed over Mexico's underground resources to the colonial powers, had so much land been signed away to foreign interests.

The new president and historic leader of the Mexican left, Andrés Manuel López Obrador (AMLO), elected in 2018 at sixty-three years of age, belonged to a generation that had devoured the first edition of *Open Veins of Latin America* during their youth and vowed to stop the hemorrage. His plans to recover some of the principles of developmentalism were inspired in the ideas of the heterodox economists from the Economic Commission for Latin America and the Caribbean (CEPAL), who we encountered in the story of iron in Brazil.

As part of his project for the so-called Fourth Transformation (the first three being independence in 1821, the period of liberal reform from 1855–1861, and the revolution begun in 1910) AMLO defended the reindustrialization of

Mexico. He set out to replace both the export of unprocessed raw materials, especially crude oil, and the failed "*maquiladora*" model that had built a manufacturing base dependent on the reassembly of imported parts from the Europe and Asia for subsequent export to the United States. The *maquiladoras* had spread south from the border towns of Juárez and Tijuana to places like Guanajuato, Aguascalientes, and even San Luis Potosí, which now had its own business parks packed with assembly plants. But turning Mexico into a global assembly platform had neither delivered growth nor development. The Mexican economy had stagnated and, with it, so had workers' wages. AMLO vowed to change the model, raise the value of goods made in Mexico, and power growth from internal demand, not just assembled exports. Both the *maquila* and the export of raw materials such as unrefined crude oil were to be replaced by industrialization. The new president, who had spent part of his youth living with the Chontal in the swamps of southeastern Mexico, was also a passionate defender of indigenous rights. He dedicated his victory speech to Mexico's original peoples at a moving ceremony in in July 2018, in Mexico City's Zocalo Square, before half a million followers.

Despite all this, he expressed support for finding a modus vivendi with the Canadian juniors and seniors. "We have to promote a bilateral agreement with Canada and so . . . achieve more investment from the Canadian mining multinationals but now with fair wages and environmental protection," he had said during the election campaign. AMLO did announce that the Mexican federal government would grant no more mining concessions but after Peña Nieto's generosity with the mutinationals, many asked why he would not withdraw the existing licences. In San Luis Potosí and Zacatecas, the two states in the high desert of central

Mexico most closely identified with colonial mining and key locations for the early chapters of *Open Veins*, the simultaneous defense of environment, indigenous rights, fair wages, oil-driven growth, and mining seemed a tall order.

Just as Dilma Rousseff in Brazil, Rafael Correa in Ecuador, and even Evo Morales in Bolivia had discovered, it was extremely difficult to maintain unity between the two broad currents of the Latin American left and, increasingly, the international progressive movement in the early twenty-first century. On one side were those who defended an interventionist centralized state committed to accelerating growth to generate employment and reduce poverty through big infrastructure projects in energy, agribusiness, and mining. While there were discrepancies within this school as to how far raw material exports could be part of the reindustrialization project, there were few doubts amongst these leftists that high GDP growth was crucial. On the other side was a social movement more closely linked to the small campesino economy, to indigenous culture, and to environmental protection whose supporters doubted that GDP growth was the panacea for fighting poverty. They defended local food production for the campesino communities' own consumption in an economy based on the small scale, food and energy security, and the use of alternative indicators of economic welfare such as the indigenous ideal of the *buen vivir* (good life) founded upon a harmonious relationship with nature and the rejection of consumerism.

So, after he won a spectacular victory in the 2018 elections, López Obrador tried hard to reconcile the two tendencies. He implemented pro-campesino measures such as the program Sembrando Vida (Sowing Life), in which one-hundred-dollar subsidies were paid to campesino communities in return for their planting fruit-bearing trees. But he also supported massive investments in the oil industry and hoped to push average yearly GDP growth up to 4 percent or more.

"AMLO lived with the Chontal from Tabasco and defended their customs and folklore, but his basic aim was for them to improve their standard of living. For that reason he wants strong growth in Mexico," said José Agustín Ortiz Pinchetti, a friend of the president and a former collaborator of his in the government of Mexico City, when I asked him about the growth versus conservation dilemma. Some activists who had supported the AMLO campaign wondered why the new president defended mining and oil sovereignty when Mexico could make a swift transition to renewable energy sources. The question that divided the left was key to the future of Real de Catorce. On one hand, there was concern about the possible contamination of underground water springs in one of the driest regions of Mexico. But, on the other, unemployment and poverty were of enormous concern in the town of La Luz, where the First Majestic mine had considerable support.

In truth, any growth driven by mining had caused more problems than solutions in Zacatecas and San Luis Potosí. Not only because of its impact on the environment or the barely visible benefits to the local economy. There were also signs that the mafias of organized crime were using violence against small farmers opposed to mining projects, and to intimidate the workers in the mines in Guerrero and Chiapas in the south. The mining multinationals had found synergies that would never be discussed at Harvard Business School, making tacit agreements with gangs that specialized in the most macabre violence, which had helped to crush opposition. There were even indications, according to the journalists who wrote *La guerra que nos ocultan* (The War That

They Hide from Us), that the disappearance of 43 students in Ayotzinapa (Guerrero), a crime that shocked the country in 2015 and sowed the seeds for Peña Nieto's demise, might be related to the existence of gold deposits in a region where Frank Giustra's Goldcorp had won mining concessions.

The students, all from rural farming families, were opposed to extractive activities on their land. "We know that drug traffickers take a slice when mining companies pay communities. I would even say that serious conversations between company employees and organized-crime leaders happen so that there is no opposition to mining," said Sergio Uribe, a mining expert at the Autonomous University of Zacatecas, when we met in the stunning, baroque city center built with the riches from the first silver boom. Whatever the degree of direct involvement of multinationals, an endless list of murders of environmental leaders, small farmers' leaders, indigenous activists, union leaders, and critical journalists supported suspicions that organized crime was clearing the terrain for the Canadian mining companies.

* * *

Maybe tourism would provide the means to square the circle and achieve environmentally sustainable growth without opening craters in the sacred ground of the Huichol, poisoning their underground springs with mercury and cyanide, or turning a blind eye to the *sicarios*.

"We've been struggling for years, and it's only because of our fight that the mine is still closed," said Cornelia Ruth Ramseier, the owner of the Hotel Real in the historic center of Real de Catorce, who had shown excellent taste by decorating the hotel walls with photographs from John Huston's *Treasure of the Sierra Madre* rather than ones of Brad Pitt and Julia Roberts in *The Mexican*—both shot in the old mining town. The anti-mining NGOs also proposed tourism as a model of alternative development. After all, without demand from cultural tourism, the incredible psychedelia of Huichol art would likely have disappeared. Thanks to the gringos, magnificent, peyote-inspired works like *Eclipse of the Huichol World* by Antonio López Pinedo or *The Skeleton of Tatewari* by Justo Benítez, which resemble crossovers between Jean-Michel Basquiat and Keith Haring, were bringing revenue to the Huichol.

So there was no reason at all for the Huichol to shy away from an encounter with global culture in Real de Catorce. But that procession of 4x4 pickups, coaches, and racers, full of day-trippers from San Luis Potosí, Saltillo, and Monterrey, along with the World War II–era Willys Jeeps heading off for the desert excursion to Las Margaritas ejido farm, was another matter. Even without the mine, the Cerro Quemado was beginning to face an extractivist threat. These tourists did not appear to be the spiritual heirs of Antonin Artaud, who was expelled from the surrealist circle because hallucinogenic drugs were deemed too easy a route to the surrealist consciousness. The peyote tours of the twenty-first century were a more packaged experience, another assimilated subversion, and the same aberrations were emerging as those of the ayahuasca trips to the Peruvian Amazon, where a Canadian traveler hooked on the hallucinogenic brew had shot his shaman-guide dead.

"There is now a business of peyote trafficking from here to the tourist areas in Cancún," said Pedro Medellín, an environmental engineer from the University of San Luis Potosí who, despite advanced cancer, had participated in that year's Huichol peyote pilgrimage. "People here are now beginning to use the term the pillage of the peyote."

PART THREE: DEPLETION

PART THREE: DEPRESSION

CHAPTER TWELVE

Avocados (Michoacán, Mexico)
Hot Dog with Guacamole

Avocado orchards had carpeted the gently undulating hills around the sacred lake of Pátzcuaro with stodgy green bushes. Here, before the cataclysmic arrival of the first envoys dispatched by Hernán Cortés from the Aztec capital over the mountains to the East, the great civilization of the Purépecha had sown maize, amaranth, zucchini, cacao, cotton, tomato, beans, a dozen types of chili, and much more. Now the monotonous "green gold" of the avocado boom had colonized the entire Mexican state of Michoacán. As the uniform landscape unfolded before us, it was shocking to think that the cause of the disaster was America's great patriotic party: the National Football League's Super Bowl.

A flurry of advertising creativity on behalf of the Mexican avocado was unleashed every year during the multi-million-dollar sports broadcast. Usually starring a Hollywood actor, the ad would habitually outdo BMW, Budweiser, Coca-Cola, Dove, Mercedes-Benz, Snickers, or Victoria's Secret. "Is your life just terrible?" asks the comic actor Chris Elliott, star of *Scary Movie 2* and *Scary Movie 4*, in the 2019 spot. "You deserve more! Spread an avocado on top of everything!" All this against a background of pizzas, hamburgers, chicken, and bacon sandwiches, topped with a thick layer of creamy guacamole.

Guacamole was now an obligatory snack for the hundred million or so Americans who watched the Super Bowl. In February of 2017, 278 million avocados—most of them from Michoacán—had been sold during the days before the game in a country whose relationship with its five million undocumented Mexicans was frankly schizophrenic.

Perhaps America's fragile identity, ever more Hispanic yet, at the same time, more xenophobic, needed the Mexican avocado mash to gel its parts together. A few days before the Super Bowl, the domestic diva Martha Stewart, fresh out of jail after serving five months for insider trading, had released on social networks her latest recipe for guacamole and nachos adapted to the palate of the New England Patriots. Gwyneth Paltrow would soon throw her recipe into the mix.

The avocado had become the star product of Mexican food production in the age of the North American Free Trade Agreement (NAFTA), soon to be rebranded the United States–Mexico–Canada Agreement (USMCA). It had led the explosive growth of vegetable and fruit exports from Mexico to the United States, from $3 billion to $20 billion since NAFTA was signed in 1994 by Bill Clinton, Carlos Salinas de Gortari, and Jean Chrétien. Sixty percent of the avocados consumed in the United States now came from Mexico, whose farmers produced sixteen times more than the formerly dominant Californian growers. The fruit (or was it a vegetable?) could even be considered a symbol of cross-border cultural integration. Those who drove through the American interior, where the Mexican diaspora now stretched as far as the Rocky Mountains of Montana to the Mississippi swamps, soon learned that the roadside taqueria and its *aperitivo* of guacamole with cilantro, lime, and onion was the only stop-off that did not involve eating in a global fast-food chain. The only real soul in the desert.

Moreover, the avocado was now classified as a "superfood"–bursting with nutritive fats that miraculously did not produce heart disease but rather improved coronary health. It contained vitamins B, C, E, and K, the last a crucial preventative treatment for osteoporosis. Fiber, natural statins, and beta-sitosterol in the avocado flesh lowered cholesterol levels in the blood. The presence of zeaxanthin in the avocado would combat ocular problems. Guacamole could help prevent colon, stomach, and pancreatic cancer. To drive home its claim to be the most super of foods, several studies had shown that consuming avocados also mitigated depression. Sales were not only soaring in the United States but in Europe and Asia too.

It had not always been like this. In the 1950s, the avocado was known unsentimentally as the crocodile pear because of its hard, wrinkled skin. Imports from Mexico were banned until 1997 due to the alleged danger of parasites from the dreaded tropical south. Nobody would have imagined in those days buying two pounds of avocados to celebrate such a truly American event as the finals of the NFL. But after those million-dollar ads and an inspired marketing campaign in which leading NFL stars sponsored different recipes for guacamole, the United States learned to love the crocodile pear.

Seizing the opportunity, more and more Michoacán producers managed to pass the sanitary tests necessary to gain access to the US market. When complete liberalization was announced in 2007, Michoacán had become an unbeatable competitor for the Californian avocado growers. The Mexican producers specialized, like their Californian rivals, in the Hass variety of avocado, more meaty than those that the Purépecha had quietly consumed over the millennia, and with a tough skin that protected the pears during long hauls in chilled container trucks to El Paso or Tijuana and then beyond to the big US consumer markets. With its resilient natural packaging, the Hass avocado was perfectly suited to the global market for overhyped super-foods. Demand and production were ramped upward to ever-higher levels. Michoacán, whose crystalline lakes had earned it the name of the "land of fish" in the indigenous language of Tarasco, would never be the same.

By 2020, 80 percent of the avocados consumed in the United States came from Michoacán, and the unmistakable signs of yet another extractive fever were visible in the lost kingdom of the Purépecha. Similar perhaps to the lust for wealth that had brought the Spanish to Michoacán soon after the sacking of Tenochtitlán, the magnificent Aztec capital, laid waste in the name of Christ and gold. Now in the twenty-first century, on the outskirts of Uruapan, the frenetic *capital del aguacate*, the new economy of agri-business took shape in an undulating expanse of densely foliated avocado bushes, glowing fluorescent green in the late afternoon sun.

Further west on the shores of Lake Pátzcuaro, the monoculture had not yet colonized the entire landscape, but the advance of the avocado seemed unstoppable. "Practically everybody here wants an avocado orchard. One person switches and it goes well for him. Others say: 'I'm switching too!' Others see them and do the same," explained Francisco Flores Bautista, a resident of the Purépecha indigenous community of Jarácuaro on the shores of the lake.

When Bautista returned to Lake Pátzcuaro after forty years working in construction in the Mexican capital, he was horrified by the extent of environmental destruction. "They pump water from the lake to water the avocado orchards and, bit by bit, the lake is shrinking. It's pillage.

Just look! Once it reached the road. Now it never rises, just falls," he lamented as we walked through dried-out reeds.

The falling water level, together with the introduction of the rapacious predator tilapia, had wiped out almost all the indigenous fish species. Of the cornucopia of marine life that had fed the Purépecha cities, only the diminutive silvery *charal* remained. The same occurred at other great freshwater deposits in Michoacán. Only Lake Zirahuén, fifteen miles to the south, had been saved from pollution and falling water levels. The Purépecha communities on the shores of the lake, a landscape of stunning beauty where dense pine and ilex oak forests met white nymphaea lilies floating on turquoise water, were girding themselves for the arrival of the *aguacateros*, avocado producers, just as their ancestors had waited anxiously for Cortés. Then, many chose to drown themselves in the Michoacán lakes. Now, Bautista had chosen an alternative strategy. He had set up a microbusiness in Jarácuaro, specialized in purifying well water with sand and gravel filters that he then sold to lake dwellers increasingly concerned about water quality.

The unstoppable advance of the avocado in Michoacán might have been the unwritten chapter of *Relación de Michoacán*, the heartbreaking chronicle of the destruction of the Purépecha civilization, written from 1539–1541 by Fray Jerónimo de Alcalá, a progressive Franciscan monk who had arrived in Mexico just in time to catch a fleeting glimpse of life amongst the pyramids on the shores of Lake Pátzcuaro.

In the polytheist societies of the Purépecha, a profound, maybe fanatical religiosity blurred the division between external reality and interior myth. Plants and animals magically merged with human beings in a mythology governed by daylight dreams of hybrid beings with jaguar heads and pumpkin bodies. The Purépecha inhabited a world of infinite biodiversity, which nourished their boundless imagination. There was in fact a greater diversity of domesticated plants in pre-Hispanic Mexico than in any other contemporary horticulture except China's. Michoacán, with its fertile volcanic soil and plentiful water supply, was one of the regions of Mexico best endowed with the rich fruits of nature.

Altitudes varied between one thousand and ten thousand feet above sea level and gave rise to a vast range of microclimates, each with its corresponding set of crops. The avocado—*ahuacatl* for the Aztec, *kupanda* for the Purépecha—was just one more element of this natural wealth reproduced in the Purépecha imagination. A native plant of Mesoamerica, it was enjoyed as a wild fruit for millennia. Although, judging by historical documents, it was not a particularly remarkable fruit for the Purépecha, never mind a superfood. Teresa Rojas Rabiela makes no mention of the avocado in her exhaustive investigation of pre-Columbian agriculture and fourteenth-century indigenous food, *Las siembras de ayer* (Yesterday's Crops).

Half a millennium later, the avocado was the only crop that mattered. Diversity was annihilated with every new plantation made to the requirements of supermarkets in Texas or Los Angeles. "Why do they crave for this gold? These gods must eat it. That is why they want it so," declared the *cazonci*, the divine ruler of the Purépecha, when the Spanish conquistador Francisco de Montaño arrived on the shores of Lake Pátzcuaro in 1522. Five hundred years later, the twentieth-century *oro verde*, the green gold, was not being eaten; it was being devoured. The avocado plantations advanced relentlessly around the shrinking lakes while the biggest players in the business amassed huge fortunes.

"They destroy the pine forest, they destroy everything, but no journalist here will tell the story," whispered Osmar, a waiter in the mezcal bar Carajo in the old center of Pátzcuaro, after we arranged to meet at closing time at a secret rendezvous point in the shadows of the baroque cathedral.

Bautista's parents, Purépecha campesinos, wearing large straw hats and woolen ponchos draped over their shoulders, returned wearily from their orchard, laden with corncobs, as a fine, tepid rain fell over Jarácuaro. We stopped to give them a ride. They spoke Tarasco, a language in danger of extinction. "The youngsters are ashamed to speak it and it is not taught in school," explained the mother. The age-old custom of making corn tortillas was also disappearing as young Purépecha chose to buy the ready-made product, she explained.

On hearing the Purépecha's ancient language I decided to try another makeshift linguistic test of the perception of taste, like the one I had used on the Aymara potato growers in Puno: "Do you have words in Tarasco that describe tastes that do not exist in Spanish?" The mother responded: "*Churipu* is the taste of fish broth; *jawas* the taste of chili." And the taste of *aguacate*? "*Chamahuelhatipua*," she replied expressionlessly. Or at least this was how I noted the word down in my pad. Then she added in Spanish, "The avocado is using up all the water." The autochthonous avocado was now considered an existential threat in the Purépecha communities. Never could they have imagined even in their most disturbing dreams that a single Purépecha fruit would monopolize the palate of the world. After all, there had been so many in their orchards, *equaros* they were called, before and after the Spanish conquest, merging the "land of fish" with Andalusia, the guava with the pomegranate, the pineapple with the grape.

Curiously, notwithstanding the knowledge of their natural environment and personal health accumulated over millennia, the Purépecha showed little interest in the miraculous health-enhancing properties of the avocado pear, discussed ad nauseam in the Sunday lifestyle magazines, from New York to Mexico City. Others did show interest, however. The new avocado millionaires in their kitsch mansions on the other side of Lake Pátzcuaro were keen readers of the superfood guides. And so were the other *aguacate* magnates in Michoacán, less easy to identify but now key players in the business. Drug traffickers and other mafias had launched themselves headlong into the new business of green gold.

As the avocado became the perfect side dish for a billion American hot dogs and buffalo wings, and as a tasteless alternative to butter spread on trillions of slices of students' toast, the avocado boom in Michoacán had turned into the target of a new generation of organized (or rather, disorganized) crime that now competed with the old Mexican drug cartels. Criminal groups with names like Los Caballeros Templarios (the Knights Templar) or Los Viagras tried their luck in the avocado business, in league with a series of corrupt governors of the state of Michoacán. It was an excellent complement to the cocaine, heroin, marijuana, and oxycodone in which they trafficked. They would soon apply their own methods of extortion, torture, and murder to the global guacamole trade.

The traditional avocado farmers of Michoacán, victims of blackmail and kidnapping, were forced to sell their orchards to the narcos at bargain prices. "They put a gun to your head and tell you to sign the deed before the notary. That's how the transfer of land is agreed upon," explained Guillermo Vargas, a sociologist at the University of San Nico-

las de Hidalgo in Morelia, as we strolled around the spectac-
ularly baroque cathedral in the Michoacán capital, formerly
a tourist destination and now a no-go area as the murder
rate soared. Likewise, the Knights Templar and the Viagras
demanded a commission for every hectare farmed or ton of
exported avocado. Those who refused to pay might end up
like one of the seven workers found in an avocado orchard
with bullet holes in the nape of their necks. The avocado
was such a coveted prize that gangs hijacked an average
of four trucks loaded with the fruit per day. Some avocado
farmers, following the example of the doctor-vigilante José
Manuel Mireles, tried to create self-defense groups to expel
the criminals from their lands. But the draw of guacamole
was now irresistible, and just as one gang was driven out of
town another appeared with more powerful weapons and
more sadistic *sicario* gun men.

Meanwhile, large exporters and avocado brokers–some
of them international brands like Del Monte–were profiting by purchasing from producers at dirt-cheap prices and
reselling to the US supermarket chains at very attractive
ones. "They pay a dollar per kilo of avocado here and sell it
for eight at a Minnesota Walmart," said Vargas.

In order not to squander such a reliable source of profits,
"transnational corporations, just like the Canadian mining
companies in Zacatecas, pay the extortion money demanded
by the narcos," he continued. Michoacán, the state of the
legendary Mexican president Lázaro Cárdenas, with its
spectacular colonial buildings and revolutionary-era
murals, had become a narco state plagued by endemic violence. Or maybe it was a guacamole state.

It was no coincidence that the first mass grave discovered by bereaved family members while searching for the
remains of more than thirty-seven thousand disappeared

Mexicans was found in Uruapan, the avocado capital of the world. Nor was it a coincidence that nine corpses were found hanging from a bridge in Uruapan in the summer of 2019 alongside a sign advising DEAR PEOPLE, CONTINUE WITH YOUR DAILY ROUTINES. Another ten dismembered bodies were found the same day stuffed into plastic bags. Police concluded it was a show of strength by the new cartel in town, the New Jalisco Generation, that had crossed the border from the neighboring state and its capital Guadalajara to claim its share of the guacamole.

* * *

The highway from Pátzcuaro to Uruapan ended with a steep and perilous descent where dead-end deceleration exits allowed trucks laden with avocados to avoid crashing when their brakes failed. GIVE WAY TO VEHICLES WITHOUT BRAKES, the signs announced enigmatically. The message seemed tailored to the avocado boom in Uruapan, a chaotic rush of investment, now unstoppable, destined to end in disaster. Further down, a truck carrying beehives had overturned and a swarm of insects buzzed in the scorching heat.

In the gentle hills around the city, thousands of geometric rows of avocado bushes rose and fell like an advancing army. There were avocado plant nurseries and plots for sale that could be paid for over thirty-six months without interest. There was a jail at the city entrance, built of gray concrete, followed by a long strip mall with a Super Pollo fried-chicken franchise, gaudy seafood restaurants, a taco joint called Taquería El Infierno, and motels whose rooms were rented by the hour. Most importantly, Uruapan was the headquarters of the Avocado Producers and Packers/Exporters Association of Mexico (APEAM), and of the three

US brokers expert in exploiting the difference between the prices paid to the producer and those paid to the retailer. According to Carlos Paniagua, economist from the Michoacán University of San Nicolás de Hidalgo, exporters and packers received 35 percent of the income generated in the avocado supply chain, compared with 20 percent for the producer, most to the large-scale avocado farms. "The people who take most risk receive the least," he said.

The first commercial avocados were planted in in Michoacán in the 1960s on already cultivated land in the valleys around Uruapan. Land liberalization during Carlos Salinas de Gortari's presidential term from 1988 to 1994 allowed the avocado orchards to scale the mountains toward the Tancítaro volcano, and then head westward. The number of hectares under cultivation rose from 3,000 in the 1960s to 180,000 by the early twentieth century. Only the coldest areas of the highest mountains, snow-peaked in winter, seemed beyond the reach of the Hass avocado. Soon even the mountains on the Tarascan plateau with its spectacular volcano would be colonized, thanks, in part, to rising temperatures and climate change that were turning northern Mexico into a desert and destabilizing rainfall distribution.

Nevertheless Michoacán appeared to have a prosperous future ahead of it. Avocados would be a driver of development in a state that suffered extreme rural poverty. "Despite all the problems, avocados create a lot of jobs and many small producers are able to escape poverty thanks to their avocado orchards," said biologist Mayra Elena Gavito in her office at the National Autonomous University of Mexico (UNAM). And since unemployment and endemic poverty were organized crime's recruiting ground, some believed avocado production could provide a solution to

Mexico's horrifying violence. Gavito also argued that if the old practice of combining orchards with other crops were resurrected, the avocado could be less destructive than other monocultures, such as corn. "The avocado doesn't have to be a monoculture," she insisted. What was needed was a sustainable production model, rather than the green gold rush. But there was little sign that the avocado industry, from California-based multinationals to the mafias in Michoacán or Jalisco, was willing to change course. As Francisco Bautista and his parents feared, falling water levels in Lake Pátzcuaro were a warning of an incipient environmental catastrophe.

* * *

I contacted Alberto Gómez-Tagle, a veteran environmental expert who had spent ten years studying the impact of the avocado boom on water supply in the Uruapan region. Perhaps to warn me of what was in store for Michoacán and Mexico, Gómez-Tagle suggested we meet on the bland outskirts of Morelia, in a Vips cafeteria, a franchise of the multinational chain allied with Starbucks, Burger King, and Domino's Pizza whose chilled, insipid guacamole was now available worldwide. Next door was a Walmart, the megadiscount store owned by the Waltons of Arkansas, the wealthiest family in the United States, who were so proud to be the icon of the low-wage economy in the United States that they had crossed the border to Mexico, where the minimum wage was less than eight dollars a day.

Specializing in water ecology, Gómez-Tagle explained to me how he had monitored the flow of an underground spring on the outskirts of Uruapan called La Rodilla del Diablo (the Devil's Knee). In the 1960s, 4,224 liters of water per minute flowed from the spring. By 2015 this had dropped to only 724 liters, 80 percent less. Gómez-Tagle sent a team of technicians to investigate and discovered that the most probable cause was the proliferation of avocado production and water pumped from wells in the Uruapan area.

The avocado expansion had caused mass deforestation of native pine trees and ilex oaks in Michoacán. Since the avocado consumed twenty-six thousand gallons of water per month per hectare, eleven times more than the orginal pines, the avocado boom was not good news at all for the environment. According to Gómez-Tagle's research, the avocado tree transpired (lost water by evaporation) eight times faster than the pine. "A pine tree is a perfect funnel to transport rainwater to the ground, but now you have thousands of hectares of avocados sucking water and evaporating it," he told me. Deforestation was also leaving small isolated forests that were more vulnerable to insects and plagues while threatening the habitat of the millions of monarch butterflies whose vibrant golden tones transformed the Michoacán landscape at the turn of the year.

While a family of less than slender Michoacános sitting at the next table in the Vips restaurant ordered an authentic American breakfast (pancakes with whipped cream and maple syrup), Gómez-Tagle described to me the crude reality of the green gold: "We are facing a force of terrible destruction and not only in Michoacán; the avocado is spreading to Jalisco and will not stop there."

Nor would it be detained at the Mexican border. Colombia had announced plans for sixty-two million hectares. Chile was expanding its own production. Such was the appeal of the American guacamole craze and the world superfood market. And while the marketing of the Super Bowl raised avocado consumption in the United States to unimaginable heights, in Michoacán the other face of cross-border integration was becoming visible. "More and more indigenous people here now shop at Walmart," said Alberto as we left Vips. And indeed, there they were. Extended families of Purépecha emerged from the Waltons' store across the street with bags of premade tortillas, made almost certainly with American wheat. There were no avocados in their Walmart trolleys, however. In Mexico the avocado was now prohibitively expensive.

* * *

White veins of lightning flashed across an ominously darkened sky behind the great pyramid of Ihuatzio, the third city of the Purépecha, once a ceremonial center for military training, on the shores of Lake Pátzuaro. The purple clouds on the horizon were so laden with vapor that a Purépecha shaman might have seen a pregnant goddess about to give birth to a giant frog. "That is a lightning fork. Now the rain is coming," said the guide José Socorro Castillo, who, silhouetted against the still intact wall of the pyramid with a wrinkled face, laughing eyes, and a toothless mouth, resembled a prophet or a shaman. Thousands of warbling crickets spread across the lawn like a living carpet laid over what was once the great plaza. Here the Purépecha warriors trained for their theatrical but no less lethal battles and staged games with hockey-style sticks and a rubber ball, often in flames. "The Purépecha ate the crickets, but we don't eat them here. Not now. The chapulines [natives of Mexico City] do eat them. Oh, yes. They don't leave anything there! Here what we have left over, we give it away," he boasted, laughing out loud while the first thunderclap crackled in the distance. The steps up to the pyramid were so tall that they seemed unfit for human beings especially for the short and stocky Purépecha.

"The Purépecha were more advanced than us. They were astronomers. They understood their cosmos. Now, all the technology comes from Japan and it is contaminated by the atomic bombs," said Socorro in a baffling monologue. The rain now fell like a curtain of warm water, and we ran toward the exit gate from the ruins. "For the Purépecha everything they ate was a god. The avocado too. Of course!" continued the prophet Socorro. "They ate snakes, armadillos, they ate the humans they sacrificed. Tasty!" he exclaimed, and another loud cackle resonated through the ruins of the ancient city.

That apocalyptic visit to the lost city of the Purépecha with José Socorro as guide seemed the perfect setting for the catastrophic denouement of the story of the Michoacán avocado. Friar de Alcalá narrates in the *Relación de Michoacán* that weeks before the arrival of the Spaniards the people of the lake spoke of strange visions that appeared in their dreams, omens that augured the end of the Purépecha kingdom. Young sapling trees bent under the weight of their fruit before they had grown strong enough to bear it; young girls became pregnant before reaching puberty; old women gave birth to flint daggers adorned with the colors of the four regions of the world. Time was close to the end. Now in Michoacán, on the shores of the fishless lakes, the same presentiment of disaster was voiced in interview after interview.

"The Purépecha, like all Mesoamerican societies before the arrival of the Castilians, had developed a sustainable system that did not damage Michoacán's fertile volcanic soil," said Guillermo Vargas after our walk through around the cathedral. The so-called *altepetl* (the hill of water) was the fundamental unit of the geography of the Purépecha, he explained. Maintaining a balance between highlands, lakes, and underground aquifers was the key goal of their philosophy of life. "Remarkably, they managed to maintain the balance for seven thousand years. Even after the arrival of the Castilian farmers and sheep herders. But now, the time horizon has been reduced to the next semester. There is no longer a cosmic worldview of nature and the *altepetl* are being destroyed. Soon we shall reach a peak of avocado production and, without water, a debacle will follow," he said. Then, as if the ghost of Eduardo Galeano had returned to the baroque center of Morelia, Vargas added: "When that occurs, the Americans will suddenly say: 'Goodbye!' And they will go elsewhere."

CHAPTER THIRTEEN

Soy (Pará, Brazil; Bahia, Brazil)
Cargill and the War of the End of the Planet

So oppressive was the heat that afternoon in Santarém that not even down by the harbor, where the Amazon meets the Tapajos, was there enough air to breathe. Top-heavy ferry boats set off for Manaus or Belém, the locals already dozing in rows of hammocks hung from the deck roofs while the tourists gazed wide-eyed at the ocean-like river and fantasized about Werner Herzog and his Fitzcarraldian adventures.

But the new reality of the Amazon was unfolding in the background. The Bahamas-flagged bulk carrier Jaguar Max had loaded several thousand tons of soybeans from a monstrous grain terminal in the privatized port run by the US commodity giant Cargill. That afternoon the ship would depart for southern Europe, where the soy would be processed into feed for pigs and chickens to be packaged as environmentally sustainable meat. With a little feverish imagination, aided by the sweltering Amazon heat, the Cargill terminal, built in 2003, without the mandatory environmental impact study, resembled an alien invader, perhaps those that terrorized humanity in H. G. Wells and Steven Spielberg's respective wars of the worlds. In Santarém, the war now underway was for the future of the planet.

With storage capacity for 114,000 tons of soybeans or corn, the terminal had transformed the logistics of the grain business in the Amazon. It would give access along the Tapajos River–and the BR163 highway once surfacing the road was completed–to five million tons of soybeans harvested yearly on the new frontier of Brazilian agribusiness a thousand miles downriver in the vast state of Mato Grosso. There, soy plantations stretched out across a horizontal landscape like a Rothko painting of alternating green and gray–a doleful monoculture where the most vibrant biodiversity on the planet had once bubbled and climbed.

Cargill bought millions of tons from the Mato Grosso soy barons after each quarterly harvest. The grain was loaded onto gargantuan barges with gaily painted white and green hulls in the agribusiness boomtown of Pôrto Velho, another strategic hub for the new extractive logistics of the Brazilian Amazon. Then as the soy reached Santarém it was transferred onto long-distance bulk carriers and transported five hundred miles downriver to Belém and out onto the Atlantic.

Other vessels with a capacity for fifty-five thousand tons of beans waited in line to connect to the system of cranes, belts, and tubes and fill their holds with the commodity most closely identified with the globalization of the food industry: soy, the wonder cereal that, as Cargill's Malthusian PR team tirelessly repeated in corporate press releases, would be humanity's only hope in the war against global famine.

Among the destinations across the ocean was the once-mighty port of Liverpool where one of Cargill's two European bean crushing plants was located. A century and a half earlier, in the classic era of the open veins, sugar, coffee, and tin arrived from Brazil and were stored at the austere Victorian warehouses of the British Empire's biggest port. Slaves bought in West Africa and sent to the New World completed the triangular trade. Now, soy from Santarém had helped resurrect Liverpool after a century of decline. But the empire that ruled in the twenty-first century was that of Cargill, the largest unlisted company in the world, with 170,000 employees and global turnover worth $100 billion.

The company's original headquarters, an incongruous replica of a Parisian château in a Minneapolis suburb, had been the nerve center for the first phase of global agri-business that had made the American Midwest the world's granary. Turning its back on Iowa's poker-faced farmers, Cargill opted for the "tropicalization" of the soybean, adapting the cereal to the climate and the soils of the equatorial Amazon. Brazil, Argentina, and their neighbors were now the biggest soy producers in the world with almost 60 percent of global exports, and Cargill would not miss the opportunity to expand business into the Amazon. Its yearly turnover was already double that of its main competitor, Archer-Daniels-Midland (ADM)—headquartered down the interstate in Chicago—where soy, wheat, corn, and pork bellies "futures" were traded on the commodities exchange in a daily orgy of speculation within which essential foodstuffs had morphed into financial derivatives.

This duo of American giants dominated the global cereals market along with two other brokers, France's Louis Dreyfus and another US company, Bunge, the latter also aggressively active in the Brazilian Amazon with a cargo terminal ninety miles downstream from Santarém in Itaituba, the chaotic metropolis of jungle extractivism. Soy was the most important of the so-called flex crops. It served as food for human beings, feed for animals, and fuel for diesel vehicles, and had even been tried as raw material for the automobile industry. Henry Ford had made plastic from soy and planned to "grow" his car components on a soybean farm in Michigan. An inspired idea perhaps, but the ruins of Fordlandia, the automobile magnate's delusional project to build a replica of a Midwest town on the banks of the Tapajos River, was now overrun by the jungle—a warning to all those who chose to reconcile nature with the fossil fuel industry.

Despite those "Feed the World" Cargill press communiqués, only 6 percent of soy production was actually used directly to nourish human beings. The rest fattened billions of animals on their short journey from the mechanical feedlot to the industrial slaughterhouse. Soy was the first link in a destructive supply chain whose final link was a packet of frozen chicken wings, or a supersized hamburger topped with crispy bacon. Of course, this was a business model entirely incompatible with the urgent need to drastically reduce global carbon emissions. But the challenge of climate change was very much a secondary matter for Cargill, whose global profits had soared by 47 percent in 2018 to $3.2 billion. The megabroker's unrivaled status as the emperor of soy produced excellent synergies with its billion-dollar business of battery chickens, the most prized "protein platform" for the twenty-first-century global food industry. Cargill was also seeking to increase its presence in the swine sector (as those pork bellies hit new highs in Chicago), which would complement its already dominant position in US beef production.

The corporate behemoth processed 1.5 million chickens in its plants in the United Kingdom and France using soy imported from Santarém as feed. Its high protein content helped fatten the poultry in record time for controlled atmospheric stunning, slaughter, and, in some cases, subsequent transformation into McDonald's chicken McNuggets produced in-facility.

Spain, meanwhile, was now the third-biggest pork producer in the world with over fifty million hogs—more than the Spanish population—crammed into nightmarish factory farms. Soy from the Santarém terminal would be processed at another Cargill plant in Barcelona, and used as feed at the pig-fattening plants. All for the production of the now globally fashionable industrialized chorizo sausage or that slithery processed ham sold in unopenable plastic packages at the Carrefour or Aldi supermarkets in the new strip malls in outer Madrid. The same process linked most advanced economy supermarket chains to the Brazilian soy producers. Cargill—dominating the transcontinental six-thousand-mile supply chain from the soybean in Mato Grosso to the KFC in Nowheresville—was the key player for globalized Big Food.

Of course, the big market for Brazilian soy was Asia, although most exports to China did not go through Santarém but through the ports of Santos and Paranaguá in southern Brazil, where deforestation had been a fait accompli since the early twentieth century. Rather than saving the world from hunger, soybeans were in fact satisfying Asia's burgeoning demand for meat as global fast food displaced millenarian cuisine, with disastrous consequences for public health. Brazil was already the second-largest soy producer in the world and, thanks to Chinese demand, it seemed a question of time before it clinched first place. Brazilian agribusiness had learned from Cargill's meatpacking model and was using soy to feed its own battery chickens. The national beef champion JBS had become the world's biggest exporter of frozen birds slaughtered in less hygienic conditions than in the United Kingdom, which had already caused a spate of food hygiene scares and potential pandemics.

The price of soy saw a meteoric rise from eight to seventeen dollars a bushel between 2004 and 2012. Seven years later, after the slowdown in the Chinese economy in the second phase of the global financial crisis, the price had fallen back to nine dollars. But Brazilian soy production continued to rise and accelerated when trade tensions between the United States and China flared, threatening US exports and pushing prices back up.

Lending support to Cargill's bid for tropical soy was the Brazilian state agricultural agency the Brazilian Agricultural Research Corporation (EMBRAPA), created by the military government in 1973, which had innovated a series of scientific advances in fertilizers, pesticides, and herbicides vital for monocultures. In the Brazilian version of the green revolution, EMBRAPA was the vehicle for Brazilian agrarian policy, and, together with the world's largest public development bank, the National Bank for Economic and Social Development (BNDES), it turned Brazilian agribusiness into a rival to the United States. An impressive achievement by state-driven developmentalism.

But here too the Brazilian developmental state had created a Frankenstein. Soon Brazil would lead the global ranking in the use of toxic chemicals for agribusiness, approving transgenic soybeans and the glyphosate pesticide needed to protect them, a carcinogenic substance that had already been detected in the breast milk of mothers in Mato Grosso. Cargill, which also supplied the pesticides, would learn to love the open, now treeless, spaces of Mato Grosso just as it had the Great Plains of the American Midwest.

A year after the Cargill terminal was built at Santarém, the deforestation rate in the north and west of the state of Pará had doubled, from fifteen thousand to twenty-eight thousand hectares. Cargill's arrival coincided with the two worst years for deforestation in the entire Amazon region since the record set in 1995, with the destruction of an area equivalent to fifty thousand soccer fields. This was no surprise. Cargill guaranteed soy farmers a steady demand and provided loans for setting up in the area. Thousands of *fazendeiro* ranchers from Paraná and Rio Grande do Sul in southern Brazil headed north to the Santarém region to plant soybeans. Raissa Macedo Lacerda Osório, a specialist in sustainable development at the University of Brasília, concluded in her doctoral thesis: "Cargill's actions in the region were the main factor that persuaded producers to migrate and settle in the west of Pará." By "migrating and settling," of course, she also meant deforesting.

This would create problems for the Minnesota giant. Soy was now endangering progress made by the first Lula government in the fight against Amazon deforestation at a time when consumers began to lose sleep over climate change. While only 10 percent of Brazilian soybeans were grown in the Amazon, almost all of it in Mato Grosso, a pioneering report called *Eating Up the Amazon*, published by Greenpeace in 2006, warned, "A powerful newcomer [is] beginning to operate at the frontier of Amazon destruction: the soya industry." The global NGO encouraged consumers to boycott foods made from soy grown in deforested areas of the Amazon. The fight against climate change was already mobilizing millions of people in Europe and the United States, many of them under thirty years old, a key demographic for a consumer brand. The corporate image of the big commodity brokers' most important customers was at stake, from fast-food empires such as McDonald's to supermarkets and discount stores like Walmart, Tesco, or Lidl.

Greenpeace and other NGOs soon realized that by targeting the big consumer brands, they could reach Cargill.

Up until then, the company had been a successful corporate delinquent with a long history of labor, human rights, and environmental abuses but little concern for its brand image. Santarém was an excellent showcase for the campaign against deforested soy. In 2005, a team of Greenpeace activists scaled the cranes and bridges at the Cargill grain terminal and displayed banners that read FORA CARGILL and STOP DEFORESTATION. The Santarém port, they denounced, was not only encouraging deforestation at the Mato Grosso soy frontier, from which 80 percent of the beans were transported to the Cargill terminal, but it was also destroying the forests around Santarém right in the heart of the Amazon jungle.

The impact of the terminal was not only evident across wider and wider areas of cleared forest, but also in a demographic explosion in the city of Santarém itself, whose population quintupled from 63,000 inhabitants in ten years to almost 350,000. Mass migration emptied the forest of people as well as trees.

"Fifteen years ago, in the Santarém region, agriculture was mainly family-run and highly diversified. We produced everything: rice, beans, coffee, sweet potato, tomato, cocoa, annatto," explained Ib Sales, an environmental activist in Santarém whom I met at an event organized to protest the construction of the big dam on the Tapajos. "But when Cargill and Bunge set up in town, most small farmers sold their land for a pittance to the soy farmers. Thousands of them moved into town. The result is chaos."

Twenty thousand landless farmers, displaced by soy, built favelas of makeshift shacks on the outskirts of the city. These displaced landless workers and farmers were the forgotten victims of the global soy economy. The favelas became incubators of crime and potentially contagious disease as the millenary rain forest and its fauna edged up against open-sewer shantytowns. "The countryside is now empty and the city is full," summarized the Franciscan priest Edilberto Sena.

"What do country dwellers know how to do? Well they know how to plant, harvest, fish . . . And if they come to the city, what are they going to do? Well, they will do shit, sell sweets in the street or collect Bolsa Família," said the marvelously profane Father Edilberto, in reference to the anti-poverty subsidy that had been an essential element of Lula's social policies. A former militant of the rural left, Sena was a tireless critic of the PT model of extractivism and social transfers. "The sons of a whore destroy the farmers' economy and then pay a subsidy to the victims," he complained.

Cargill's corporate image–already damaged by a case of poisoned meat from animals industrially dismembered in its hellish US slaughterhouses–went up in flames. McDonald's, in the midst of an opportunistic eco-rebranding as its First World logos switched from red to green, demanded that its principal supplier remove deforested soy from its supply chain. Other global brands followed suit. In 2006, Cargill and the other brokers signed the historic Amazon-soy moratorium, which vetoed production in deforested areas. The result was spectacular: deforestation caused by newly planted soy fell from 30 percent to 1 percent between 2006 and 2008. Ten years later, the moratorium had entirely eliminated Amazon deforestation directly related to soy, concluded a University of Wisconsin study.

The outcome was even more positive for Cargill and its rivals. Soy output had risen dramatically in the Amazon despite the moratorium, thanks to productivity improvements and the use of already deforested land. "The moratorium showed there are millions of already deforested hectares where soy can be planted without affecting producers' incomes," explained Glen Horowitz, CEO of the NGO Mighty Earth, set up by former congressman Henry Waxman, with an office especially located to keep tabs on Cargill in Minneapolis. Of course, the missing signatories to the moratorium were meat-packers like the gigantic JBS, and its main rival in the Brazilian beef business, Marfrig, whose support was needed to control massive cattle-driven deforestation, which often trailblazed the arrival of soy. But few doubted that the moratorium was a historic achievement for the protection of the Amazon forest.

* * *

Following the Amazon moratorium, the soy industry (and Cargill in particular) was forgiven and exonerated of guilt for deforestation. The enemies of humanity were no longer corporate soy producers, but cattle ranchers, loggers, and *garimpeiro* miners. It was fancy footwork worthy of Neymar by the Cargill marketers. But in the vast area of Brazil known as Cerrado—a savanna ecosystem to the south and southeast of the Brazilian Amazon, far less discussed in National Geographic documentaries despite its astonishing biodiversity and critical role as a carbon store—the miracle commodity was quietly continuing to cause massive deforestation.

Covering an area greater than the surface area of Mexico, from Mato Grosso in the south to Bahia in the east, the Cerrado was disappearing at dizzying speed. A staggering twenty-eight million hectares of forest had been destroyed since 1985, eliminating half of the native vegetation. All to pave the way for monocultures, including cotton and corn but predominantly soy. Incredibly, most of this deforestation was legal. Under the Brazilian forest code, only 20 percent of privately owned land in the Amazon could be deforested. But, in the Cerrado, which was home to 5 percent of the planet's animal and plant species, forty-eight hundred of them unique to the region, often absent *fazendeiro* land-owners could destroy native vegetation across no less than 80 percent of the surface area of their property.

Instead of the 100-foot-high leafy canopies and tow-ering trunks of the Amazon, the Cerrado was a forest of smaller bushes and trees: *byrsonimas* or *perobas*. The roots of its plant life, however, mirrored the Amazon's heights. They burrowed up to a hundred feet underground, as far as the giant subterranean aquifers that supplied the rivers of the Amazon basin, and were crucial to environmental equilibrium of the whole región.

During a visit to the west of the state of Bahia in August 2019, I drove through a landscape similar to the now-deforested Mato Grosso Cerrado, with vast plains of soybean and cotton. But in Bahia, lush vegetation on table-shaped plateaus that were still untouched by agribusi-ness were a visible reminder of an alternative to the mono-culture on the flat plains below. As I drove north toward the Amazon, the alternating landscapes of Big Food and native Cerrado that flashed by the highway merged eventually into a hundred-mile inferno. Walls of flames stretched across the landscape and smoke columns rose from small islands of forest that remained amongst the soy fields. After a 200 percent rise in the number of fires recorded in Brazil during Jair Bolsonaro's first seven months in power, millions of the compact shrubs of the Cerrado were now grotesque blackened skeletons. Unlike in the Amazon, fires ocurred naturally in the Cerrado biome but not on this scale. Some of the fires were lit by small farmers clearing forest in the burning season, perhaps encouraged by Bolsonaro. But the most likely cause of the conflagration was the burning of brush wood by soy farmers on deforested land that then ignited the forests beyond. Convoys of trucks loaded with soybeans dodged the flames on their way to the Cargill and Bunge processing plants in Barreiras, a town known as the soy capital. In the midst of the charred landscape, a solitary mammal, perhaps a jaguar or a long-haired wolf (I lacked the expertise to say for sure) prowled aimlessly like a lone survivor of the apocalypse.

Cargill and the other transnational commodity brokers generously congratulated Greenpeace and themselves for the success of Amazon soy moratorium and placed self-serving ads in the global media. But they flatly refused to implement a similar arrangement in the Cerrado. "Cargill is committed to the goal of eliminating deforestation in its supply chain," replied the communication manager of the US company in São Paulo when I brought up the question of the Cerrado. "But removing suppliers from the supply chain in the Cerrado would not solve the problem, it would simply transfer it to other companies." Of course, a Bunge spokesperson would say exactly the same. And the other brokers would too. Obviously, the secret to the success of the Amazon moratorium was avoiding free riders. All parties signed the agreement just as they could have done in the Cerrado. The consumer brands who had shamed the brokers into action in the Amazon remained silent where the Cerrado's future was at stake.

In general, no one in the Big Food industry seemed particularly interested in halting deforestation in the Cerrado region that now provided more than 50 percent of Brazil's soy. For once the United States was not the main culprit, since most American soy was domestically sourced, and although China was a big importer of Brazilian soy, most came from the already deforested areas from the colder climes of southern Brazil. Despite its green credentials, it was Europe that was the prime culprit. By 2020, according to research published in *Science*, 20 percent of Brazilian soy exported to the old continent was sourced from deforested land, mostly from the Cerrado. The carbon footprint of European-consumed soy was six times greater than China's.

Finally, concerned by their customers' growing awareness that Big Food and its hypermarket distributors were driving humanity toward the cliff edge, British supermarkets took the lead in warning of possible boycotts of Brazilian soy if action was not taken to stop deforestation. These included chains like Tesco, Sainsbury's, and the then Walmart-owned Asda. But there was reason to be suspicious of corporate social responsibility posing as the savior of the Cerrado. One of the signatories of a letter sent to Brazilian Congress in protest to deforestation was the UK subsidiary of Burger King.

* * *

Visitors who arrived at the tiny airport of Barreiras realized at once what was at stake in the expansion of agribusiness across the Brazilian Cerrado. Dozens of species of birds–flashes of color, from the fluorescent green of the parakeets to the crimson heads of the cardinals–spiraled around a fig tree outside. But beyond the aerodrome access road, vast harvested soy fields, as gray as concrete, stretched out toward the horizon. This was indeed the "construction of a 'neo-nature,'" as Susanna Hecht, professor at the University of California, Los Angeles's Institute of the Environment and Sustainability, has described soy in Brazil. These lifeless squares of dead earth would soon be sown with seeds patented by Cargill, Dow Jones, or Bayer and sprayed with the same companies' pesticides. The so-called MATOPIBA program, which guaranteed federal support for agribusiness in four states bordering the Amazon (Maranhão, Tocantins, Piauí, and Bahia), encouraged deforestation in the Cerrado as well as the intensive use of chemical fertilizers to combat the acidity of the earth.

As the commodity bubble inflated, soybeans traded higher and higher and the Cerrado became a magnet for national and global investors. The landowners were no longer just the old soybean barons, experts at milking Brazil's patronage-ridden political system. The Cerrado soy belt was now a cross-border business, a diversified asset for portfolios sold in financial centers from São Paulo to Wall Street. Managers of American investment funds such as BlackRock, specialized in asset stripping and real-estate speculation across the five continents, headed for the west of Bahia in search of double-digit returns unavailable in the United States. Harvard University's controversial endowment-fund managers bought up land and chopped down trees.

"For agribusiness, the Cerrado is a highly desirable area with a mild climate, great plains where the biggest machines can operate, and cheap naturally irrigated land," said Martin Mayr, an Austrian priest who had lived in Barreiras for thirty years helping small farmers to resist the advance of soy and the big *fazendeiro* landowners from the south. "But for us the Cerrado is a desirable area because it is a crucial reservoir of water. That's the difference of vision between ourselves and them," he added while chain-smoking and sipping at his beer. Like Edilberto Sena in Santarém, Mayr was an unorthodox cleric, and like Sena he was suspicious of the agribusiness lobby's insistence (at times repeated by Lula and Dilma) that soy was the solution to Brazilian and world hunger. "I agree with Amartya Sen that the problem is not the amount of food, but how it is distributed," he said, in reference to the Indian economist and Nobel laureate.

Mayr's point was driven home by the resurgence of hunger in Brazil when the COVID-19 pandemic sank the economy even further. By mid-2020, with exports of soy at all-time highs thanks to US-China trade tensions and a competitive real, ten million Brazilians interviewed in a poll could not say with certainty that they would have enough food to get through the week. One in ten of them was in northern Brazil where the new soy frontier was wiping out traditional farming.

And it was not only the Cerrado forests that were falling before soy's relentless advance. In Barreiras, I met André Guedes de Souza and Fernando Ferreira, two young Afro-Brazilians from the farming communities that had been entrapped within the perimeter of the gigantic soy estate Fazenda Estrondo. The two *geraizeiros*, as people called the independent small farmers in the west of Barreiras, were living proof that in the conquest of soy, first came the chain saw, and then the bullet.

"We were riding to collect our cows; I was on a mule and Fernando, a horse. It was an area where on previous occasions we had been able to move freely," explained the twenty-three-year-old Guedes de Souza, who had traveled to Barreiras to testify before the state prosecutor. "An SUV from the Estrela Guia security company approached with two armed guards, employees of the *fazenda*. They told us to show them our documentation. Walking around there was forbidden, they said, and we could not return to the grazing land. So we began to argue. Then the guard pulled out a gun. We ran, but Fernando was shot." The younger of the two *geraizeiros* lifted his pants and showed me the bullet wound in his right thigh. It was the second time in six months that a small farmer on the land appropriated by Fazenda Estrondo had been the target of shots fired by security guards.

The Fazenda Estrondo, which occupied some two hundred thousand hectares of Cerrado, was located in the municipality of Formosa do Rio Preto in the west of the state of Bahia, the new frontier of Brazilian soy expansion. Taking in the headwaters of various tributaries of the great San Francisco River, this was Cerrado land of enormous environmental value. Between 1993 and 2004, a hundred thousand hectares (50 percent of the surface area) of Fazenda Estrondo had been deforested and replaced mainly by soy. The *fazenda* management had requested authorization to clear an additional twenty-five thousand hectares of woodland under instructions from the leading shareholder in the business, a notorious Rio de Janeiro banker and real estate mogul named Ronald Guimarães Levinsohn. But seven *geraizeiro* villages thwarted the investors' plans.

Just forty-seven families lived on the land occupied by Fazenda Estrondo, but their roots in the western Bahia were as deep as those of the Cerrado's brush forest. They had arrived in western Bahia in the late nineteenth century after participating in the Canudos rebellion in 1896. As readers of Mario Vargas Llosa's novel *The War of the End of the World* might remember, Canudos became a symbol of the tragic heroism and messianic faith of the people of northeast Brazil. Under the leadership of an apocalyptic prophet known as the Counselor, a community of small farmers, runaway slaves, and indigenous tribespeople resisted for two years under siege by Brazilian federal troops. In the end, almost nothing remained of the town. Vargas Llosa describes the final scene after the resistance fell: "It was only when they made their way down the drab, stony slope . . . that they realized that the sound was that of the flapping wings and pecking beaks of thousands upon thousands of vultures . . . [W]hat neither dynamite nor bullets nor fires had been able to reduce to dust: those limbs, extremities, heads, vertebras, viscera . . . these rapacious creatures were now crushing to bits, tearing apart, swallowing, gulping down . . . [It was] '[t]he end that Canudos deserved.'"

But not all of the Canudos rebels were devoured by vultures. Some fled west and established new farming communities in Formosa do Rio Preto on the banks of the eponymous river, a tributary of the mighty San Francisco. Self-sufficient, they raised livestock, cattle, and pigs, and grew traditional crops such as beans and cassava, as well as continued the ancient craft of weaving *capim dourado*, the extrraodinary gold-colored grass that is common in the north of Brazil. They had cohabited harmoniously with the Cerrado forests for nearly a century.

But in the 1990s, Levinsohn arrived on the scene. After wiping out the savings of thousands of unsuspecting depositors when his Rio-based bank Grupo Delfin failed, the financier purportedly appropriated the Canudos survivors' land with the help of Brazil's notorious *grileiros*, land-grabbers who specialized in the falsification of property titles. The *geraizeiros*, who under Brazilian law possessed de facto property rights by virtue of living on the land for more than a century, responded by claiming forty-three thousand hectares that they used for grazing their livestock.

This would not lead to the destruction of Cerrado forest, as in the case of the big cattle ranchers, since the *geraizeiros'* herds were small and their pasture was self-replenishing.

Facing the resistance of the descendents of the Canudos revolutionaries, Levinsohn and his business partners in the Fazenda Estrondo first attempted the strategy of the carrot. "They turned up and organized parties in the town. They put on firework displays, but nobody sold them their land," said Guedes de Souza. Then, after a series of conflicting court decisions, came the stick. The *fazenda* employees erected barbed-wire fences, dug trenches ten feet deep, and built sentry boxes with guard towers manned by the Guia Star armed guards. The dirt roads that the *geraizeiros* used to get from one community to another were blocked.

"We are practically fenced in now. Soy has brought many problems: armed sentry boxes, fenced-off land, and poison in the river when it rains," explained Guedes de Souza in a video that I recorded with my mobile phone in the garden of a church-owned cultural center in Barreiras where the two *geraizeiros* were staying. After cutting off each community with roadblocks and barbed-wire fences, the police harassment had entered a new phase. The security guards began shooting. When Ferreira finally drummed up the courage to speak, his remark was graphic. He raised his crutch to the camera and spoke solemnly: "We are living amongst gunmen, waiting for the tractors to come and destroy our homes." But the *geraizeiros* would not budge.

Back in Rio de Janeiro, Fazenda Estrondo's management countered that everything was above board. "No public highway has been blocked, and armed guards are necessary because the *geraizeiros* destroy the sentry boxes and steal the machinery," said the administrator Daniel Ferraz in an interview held in the offices of Levinsohn's PR agency in downtown Rio. The Estrela guard who shot Ferreira claimed that the two young *geraizeiros* were also armed, an accusation they emphatically denied. Faced with allegations that illegal deforestation had taken place in Estrondo, Ferraz replied that the legal requirement to preserve 20 percent of protected land had been met. But it was a specious argument. By removing the original inhabitants, Levinsohn and his partners intended to free up land that could then be registered to meet the 20 percent conservation requirement. "What we have here is a kind of environmentally correct eviction policy," said Martin Mayr. Even after Levinsohn's death in 2019, the battle for the *geraizeiros*' land rights continued.

Of course, Cargill was no stranger to the Fazenda Estrondo. Outside the wire fences that enclosed the vast fields of soy, stood two warehouses where the soybeans were stored. One was owned by Cargill, the other by Bunge. Trucks leaving Fazenda Estrondo went to Cargill's processing plants, one forty miles north and the other in Barreiras, one hundred miles south. Obviously, without the processing and exporting infrastructure provided by Cargill and Bunge, Estrondo would not have been able to continue operating as it did. A minimal amount of pressure from the multinational broker would have been enough to guarantee the rights of the *geraizeiros*. But at Cargill's headquarters in São Paulo and Minnesota the response to my inquiries was one of absolute indifference. "Cargill has no engagement with the conflicts," declared the company PR team in a written response. "We are working to find solutions that balance the need to protect forests with the need to help communities and farmers thrive and nourish the world."

CHAPTER FOURTEEN

Beef (Pará, Brazil)
The Capital of the Ox

Preparations were well underway for the Xinguara annual agricultural fair held in September in a once densely forested area of the Brazilian Amazon. Formerly populated by jaguars, sloths, and spider monkeys, it was now the regional center of beef production with several million heads of cattle and three industrial slaughterhouses. XINGUARA: WELCOME TO THE CAPITAL OF THE OX, announced the sign at the town entrance.

It had been the worst year of the decade for forest fires in the state of Pará, and Jair Bolsonaro's nine months in the presidential palace in Brasília did not seem unrelated to an environmental disaster that had made global headlines and sparked a diplomatic row with the French president, Emmanuel Macron. Dense clouds of gray smoke floated over what was left of the forest around Xinguara, where herds of zebu, white dots on the blackened landscape, chewed plaintively on the occasional green shoot.

The big cattle ranchers would soon fly in from São Paulo, Rio de Janeiro, Brasília, or Belo Horizonte to attend the fair. The Quagliato brothers from São Paulo were owners of the immense Fazenda Rio Vermelho, twenty miles south of Xinguara, where more than 150,000 oxen grazed on the lush Amazon pasture. Despite the judicial orders from Brasília or Belém that turned up from time to time in the Quagliato mailbox with accusations of illegal deforestation or even the use of slave labor, the family were now the biggest ranchers in Brazil and, by deduction, the world. After all, Brazil, with eighty-five million heads of cattle, had just overtaken the United States and Australia as the leading beef producer on the planet.

The Quagliatos had bought their Xinguara properties at bargain prices from the military government in the 1970s as part of the junta's Amazon colonization project implemented under the slogan *Terra sem homens para homens sem terra* (Land without men for men without land)—a slogan that not only erased from history more than a million indigenous inhabitants of the Amazon, but also the entire female popualtion of Brazil. For the men in uniform, a vast bovine infantry of stomping hooves would be the ideal vehicle to conquer nature's wildest terrain and, at the same time, secure the borders of the Brazilian Amazon, a an area of 1.5 million square miles (equivalent in size to the whole European Union) that accounted for 60 percent of the Amazonic biome in South America.

A representative of the family of Daniel Dantas, a Rio-based banker and president of the AgroSB (Agro Santa Bárbara) group whose Amazon *fazenda* occupied twenty-five thousand hectares of former forest in western Pará, would also attend the Xinguara fair. Dantas was one of the most controversial Brazilian tycoons. Enriched in the 1990s during the privatization of a swathe of public assets under the governments of Fernando Henrique Cardoso, he had spent time in prison for bribery, money laundering, and tax evasion. Despite this, his net worth now approached $1.5 billion, thanks mainly to the lucrative meat industry. Dantas's multimillion-dollar Opportunity Fund had acquired half a million hectares of land for cattle ranching in Brazil, most of them in the Amazon, and like Ronald Levinsohn, the soy king at the Fazenda Estrondo, he soon adapted his skills in financial skullduggery to the art of ranching. As preparations were made for the 2019 Xinguara fair, news broke that he was under investigation for selling animals that had grazed on illegally deforested areas in his *fazendas* to local meatpacking plants owned by JBS, a company that rivaled the infamous construction firm Odebrecht for its willingness to grease the palms of Brazilian politicians.

The *fazendeiros* attended the parades of humpback zebu that made up the most numerous herds in Brazil–their Indian origins equipping them well for the tropical heat. Other attractions at the fair were wild-pony rodeos, cattle auctions, churrasco and *picanha* barbecues, and concerts performed by artists from the latest wave of "university" *sertanejo*, the Brazilian answer to mainstream country and western with sentimental lyrics and choruses that everyone in Xinguara knew by heart. A cowgirl beauty pageant was held and Rissy Rais, sporting a checked shirt tied in a knot over her navel, appeared on the billboards as the star entry.

State-of-the-art fattening lots designed to maximize the number of oxen per square foot were displayed alongside a range of tractors useful for clearing forest. The organizers had invited the best genetic engineers in the Brazilian meat-packing industry to explain the latest techniques of cross-breeding and several exchanges of semen were performed in situ. The excitement in the city was palpable. "It is the event of the year. There will be a lot of drunkenness, a lot of music, and probably some shooting," explained a young university student in the town center.

There was good reason for Xinguara to celebrate the cattle fair with such abandon. Beef had turned a sleepy village in the middle of the jungle into an urban center with forty-five thousand inhabitants, a churrasco restaurant (located inside the Petrobras gas station), a small shopping mall, and a four-star hotel fully booked during the fair, even though the ranchers and their guests stayed on their own *fazendas.*

Beef was a burgeoning business on a planetary scale. According to Food and Agriculture Organization (FAO) forecasts, world meat consumption would increase by 76 percent between 2018 and 2050 and beef specifically by 69 percent. On paper, Brazil was well positioned to capitalize on the growing appetite of the emerging middle classes in the Global South, especially in Asia, for a juicy T-bone steak or a Big Mac. But 80 percent of Brazilian meat was still consumed within Brazil, and the Xinguara ranchers were acutely aware of the need to internationalize their market.

The globalization of Xinguara beef was not an easy undertaking. International NGOs never tired of denouncing cattle-driven deforestation in the Amazon and called for boycotts on Brazilian meat products. Worse still, a growing scientific consensus held that meat consumption would have to be reduced, not increased, if the world was to avoid an environmental catastrophe caused by the meat industry's huge carbon footprint and profligate water consumption. Other research linked heart disease and cancer to an excessive consumption of red meat. Silicon Valley's new nanotechnology companies specializing in synthetic beef posed another challenge. Even Burger King, the most politically incorrect of fast-food chains under its Brazilian management team, had announced the Impossible Whopper, a veggie burger that not only tasted like meat but "bled" like a real Whopper thanks to a soy compound added to the mass. All of this caused blood pressures to rise both at the

Xinguara fair and in Brasília, where Bolsonaro's eccentric chancellor Ernesto Araújo–a disciple of Olavo de Carvalho, the far-right guru and astrologer whom we had the misfortune to chance upon in the esoteric world of niobium–had denounced a conspiracy of "cultural Marxism" to "criminalize Brazilian red meat."

While the Xinguara crowds sang along with the latest *sertanejo* hits from the Bolsonaro-supporting two-piece Cleber e Cauan, the ranchers held meetings behind closed doors. The first item on the agenda was a communications strategy needed to counter the damage caused to their global export plans by thirty thousand wildfires detected in the Amazon that June, an increase of 60 percent from the same month in 2018. International media highlighted a probable correlation between the fires and the 200 percent increase in deforestation in the first six months of Bolsonaro's presidency, as reported by the respected National Institute for Space Research (INPE), whose director was summarily dismissed after the publication of the figures. The data, obtained by satellite image, sparked outrage in Europe, and Bolsonaro did not help matters by first blaming foreign NGOs, whom the president accused of provoking the fires in order to denounce them, and then pointing the finger at the Amazonian indigenous leaders.

"We are in the eye of the hurricane. Bolsonaro has made a rhetorical error," complained Joel Lobato, president of the cattle ranchers association of Xinguara, in an interview we held at the organization's flamboyant offices in the center of town. Lobato was especially hurt by French president Emmanuel Macron's statements. "It's not fair. If I go for a coffee on the Champs-Elysées they will throw stones at me, but no one in the world has to conserve their land without compensation," he protested. As it had for other members of Brazilian elites, historic or emerging, the mere thought of being the object of scorn in Paris traumatized Lobato, whose office was adorned with chandeliers, silver-plated sculptures of horse heads, a table embedded with a selection of precious woods, and a reproduction of *Napoleon I on His Imperial Throne* by Ingres.

"If you want to pay me for not producing like the European ranchers do, I will sell all my oxen, I will plant native trees, I will water them every day, and I will kill all the termites," he said petulantly, perhaps with sarcasm, perhaps not. "I would only charge eighty-seven thousand euros a year."

According to the National Wildlife Federation, an American NGO specialized in analyzing the relationship between the beef industry and deforestation, two-thirds of the Amazon forest destruction, mostly illegal, had paved the way for the zebu. There was now little forest left in the southeast of Pará, a vast state whose total surface area exceeded that of France, Spain, and Portugal taken together. In Xinguara, the landscape was more reminiscent of the pastures of southern Brazil, a land of gaucho cowboys since the nineteenth century, than of the Amazon. Only on the hills to the south of the town was there any visible forest left, and that was where the fires now raged. "But this is not the Amazon. That starts much further west!" replied the young hotel receptionist when I mentioned that the reason for my visit was to report on Amazon deforestation.

Further west, indeed, a wave of destruction was advancing through virgin rain forest, despite the Brazilian forest code that required landowners to conserve 80 percent of the native vegetation on their *latifundios*. A study by Trase, based on detailed satellite images, highlighted the critical role of meat in the latest wave of Amazon deforestation. Between 2015 and 2017, 580,000 hectares of rain forest had been destroyed in Brazil, most of it in the Amazon, the equivalent to sixteen hundred soccer fields every day. Cattle almost always followed the chain saws and tractors. One out of every three forest fires recorded in 2019 in the Amazon had occurred on privately owned land and the Trase researchers suggested the most likely cause was to clear recently deforested areas of brushwood in preparation for livestock.

Bolsonaro tried to counterattack, this time arguing that the 2019 fires were the inevitable result of the dry season and uniquely high temperatures linked to the cyclical El Niño weather phenomenon. Small farmers regularly burned plots in August before the planting season and this year the collateral damage had been more extensive than usual. But the Amazon Environmental Research Institute (IPAM) published more satellite images of fires on recently deforested land in the big private ranches. "The *fazendeiros* cut down the trees and then burnt the stubble for cattle; rain forest does not burn just because of high temperatures," Ane Alencar, one of the IPAM scientists, told me. "What's more, the fires are clearly linked to Bolsonaro's policies and statements," she added.

This was not an exaggeration. Bolsonaro's railing against an alleged excess of restrictions on commercial activities in the Amazon–that imaginary "fines industry" that had enraged the *garimpeiro* miners–empowered local politicians, cattle ranchers, timber merchants, poachers, and other extractive business interests to seize the moment. One local mayor in western Pará actually placed an ad in a local paper inviting patriotic Brazilians to show loyalty to Bolsonaro by burning down as many trees as possible. "Let's demonstrate to the president that we want to work," it urged.

The result was the so-called *dia de fogo* (day of fire) a week before my arrival in Xinguara in August 2019, when thousands of fires burned across the region in an aptly infernal homage of flames to the president. Bolsonaro's slick libertarian environment minister, Ricardo Salles, meanwhile, sent out more shock waves when he remarked in a BBC HARDtalk interview that the new government had devised a daringly original plan to combat illegal deforestation: it would legalize it. "The laws are too restrictive. People just ignore them. Capitalist solutions are needed," he concluded. A few days later Salles provided more details of this innovative free-market environmental strategy researched perhaps during the minister's business administration degree at the Mackenzie Presbyterian University in São Paulo: We have to "monetize" the Amazon to save it, he proposed, suggesting placing market value on the forest in an interview with *Financial Times*. It was an idea that not even the global business daily felt comfortable with. Months later, when COVID-19, a mere *gripezinho* (sniffle) for Bolsonaro, swept across Brazil filling thousands of unmarked graves in the Amazonian capital of Manaus, Salles said in a cabinet meeting that the pandemic would be the perfect opportunity to push through the Amazon deregulation plan since the media "now only talks about COVID."

Salles even launched an attack on those who described the Amazon as the "planetary lung" in an attempt to discredit Macron, who had used the term in one of his tweets. The Amazon did not produce oxygen like a lung, said the minister, and the message careened through the Bolsonarista social networks. But of course Macron and most of the international media did not mean literally that the forest generated enough oxygen for the planet but rather chose the metaphor because of the Amazon rain forest's extraordinary capacity to absorb CO_2. Of the 2.4 trillion metric tons of greenhouse gas pumped into the atmosphere by the fossil fuel economy, the Amazon had absorbed around 2 billion per year for decades before the turn of the century. But Salles was right in one sense. The Amazonian lung was close to collapse. Deforestation, and the replacement of mature vegetation for new growth, had drastically reduced the forest's importance as a carbon sink.

The Brazilian Nobel Prize winner Carlos Nobre calculated that the annual CO_2 absorption rate had fallen to around one billion tons and that, as the fires spread, 20 percent of the Amazon was emitting more carbon than it absorbed. Nobre warned that if the rate of deforestation registered that year were maintained over the next decade, with forest fires acting as a tipping point, the humid Amazon biome that had been unchanged for millennia would morph by 2035 into the drier Cerrado ecosystem, with catastrophic consequences for Brazil, the western hemisphere, and the planet. By that time, of course, Big Soy would have turned the existing Cerrado into "neo-nature."

With Bolsonaro at the helm there seemed little reason to believe that the rate of destruction would slow. The government, packed with libertarian neoliberals like Salles, neoconservatives like Araújo, and nostalgic old generals such as Augusto Heleno, a veteran of the junta's "land without men" policy, appeared on the Amazon horizon like the cast of *The Texas Chain Saw Massacre.*

The sad truth was that destruction of the forests in Xinguara and the rest the southeast of Pará was by then a fait accompli. "Thirty years ago, there were one hundred and fifty tractors pulling up trees on the Quagliato *fazendas* and we had twenty-two sawmills in Xinguara," explained Ana de Souza, director of the Xinguara office of the Pastoral

Land Commission, a progressive Catholic organization that defended human and labor rights in the countryside. "The same is now occurring to the west. If it is not controlled, in ten years western Pará will be the same as Xinguara," she warned.

But there was no indication that the lesson from Xinguara had been learned. On the contrary, with Bolsonaro now in office and Salles designing a libertarian conservancy strategy, those ranchers intent on clearing the jungle believed they could enjoy absolute impunity. The new frontier of paraffin and chain saws advanced to the south of Itaituba, where the Munduruku indigenous territories were already buckling under intense pressure from extractivists: first loggers, then ranchers, and finally, soy farmers. The weak point of the soy moratorium, after all, was the substitution effect, and soy was now expanding on deforested land for livestock that did not enter into the agreement.

Preventing the end of the Amazon was not impossible. Recall that between 2003 and 2011, while Lula was in power, deforestation in the Brazilian Amazon had fallen by 80 percent thanks to more effective systems of control coordinated by the environmental agency the Brazilian Institute of the Environment and Renewable Natural Resources (IBAMA) in tandem with new satellite technologies that tracked deforestation in real time. The experience of the soy moratorium suggested too that if the major consumer brands put enough pressure on their suppliers in the meatpacking industry, deforestation could be drastically reduced. However, agreeing to a solution with the ranchers had proven much more difficult than with soy. Greenpeace attempted to broker a moratorium on meat from deforested areas with JBS, its São Paulo–based rival Marfig, and other big meatpackers. But, despite expressing their support in public, the slaughterhouses managed by the two Brazilian giants had bought animals that grazed on illegally deforested land. Daniel Dantas was just one of the lawbreaking ranchers. Moreover, budget cuts to federal entities responsible for combating deforestation, such as IBAMA, had enhanced the deforesters' sense of impunity.

And just as in the Cerrado, trees in the Amazon were felled first and human beings later. Hired killers gunned down indigenous leaders, environmentalists, and landless workers who had occupied unproductive land on the ranches, as was their constitutional right. "The method of concentrating land ownership in the Amazon has always been through violence. First they identify the leaders and then they choose the target for the gunmen," said de Souza. "There have never been so many simultaneous attempts to expel settlers from the latifundia."

The terrible truth behind this statement became apparent when I drove west from Xinguara along a potholed road toward the still-smoking deforestation frontier. At the entrance to the town of Ourilândia do Norte, a hand-painted sign warned: FAZENDA 1200: PREMISES GUARDED 24 HOURS. DO NOT ENTER. The ranch was owned by Eutimio Lippaus, an eighty-two-year-old native of Espírito Santo, who had appropriated five thousand hectares of jungle, fifteen hundred of which were originally owned by the federal state and therefore not legally his. On acquiring the property, Lippaus lost no time clearing the way for the zebu invasion by felling thousands of trees across an unspecified number of hectares. Like the Quagliato brothers he was soon fined for illegal deforestation and for using slave labor to remove the trees.

A new obstacle arose in 2006 when a hundred landless families settled on the formerly state-owned area of the *fazenda* with the support of the National Institute for Colonization and Agrarian Reform (INCRA), a federal agency that had managed Brazil's timid agrarian reform. Launched in the 1980s, INCRA compensated landowners by buying land that had been legally occupied. The landless rural workers used maps drawn by INCRA to ensure that the land they occupied was in the formerly state-owned area.

For Lippaus it was a question of oxen versus impoverished rural workers, and the animals fetched a higher price. After first cooperating with INCRA and recognizing the settlements in return for payment for land that was legally not his, the aging *latifundista* changed plans after Bolsonaro's victory. Here was the long-awaited opportunity to expel the settlers who had planted cacao, eucalyptus, teak, and banana for their own consumption, reforesting four hundred hectares of the estate and denying pasture to the megaherds.

One early morning in the spring of 2019, two gunmen rode into the community on motorbikes and, after firing several shots, set fire to two homes. Nobody was hurt. But from that moment, Paulino da Silva, who had helped organize the original occupation of the Lippaus ranch, lived under a permanent threat of death. "Every day, on the street, someone shouts to me: 'Hey Paulino! Eutimio wants you dead. He's paying fifty thousand reais!'" da Silva explained to me in the backyard of his small timber house near the Lippaus ranch. "It could be a lie or it could be the truth but these days I don't go out much and I go directly home after work," he added while hens pecked, a cock crowed, and, in the background, a *papagayo* trained to mimic its owner perfectly reproduced the chorus of a melancholic Brazilian folk song. A poster from the union of rural workers, FETAGRI, was nailed to the wall of the shack.

"Who is responsible for the attacks against the communities?" I asked da Silva, nicknamed Paulino do PT for his previous work as a local councillor for the Workers' Party. "Without a doubt, gunmen, cowboys, under orders from the rancher," he replied. "Eutimio denies it, but it must be him." And why now? "Because he has the backing of the federal government."

Da Silva displayed few signs of fear during our meeting but his wife fidgeted nervously as we conducted the interview. I suggested that by publishing his story he might be better protected and he agreed. But five months later, on February 22, 2020, the Belém office of Globo News broke the story that the "former councillor [was] shot dead from a bullet to the head": "Raimundo Paulino da Silva, Jr., fifty-one years of age, known as Paulino do PT, was murdered in Ourilândia do Norte on Saturday. An investigation will be launched into the circumstances of the crime."

In a tragically Brazilian twist, the prime suspects were *garimpeiro* miners who had begun to pan for gold on the *fazenda*. But the shadow of Lippaus flickered behind the gold diggers. "Paulino was against the gold mining," said Ze Aria, a comrade of Paulino do PT in the local branch of the rural workers' union in Ourilândia. "But the conflict with the gold prospectors just accelerated a process already underway. The real motive for the murder was the invasion of Fazenda 1200," he said.

Da Silva was one of a dozen of Ourilândia residents murdered in the months after Bolsonaro was sworn in as president. "With Bolsonaro, the situation is 80 percent worse than it was before," said Aria. "Paulino is just one more death for the statistics of unsolved murders."

Further west, in the municipality of São Félix do Xingu, the Xikrin had taken up arms against groups of *grileiros*, who, emboldened by Bolsonaro's rhetoric, were trying to falsify property titles in the reserve and so allow loggers and cattle ranchers onto constitutionally protected land. Bolsonaro-backed legislation known as the *lei do grileiro* recognized illegal land grabs of state-owned forest of up to fifteen hundred hectares. Since they invariably were followed by deforestation, the law "will create incentives for more fires and destruction. It makes a crime legal," said Marina da Silva, Lula's first environmental minister, when I interviewed her as the 2019 fires raged.

On the banks of the Xingu River, São Félix was now the fourth-most-deforested town in the Brazilian Amazon. Studies showed that *fazendas* there—some of which were suppliers to JBS and Marfig—were enthusiastic participants in that infamous *dia do fogo*. São Félix do Xingu also had the largest bovine herd in the country, with more than two million heads of xebu oxen, many of them grazing on ranches owned by Daniel Dantas.

News arrived in Xinguara that the billionaire chairman of Opportunity Fund had chosen not to attend the fair. The decision was perhaps due to the negative publicity generated by the JBS scandal. Or perhaps it was because Dantas, like his rival in the murky financial world of Rio de Janeiro, Burger King's Jorge Paulo Lemann, had stopped eating meat and declared himself a vegetarian.

CHAPTER FIFTEEN

Oil (Venezuela; Brazil; Mexico) Petrosocialism and Counterattack

Venezuela

Deep below the surface bubbled a black El Dorado. Three billion barrels of crude oil, the world's largest known reserves. But, above ground, along the Orinoco Petroleum Belt that skirted the huge Amazonian river as it flowed toward the Atlantic, the landscape was one of chronic shortage, black-market chicanery, and Venezuelans at the end of their tether.

In the José Petrochemical Complex, on the outskirts of the coastal city of Barcelona, one solitary orange flame flickered at dusk above the steel chimneys silhouetted against the ocean. These were the "upgraders" built by Exxon and other Big Oil multinationals in the 1990s to refine the Orinoco Belt's heavy, unconventional crude oil, as thick as molasses when pumped up from the subsoil. But most were inoperative after years of neglect and underinvestment. The plan for new upgraders with Chinese, Korean, Russian, and European capital had been shelved. The door to a new phase of petrosocialism slammed shut. Output from the Orinoco Belt had dwindled to close to zero. Even worse, production at the old conventional fields of a lighter class of oil on Lake Maracaibo eight hundred miles to the west had collapsed too.

The hydrocarbon utopia of twenty-first-century socialism evaporated into thin air in one single year, 2014, when the international oil price plummeted from $120 to $30 a barrel. Oil-generated foreign exchange, essential to buying basic necessities such as food and medicine, vaporized too. Crude output collapsed from 3.3 million barrels a day to half a million—a 75 percent drop, which triggered a depression that wiped out 60 percent of the Venezuelan GDP in six years. Such economic devastation had never been witnessed anywhere, even in times of war.

The richest country in the region was now prostrate and, according to United Nations data, seven million Venezuelans needed humanitarian aid. After the extraordinary achievements of Hugo Chávez's governments in the first decade of the twenty-first century, when destitution and inequality dropped to the lowest levels on the continent, poverty soared to 80 percent of the population. Only government food programs prevented mass starvation. The vicious circle tightened further as it became impossible to pay for the maintenance and repair of existing oil infrastructure. It was the cost of Venezuela's historic dependence on oil, a compulsive habit that not even Hugo Chávez's Bolivarian Revolution had been able to shake off.

Nicolás Maduro had to take some of the blame for the collapse. Taking over after Chávez's sudden death in 2013, he had maintained public spending at levels incompatible with such low oil prices. Many in Caracas, even loyal Chavistas, questioned the competence of the government's economic team. But the rot had set in well before due to the erratic management of the state oil company Petroleum of Venezuela, S.A. (PDVSA), under chairman Rafael Ramírez, who amassed a personal fortune in highly suspicious circumstances during the boom.

When the Trump administration announced sanctions in 2017, it compounded PDVSA's crisis by denying access to international markets. Even when oil prices rose in late 2017, Venezuelan production continued to plummet. Maduro accelerated the collapse by packing the PDVSA management with hundreds of loyal military officers and bureaucrats with little knowledge of the oil business. In order to avoid suspending payments on PDVSA's massive debt, the government also reduced the imports of essential goods. Many asked why the Bolivarian Revolution would choose Wall Street bondholders over hungry children and hospital patients. The answer was simple. Maduro was aware that if Venezuela defaulted, PDVSA assets in the United States would be seized.

The most important was CITGO's chain of gas stations and refineries in the United States, which the Venezuelan government had just sold to the Russian oil company Rosneft. In danger of losing these assets as US sanctions kicked in, Rosneft negotiated to exchange them for oil fields in the Orinoco Belt. Here was Venezuela's own peculiar version of the curse of raw materials: driven to desperate measures by Washington's sanctions, it was forced to sell its oil assets to Moscow and even consider the partial sale of PDVSA to the United States' geopolitical rivals. After all, only Russia and China were prepared to invest in the Venezuelan oil sector, and provided the credit Venezuela needed in exchange for oil assets. China had granted loans of no less than $50 billion to Venezuela in exchange for securing a long-term source of crude oil supply and the participation of Chinese companies in infrastructure works.

Under pressure from China, extraction of heavy crude from the Orinoco Belt was given priority over the Maracaiba conventional fields. This would prove a costly concession.

Whereas Maracaibo's oil was easy to extract and could be refined in Venezuela, much of the Orinoco heavy crude was exported (mainly to the United States) for refining. This heightened the need for imports to meet demand for gasoline in a country where, thanks to subsidies, the cost of filling the tank was less than a dollar. Paradoxically, in the land of black gold, imports of oil soared in five years from 70 billion barrels a day to 250 billion, using up precious foreign exchange and forcing even more cuts in supplies of imported food and medicine.

Tying the future of Venezuela to Moscow and Beijing would disturb the eternal sleep of the *liberator*, Simón Bolívar. But there were indications that with Chinese and Russian help, the collapse of Venezuelan oil production could be reversed. A joint venture between the Chinese oil company CNPC and PDVSA had helped double oil output in 2018. Perhaps this was the real reason behind the Trump Administration's decision to move in support of immediate regime change.

Geopolitical tensions between the United States, Russia, and China had tightened to breaking point. When Maduro tried to sell more oil assets to Rosneft in 2018, the opposition majority in the Venezuelan parliament, closely coordinated with Washington, blocked the sale. This forced the Maduro government to suspend the Venezuelan assembly, provoking a wave of violent protests against the government in the streets of Caracas. Accusations that Maduro had violated the separation of powers became the pretext for the US decision to support a new attempt at a coup d'etat. Despite the humanitarian PR, concern in Washington was perhaps not that Venezuela would sink further into chaos and scarcity, but rather that it would emerge from it with China and Russia's support.

Juan Guaidó–a young opposition leader and ex–street fighter, who was trained in his student days by the United States Agency for International Development (USAID)– was selected to lead the assault on power. Guaidó's bizarre self-proclamation as president in January of 2019 had been approved by Secretary of State Mike Pompeo, National Security Advisor John Bolton, and Miami Senator Marco Rubio. Trump went along.

One of the first assets to be handed over to Guaidó's new parallel government were those of CITGO, worth some 10 billion dollars, and these were soon distributed to the Venezuelan company's US bondholders.

If Venezuelans believed they had reached the bottom of the pit, the worst was yet to come. Advised by Bolton and Rubio, Trump added teeth to his support for Guaidó's attempted coup early in 2019 by announcing a total embargo on sales of oil to the United States. Until then, the United States had been the market for almost 40 percent of Venezuelan crude exports. The move shocked US refiners and companies still active in Venezuela, like Chevron. The embargo led immediately to a further collapse in oil production, now compounded by the power outages. The entire country spent a week without electricity in March 2019, and only Caracas managed to regain a reliable supply afterward.

Worse still, the blackouts forced the closure of the few remaining upgraders in the Orinoco Petroleum Belt while the embargo made it difficult to import the diluting agent necessary to refine the heavy crude oil of the Orinoco. Oil output slumped further and imports of essentials collapsed, too. Francisco Rodríguez, a Venezuelan economist based in New York, warned that Trump's embargo would cause mass famine in Venezuela. Jeff Sachs, an economist at Columbia, and Mark Weisbrot, a director at the Center for Economic Policy Research in Washington, noted that the first round of sanctions had probably already killed some forty thousand people.

During a visit to Cúcuta on the Venezuela-Colombia border, the scale of the disaster became apparent to me too. A steady flow of migrants crossed the border bridges fleeing penury in Maracaibo, Maracay, Valencia, Barquisimeto, and other cities more seriously affected by the blackouts and shortages than Caracas. "Before, only food and drugs were lacking. Now there is also a shortage of electricity and water," explained a mother from San Cristóbal in Táchira as she stood in line at the Colombian immigration office with her daughter to join more than four million Venezuelans (in a country with thirty-two million inhabitants) fleeing from the shortages. Within a year another million had left.

Outside, in the midst of the chaos, hundreds of young Venezuelans fought amongst themselves for the opportunity to carry the immigrants' suitcases and earn a few bolivares, or to help the old and sick cross the bridge in their wheelchairs. Two Venezuelan women were waiting at an outdoor barber shop in the middle of the chaos. Like Fantine in Victor Hugo's *Les Misérables*, they had decided to sell their hair, twenty inches long, for five thousand bolivares (just over a dollar).

* * *

At one stop along the Orinoco Belt, the manager of a gas station in Ciudad Guayana, with its ghoulish skyline of abandoned steel and aluminum plants, offered to sell me bolivares for dollars. We arranged to meet at my hotel, overlooking the mighty Orinoco River that swirled powerfully through the city.

The manager, Joel, was carrying three large plastic grocery bags full of bolivar notes. Sitting in the hotel bar, he counted the money with the nimble fingers of a bank teller from a lost era. I handed over two twenty-dollar notes. The exchange rate that day had reached four thousand bolivares per dollar, almost double that of the previous week, as inflation approached 500,000 percent. (In the coming months it would cross the one million mark.) Joel had received some of the new five-hundred-bolivar bills that were still unobtainable in most of Venezuela, which he kept in a thinner bundle. But the rest of the sixteen thousand bolivares came in huge wads of old hundred-dollar bills that he took from the bags like paper bricks. Keen to migrate to the United States as soon as he could afford to, Joel had decided to enter the illicit currency market because selling gas did not pay: "Gasoline is almost free in Venezuela. The government pays me to sell it, but that's not enough to live on." That day, a liter of gasoline cost three cents.

For everything else, inflation became hyperinflation, a perverse consequence of Venezuela's multiple exchange rates and price controls. In the midst of the chaos, a Miami-based internet portal known as Dolar Today had somehow gained control over the unofficial exchange rate by setting a daily benchmark for those, like Joel, who bought and sold dollars on the black market. The problem was that Dolar Today was not a neutral broker. Managed by a group of Venezuelan expats in Florida with links to the most extreme elements of the right-wing opposition, its aim was to dynamite Chávez's twenty-first-century socialism by any means necessary. Every morning Dolar Today published a wildly inflated exchange rate that doubled or tripled that of the previous day. This further fueled the dizzying hyper-inflation that tore through Venezuelans' pockets. Dolar Today did not hide its desire to sink the Maduro government. Its "estimates" of the bolivar-dollar exchange rate were accompanied every day on the Miami portal's home page by hysterical articles denouncing "Castro-Chavism" alongside homages to Leopoldo López, the millionaire opposition leader who, unable to dislodge Chávez in the elections, had supported a string of coup attempts against him.

In Cúcuta, where Richard Branson, a handful of *reguetón* stars, and the Southern Command of the United States Armed Forces would later organize the regime change–supporting Venezuela Aid Live concert, I spoke with Julio Vélez, one of the Colombian foreign-exchange market traders clustered around Parque Santander in the old city center. A veteran of the dollar-trading business in the chaotic Colombian border town, Vélez was not exactly a fan of the Bolivarian Revolution. He despised Maduro and defended the return to market-driven capitalism in Venezuela. Despite this, he railed against "the sinister Dolar Today website, which does so much harm to our Venezuelan brothers. People think that what they say is what the bolivar is really worth, but it's a lie, they want to destabilize the Venezuelan economy."

One indication of the political bias of Dolar Today's exchange rate was that the bolivar's depreciation accelerated fiendishly during election campaigns when the Chavistas looked like the winners, as the Venezuelan economist Pasqualina Curcio pointed out in her book *The Visible Hand of the Market: Economic Warfare in Venezuela.* For example, in October 2012, when Chávez won his last presidential election, the bolivar collapsed every day on the Dolar Today benchmark. Then in 2013, when Maduro ran for the first time and won narrowly, the bolivar went into a headlong slide. When the opposition won the elections to the National Assembly in 2015, however, the depreciation led by the Dolar Today team in Miami miraculously slowed down. Hyperinflation too.

The Miami financial portal did much more damage than did the opposition street protests or Guaidó's attempts to organize a coup . Bolivarian banknotes lost their value in a matter of days. The best-selling souvenir during Branson's festival in Cúcuta were origami sculptures of humming-birds made with hundred-bolivar bills.

Controls on the prices of imported essential goods, such as rice, pasta, bread, detergent, and medicines, had created fertile terrain for black market profiteers called *bachaque-ros* who, like Venezuelan reincarnations of Harry Lime in *The Third Man*, bought up scarce goods and resold them at massively inflated prices. Grim-faced strangers appeared at the front of endless lines at neighborhood stores, supermar-kets, and pharmacies.

"We call them *bachaqueros* because of an insect of the same name," said the poet Guiomar Camino, who had gra-ciously invited me to his home in Táchira on the other side of the Colombian border from Cúcuta, as he admired one of the five-hundred-bolivar notes I had obtained from Vélez.

In towns on the banks of the Orinoco and further north, lines of resigned shoppers appeared every morning at bak-eries, grocery stores, and supermarkets. At a pharmacy near Barcelona, I saw two women wrestling on the ground for a place in a line until the younger of them surrendered as blood poured from a wound in her head. At the Antonio Patricio de Alcalá hospital in Cumaná, on the Caribbean coast, there were shortages in every department, from rubber gloves to syringes, paper towels to electric light. Not to mention most basic medicines. US sanctions were beginning to bite, turning crisis into catastrophe.

"If you want to see something shocking, go to the morgue, behind the emergencies department. There is no air conditioning and the corpses sometimes swell and burst," explained a thirty-year-old laboratory technician who was waiting for his next shift at a kiosk that sold soft drinks, arepas, and . . . syringes.

Yet, as always in Venezuela, the obligatory media narrative that pitted a cruel Chavista dictatorship against a suffering people, united in its opposition to the Maduro regime, did not tell the whole story. Or even part of it. A family of about thirty members (nine children and the rest sons-in-law, sisters-in-law, grandchildren, and nephews) had camped out behind the hospital while their grandmother recovered from pneumonia. Some slept in hammocks hung from a tree. Others prepared arepas in the back of a dilapidated pickup truck. "We're going to have to try and find antibiotics for my mother and syringes too," one of the daughters said resignedly. Then, in case I had misunderstood, she added: "We are one hundred percent Chavistas, the whole family! I owe everything to the government: my food, my job, my house." They were from Barbacoa, a shantytown half an hour from Cumaná by road, where at the entrance a sign written with stones placed at the side of the road announced: SOMOS CHÁVEZ.

Aware that Dolar Today was feeding hyperinflation while the *bachaqueros* compounded the shortages, Maduro changed tack. He lifted the controls on regulated prices and, in late 2019, merged the official and market exchange rates. Soon local cash would effectively disappear from the economy and the resourceful citizens of Venezuela would switch to buying even the smallest of items with their bank cards, as if Caracas had been moved to Scandinavia. But the problem of scarcity simply turned into a crisis of affordability. Hyperinflation continued and the government no longer subsidized essentials, choosing to send monthly or bimonthly food parcels to the barrios and the ranchos instead. A kilo of meat now cost the equivalent of a fortnightly minimum wage.

On the highway to Brazil, where the Pemon were battling with the army and criminal gangs for control of the gold and coltan mines, there were also lines at the gas stations. Why, I wondered, seeing as gasoline was the only thing that was cheap and plentiful in Venezuela? "Many people here earn a living by smuggling gasoline. You can earn more selling a tank full for Brazilian reais than in a week of work if you are paid in bolivares. Others resell gasoline in the mining towns," explained Nelson, a partner in a company that organized cosmetic surgery trips to Ciudad Guayana for Brazilian women.

As the crisis deepened, gasoline shortages became widespread throughout the country. When Maduro finally eased price controls on gas too after a further collapse of world oil prices during the COVID-19 crisis, smuggling fuel across the Colombian borders became much less profitable. But the liberalization had sent prices soaring at the pump and drivers now had to spend the night in lines at gas stations for their subsidized quota of gas.

* * *

All of which begged the question: Why did Chavism not reduce its dependence on oil before it was too late? As the source of 95 percent of Venezuela's foreign exchange, not only did oil make Venezuela perilously vulnerable to falling prices on the international market but also to the plans for regime change drawn up with the support of Washington since Chávez's first electoral victory in 1999.

A 2002 coup in which Chávez was briefly kidnapped was followed by an opposition-supported strike by PDVSA that brought the country to its knees. But despite being acutely aware of the danger, Chávez was never able to diversify the economy. Like other presidents who had tried to industrialize in order to combat dependence on oil rents, he announced a string of state plans for establishing new agricultural, manufacturing, and pharmaceutical industries. But instead of decreasing, dependence on oil exports deepened, and the rentier culture, which had corrupted Venezuelan elites since the first large-scale extraction of oil at the beginning of the twentieth century, was inherited by the new *boliburguesía* of nouveau riche Chavistas.

Maybe *chavismo* was a victim of its own success. In 2007, after adroitly using oil diplomacy in the Organization of the Petroleum Exporting Countries (OPEC) to cut world supply and increase the price of crude, Chávez forced multinationals to pay higher royalties to the Venezuelan state and guaranteed PDVSA a 60 percent stake in the exploitation of the Orinoco Belt. The plan worked wonders for a decade. Exxon, which had built the first upgrader in the José Complex, refused to pay and abandoned the country under orders from CEO, Rex Tillerson, who would be Trump's first short-lived secretary of state. But other Big Oil giants—Chevron, Total, BP—stayed, and were joined by European, Chinese, and Russian companies.

Chávez reckoned that the US oil lobby, especially the refineries on the coast of Louisiana and Texas, would need Venezuelan crude so badly that it would never allow Washington to implement an embargo. As long as Venezuela did not suspend payments on its debt, oil exports to the United States were safe, concluded the Chavistas. But by 2019 global geopolitics had shifted tectonically as globalization retreated. An embargo could perhaps achieve one of the objectives of the new Trump Doctrine: to warn China and Russia that Latin America was once again an exclusive sphere of US influence. During the Lima Summit of the Americas in 2018, a report by the neoconservative Washington Center for Strategic and International Studies warned that China and Russia in Latin America supported corrupt and undemocratic regimes. "China is propping up Maduro's undemcratic and repressive narco-regime," it alleged. Such a hardline seemed now to be Washington's official strategy.

Of course, Trump's new Monroe Doctrine was not just geopolitical in nature. Regime change would create business opportunities. Bolton had remarked frankly: "It will make a big difference to the United States economically if we could have American oil companies invest in and produce the oil capabilities in Venezuela." Trump oscillated wildly between negotiating with the "tough cookie" Maduro and ordering an armed invasion. But oil was on his mind. As ex–FBI agent Andrew McCabe noted in his book, *The Threat*, the president had remarked at a confidential meeting soon after taking office that Venezuela was "the country we should be going to war with . . . They have all that oil and they're right on our back door."

Guaidó intended to deliver immediately. When I attended one of his first appearances at the Central University of Venezuela in Caracas, days after his self-proclamation in January 2019, the young opposition leader was received like a *reguetón* star by thousands of middle-class students. His speech emphasized the need to attract billions of dollars of private investment to reverse the collapse of oil output. Oil would be the key to Guaidó's Plan País (Country Plan) for national reconstruction. "We need $30 billion of investment per year, for seven years," said José Toro, Guaidó's advisor on oil policy. "This capital is available, but the state does not have it. It will be private," he added at the presentation.

Reluctant to strengthen the impression that Guaidó was Washington's puppet, Toro denied that the plan was to privatize PDVSA per se. But reading between the lines of the neoliberal Plan País, few could doubt that this was the goal, even if it was a gradual and covert privatization. That said, some sections of the US oil lobby mistrusted the regime change plan and Bolton's less than subtle views of foreign policy, fearing that the loss of Venezuelan business would come back to haunt Houston.

By 2019 many Chavista technicians emphasized the urgent need to diversify and industrialize, just as Chávez had desired from the beginning. As the crisis deepened and oil production slumped further, the government announced a national production plan that would reduce the need to import food and medicine. "Venezuela is advancing in a process of economic liberation that will make us a great productive and self-sustaining power," Maduro tweeted in late 2019.

But it was too late. In the midst of such a deep economic crisis, the "productive transformation" was a fantasy. The only conceivable way out of the economic catastrophe would be through a recovery in oil production. That was the grim lesson from Luis Salas, the economist and ex-minister in the Chávez government who had unsuccessfully urged the diversification of the economy during the bonanza.

I met Salas in Caracas during the spring of 2019, after the failure of a second coup attempt in three months–this time with a photo op at which Guaidó and Leopoldo López appeared with gun-toting soldiers in combat gear. Despite the incessant tweets from Bolton and Rubio and the headlines in the international media, there was barely a crack in the loyalty of the armed forces. The Guaidó-led regime change had failed. But Maduro's tenacity did not hide the underlying problem. Venezuela depended on crude oil and the embargo was tightening the vice every month.

Nor was there much evidence that a democratic administration under Joe Biden would loosen the screws. It was impossible to diversify the economy to make it self-sufficient. "The government's plans for a productive economy are not viable. In order for Venezuelan private sector companies and non-oil exports to spearhead a recovery, we would have to increase our productive capacity by more than 350 percent," Salas explained as we walked under the statue of the *libertador* in Plaza Bolívar. Even if local companies started up, there would not be enough energy to supply them with electricity. "We have come to oil post-rentism," said Salas. "We have nothing tangible in the medium term to replace oil revenues."

Brazil

The first time I met Sergio Gabrielli was at Davos. We spoke in a private room at his hotel during the 2010 annual meeting of the World Economic Forum, an unmissable event for the global business elite. CEOs from hundreds of Wall Street multinational companies and investment banks slithered on icy streets from one brainstorming session to the other and networked frantically on the ski slopes of the alpine resort. That year the Davos men still bore some symptoms of post-traumatic stress after the megacrisis of 2008 and the near-collapse of the neoliberal model of globalization. But Brazil, like other large emerging economies, was the object of admiration and respect. The biggest economy in Latin America still appeared to have weathered the storm at the time.

Bearded and with a warmer, less messianic gaze than most of the Davos participants, Gabrielli was not the typical corporate-multinational CEO. His company was Petrobras, Brazil's state oil behemoth whose spectacular profitability stimulated the salivary glands of the emerging market investment fund managers in Davos even more than the schnitzels at the Schatzalp ski resort. After discovering the so-called *pré-sal* oil reserves–billions of barrels of high quality crude buried under a layer of salt thirteen thousand feet below the Atlantic–Petrobras was the world's third-largest oil company by market capitalization even with only half of its shares publicly traded. Its turnover exceeded $200 billion.

Petrobras had invested the same amount in only five years to explore and drill in the *pré-sal* reserves, an ambitious plan that involved running up billions of dollars of debt. But Brazil was adored by global financial markets and Gabrielli had seized the moment. He had just carried off a bond issue of $40 billion, financed mainly by the giant Brazilian public bank BNDES and the Chinese national development bank. Private investors like those who clapped enthusiastically at the close of the Brazilian CEO's Davos conferences were also fully on board and contributed $6.5 billion. After the issue, Petrobras's debt would exceed $100 billion.

Petrobras engineers had discovered *pré-sal* oil after years in which foreign multinationals had failed to find a drop beneath the 650-foot-wide salt deposit at the bottom of the ocean. Petrobras's ten-story floating platforms were equipped with GPS systems that kept the three-mile-long drill in a vertical position. Instead of a conventional anchor, company engineers had innovated a system of torpedoes attached to a polyester rope to fix the platform to the ocean bottom with greater flexibility. Petrobras used underwater robots whose design was inspired by the propulsion system of the common tadpole. One in three exploration platforms had struck oil in the *pré-sal* area, a degree of success described as "staggering" in an article published in 2007 in *The Wall Street Journal* headlined "How a Sleepy Oil Giant Became a World Player."

Petrobras was beginning to fulfill the dreams of Brazil's iconic developmentalist president Getúlio Vargas, who founded the oil company, then entirely state-owned, in 1953. Vargas imagined a vertically integrated state enterprise, an oil company "from *poço a posto*" (from the well to the gas station).

Gabrielli had the same idea. The company's reach extended from the *pré-sal* platforms five hundred miles offshore in the Atlantic to a million gas stations scattered across the vast country, from the megalopolis of São Paulo to remote towns on the Trans-Amazonian Highway, all with the unmistakable green BR logo of Petrobras. Construction of two new megarefineries was underway, one in Rio de Janeiro, the other on the northeast coast where Hugo Chávez had helped choose the site. Endless Petrobras oil and gas pipelines meandered across the vast country.

Investments had even begun in renewables, especially biofuels (most Brazilian cars refuel with a mixture of gasoline and ethanol) and fertilizers for synergies with the other leg of Brazil's commodity economy: agribusiness. Petrobras employed almost 150,000 people.

Moreover, national content rules for Petrobras suppliers meant that new refineries and drilling platforms were built in Brazil, a form of state-run industrial policy designed by the new economic heterodoxy of the Latin American left. This, said Gabrielli, would help Brazilian engineering and infrastructure businesses compete despite the overvaluation of the exchange rate. "We give preference to Brazilian technology companies to avoid the problem of Dutch disease," explained Gabrielli, in reference to the plague of the commodity economy discussed in the story of Brazilian iron.

Gabrielli looked forward to the future with optimism and security. He forecast an average annual growth for the Brazilian economy of 4 percent until 2020 and described a virtuous circle in which Petrobras, focused on supplying energy to the Brazilian market instead of exporting crude, would satisfy internal demand that would expand thanks to anti-poverty programs, subsidized credit, and minimum wage increases all implemented by the Lula governments.

"Two million poor people's homes are going to be connected to the electricity grid. That will create demand for a million televisions and refrigerators, which will generate more energy demand for us," he explained at a Davos summit where the model of neoliberal globalization seemed to be in retreat, while the "pink tide" of the Latin American left continued to rise after ten years of power.

As Gabrielli and his advisors escorted me out after the interview, I noticed the admiring, perhaps envious, glances of the Davos men who hurried back and forth. It was strange to see. Gabrielli, after all, was a veteran of the Brazilian Workers' Party, one of Lula's closest allies during the PT's long march to power. But, of course, at that Davos summit he avoided talk of the Brazilian left. These were times in which Lula appeared to have shown that it was possible to give to the favela with one hand and to the Davos men with the other.

My second meeting with Gabrielli was held in January 2017 in his city of birth, Salvador da Bahia, on the Atlantic coast of the Brazilian northeast. Gabrielli was at that moment the latest target of the *Lava Jato* witch hunt, accused without any real evidence of being an accomplice to a network of corruption whose nerve center was Petrobras. The intrepid prosecutors of the *Lava Jato* probe had uncovered a network of bribes and kickbacks that spanned the breadth of corporate and political power in Brazil and in many cases were executed through construction company Odebrecht, which had overcharged Petrobras in order to bribe politicians. Top executives at Petrobras had been tried and jailed. The accusations against Gabrielli would fall on deaf ears, but Lula was now Lava Jato's number-one target and would soon be sentenced and jailed for alleged crimes of corruption and money laundering.

Far from growing at a rate of 4 percent per year, as Gabrielli had forecast, the Brazilian economy was mired in the deepest recession in its history and there were no signs of recovery. Petrobras's stock had collapsed partly because of the drop in oil prices between 2013 and 2014 and, to a greater extent, due to the damage caused by the anti-corruption investigation. The new management appointed by interim president Michel Temer announced a bargain sale of Petrobras assets with the alleged aim of reducing debt. Gabrielli's vertical integration strategy, "from the well to the gas station," was swiftly abandoned. As the guidelines of vintage neoliberalism were resurrected at an ideal moment for what Naomi Klein would surely have called the "shock doctrine," Petrobras's refineries, pipelines, and gas stations were placed on the auction block together with all of its assets in renewable energy. The state oil company would maintain only the Atlantic drilling operations. Investment in exploration was cut by 75 percent.

Petrobras assets worth $14 billion had been sold at fire-sale prices. And that was just the beginning. Further privatization was expected to raise $27 billion more by 2023. Several highly profitable oil fields had also been put up for sale. Statoil (now Equinor), the Norwegian state-owned company (ironically, a model of vertical integration), took control of the productive Roncador field off the coast of Rio de Janeiro at a bargain price. Shell had been offered another lucrative concession. Exxon increased its *pré-sal* presence from two to twenty-six fields in the two years after Dilma's impeachment. The *pré-sal* business was opened up to foreign companies without the need even to partner in projects led by Petrobras, since the single-operator regime legislated under the Lula's first government had been revoked. Rather than refining its own oil in order to drive national development, an increasingly large share of the *pré-sal* was now exported directly as crude oil, often benefiting foreign companies and not the Brazilian state. Rather than a vertically integrated international player equipped to lead the Brazilian economy along the path of industrialization and technological advancement, Petrobras was now a solitary platform in the middle of the ocean.

That day in Salvador, with its crumbling baroque churches and Afro-Brazilian candomblé percussion bands that marched through the streets until dawn, the atmosphere could hardly have been further from Davos. We ordered a *moqueca*, a delicious fish and coconut stew from the Brazilian *nordeste* that, to use a word beloved of Brazilian sociologists, syncretically blended Portugal and Africa. The old center of Salvador remained a city in ruins while huge favelas like Liberdade, with eight hundred thousand mainly Afro-Brazilian inhabitants, remained slum cities to the north. But the years of PT governments had transformed the historically poverty-stricken *nordeste* economy from when 30 million destitute emigrants had fled to the big cities in the south during the 1960s and '70s. Unlike in Rio or São Paulo, few Bahianos demonized Lula or Dilma, yet everybody knew the years of PT dominance belonged to the past, as did Gabrielli's vision of a Petrobras capable of driving economic growth while correcting social injustices.

He summarized without drama: "They are implementing a Jack the Ripper policy at Petrobras. It will end up as a small company with no capacity for exploration and prospecting and this means that in the long term it will die." I asked him if he thought that the historic Latin American "pink tide" was now in retreat across the region. "Yes. I think it's over. And I don't think it's a coincidence. I'm not paranoid, but it seems to me that the United States and the CIA are involved in all this," he replied between bites of *moqueca*.

He ventured that Washington–first with Obama and then Trump–had orchestrated the collapse in oil prices to "destroy Venezuela and Russia." The expansion of fracking and unconventional oil production in the United States had boosted the global oil supply and triggered a devastating slide in the price. The *Lava Jato* probe, meanwhile, had political objectives, he went on, and had been conceived with the support of the United States Department of Justice. Dilma's impeachment had, too. "It's a strange coincidence that the coups d'état in Paraguay and Brazil all occurred with the same US ambassador," said Gabrielli. It was not exactly what one expected to hear from a former multinational CEO twice invited to the Davos World Economic Forum.

Gabrielli's thesis sounded to me during that lunch in Salvador like a conspiracy theory, the last desperate resort of a man of the left who had witnessed, in two epoch-changing years, the destruction of everything he believed in. A doctor in economics from Boston University and the London School of Economics who spoke impeccable English, Gabrielli was not a likely convert to the crazed paranoia that ricocheted through Brazilian social networks, courtesy of Olavo de Carvalho on the right and, on occasions, the left too. But the idea that the end of Petrobras had been hatched at some secret meeting at the US embassy in Brasília seemed far-fetched. Perhaps, just like me, Gabrielli had reread that detailed description in *Open Veins of Latin America* of the role of Hanna Mining, US Steel, and Operation Brother Sam in the 1964 coup and, in an attack of anguish, had extrapolated too much from it in order to explain events half a century later. After all, in our first interview at Davos, Gabrielli had underestimated the danger of contagion from the 2008 crisis for developing countries so dependent on the export of raw materials, including, of course, Brazil.

Besides, the Dilma government had committed a sort of hara-kiri by choosing the Chicago Boy Joaquim Levy as minister of finance in a futile attempt to calm the markets, giving the green light to a disastrous austerity program that decimated public investment just when the economy needed it most. And, as the reader will remember from the history of iron, the Brazilian elite had always been perfectly capable of organizing their own coups d'état without any outside support. The Workers' Party's redistribution measures had begun to bother the São Paulo and Rio middle classes, who, forced to share beaches and airport lounges with those favela-dwelling masses from *nordeste*, feared for their historical privileges. They needed no US-designed plot to take to the streets in protest at Lula and Dilma's corruption and communist plans to turn Brazil into Venezuela. The support of Brazil's big business represented by the Federation of Industries of the State of São Paulo (FIESP), which provided large inflatable ducks for the pro-impeachment demonstrations, was quite enough.

However, as the years went by and the debacle of the Latin American left became more and more evident, Gabrielli's thesis concerning a US-devised regional destabilization strategy seemed more and more credible. The end of the PT had indeed become a prerequisite for opening up the Brazilian oil sector to international capital as requested by those very same fund managers and energy sector CEOs at the Davos summits, all so much more at home on the ski slopes than Gabrielli could ever be.

There were compelling reasons to take Gabrielli's conspiracy thesis seriously. For one, the "Jack the Ripper"-style stripping of Petrobras's assets did not seem necessary or desirable from the point of view of the oil company's own long-term health or, for that matter, the health of the Brazilian economy. It seemed explicable only if the real goal was to benefit foreign multinationals and, specifically, the giants of Big Oil from BP, ExxonMobil, and Chevron to Shell, Conoco, and Total. After all, in 2018 Petrobras had the highest gross profit margin in the world, with the exception of Statoil.

As Petrobras was put on the block, it was surely no coincidence that the first sight that caught the attention of visitors to the 2016 Olympics when landing at Rio's Galeão Airport were not the photos of the surfers on Ipanema Beach but rather the huge billboards advertising Total. The sale of eight of the thirteen oil refineries and the privatization of Petrobras's gas stations, far from helping Petrobras out of the crisis, actually undermined its ability to offset further decreases in the price of crude oil. Felipe Coutinho, president of the Petrobras Engineers Association in Rio, showed me a revealing graph of the disaster that the "Jack the Ripper" business plan would entail. Refinery and marketing revenues had actually risen in 2015, offsetting the drop in oil prices for production activities. The "*poço a posto*" structure had been a key element of Brazil's energy security in times of declining resources and volatile prices. "Vertical integration helped Petrobras protect its income whatever the international oil price or the exchange rate; this will no longer be so," forecast Coutinho.

What's more, the privatization of refineries and other Petrobras divisions would mean losing billions of future state revenues. Coutinho estimated that losses would amount to $2.8 billion per year, which would soon nullify the revenues from the sale of such valuable assets. "Petrobras is a highly profitable company. The company's debt would have fallen without the need to sell all this," he explained. Then he made a striking statement in defense of the Gabrielli thesis: "You must understand that the cause and the effect have been reversed. Petrobras has not been privatized to reduce the debt, but rather a debt crisis has been invented to justify the privatization of Petrobras." Once in the presidency, Bolsonaro, forgetting the petronationalism that he had defended in the past, appointed a new Petrobras CEO, Roberto Castello Branco, who in his first interview with the Brazilian press confessed that his dream was "to privatize Petrobras."

There were other reasons to think that the United States might be interested in a regime change in Brazil as well as Venezuela in order to free up oil assets. In the summer of 2009, WikiLeaks had leaked a statement from the US consulate in Brasília to the State Department in Washington entitled "Can the oil industry defeat the *pré-sal* law?" It was proof of the dissatisfaction that executives of Chevron, Exxon, and other multinationals felt toward a Lula-era law that gave Petrobras priority in the exploitation of newly discovered Atlantic reserves. Patricia Pradal, a Chevron executive in Brazil, complained that the law, which provided Petrobras with sole operator status, would exclude all western companies from the business and give China's Sinopec an advantage. "The Chinese can make better offers than anyone else," she explained. Why? Because Chinese companies, unlike Chevron, were not in search of short-term profits. "As long as there are no losses, it will be attractive to them. They just want the oil," complained Pradal, a striking confession of the difference between profit-seeking Houston and the strategically minded Chinese state oil companies.

As had occurred in Venezuela, Washington appeared concerned that Lula's PT, which the Wall Street banks and the think tanks on Pennsylvania Avenue had so admired during the previous decade, was now too close to its emergent geopolitical rival. When Rousseff was dismissed, the Temer government promptly quashed the law that gave preference to Petrobras. "There is an international geopolitical dispute over access to energy resources. China depends on imported oil and the United States intends to block its access. I believe that the fight against corruption here has been used for that purpose," said Coutinho, noting how the initial impulse for the anti-corruption probe had come from the US Department of Justice.

When the crusading *Lava Jato* judge Sergio Moro joined the new Bolsonaro government, the feeling that a political agenda supported by Washington was behind the investigation gained strength. No one could deny the scale of the corruption scheme involving Petrobras. Bribes and illegal financing had been endemic in Brazil for decades or centuries. But that only the Workers' Party had paid the price for a system of patronage seemed suspicious in the extreme.

The *Lava Jato* attorneys' weakness for US-style plea bargaining (offering reduced sentences and in some cases monetary rewards to the accused if they implicated others) heightened the sense that the investigation was selective and politicized, the pioneering case of a new strategy of lawfare that would be used to criminalize other progressive leaders in the region, such as Rafael Correa in Ecuador and Evo Morales in Bolivia. Private media groups, such as the all-powerful Rede Globo, also seemed to have a clear anti-PT agenda. Leaks of conversations between Moro and his prosecutors, published by *The Intercept*, would confirm these suspicions. That *Lava Jato* had ushered in the privatization plans of Temer and Bolsonaro, with the jewel in the crown, Petrobras, at the top of the list, seemed much more than an accident of history.

On a visit to Curitiba, the nerve center of the *Lava Jato* investigation and where Lula was now imprisoned, I met other Petrobras experts who also interpreted events in Brazil as a coup d'état designed to deliver the oil to the Davos men. "Vargas's suicide in 1954, the coup d'état in 1964, and the 2014 coup are all related to Petrobras," suggested the veteran journalist José "Zé" Augusto Ribeiro, who, despite being confined to a wheelchair, had gone that day to support a nightly vigil for Lula a few feet from the federal police jail where the former president had been locked up for six months in a 161-square-foot cell. "Good afternoon, Mr. President!" they shouted every day at eight o'clock in the evening, and Lula, a consummate politician even from his prison cell, told the media that he heard the chants.

According to Ribeiro, Petrobras was the main reason Getúlio Vargas had decided to shoot himself in the heart that August day in 1954 in the presidential palace of Catete when Rio was still Brazil's capital. He had been put under unbearable pressure to privatize the new state oil company from the powerful "media king" Assis Chateaubriand, who had smeared the president mercilessly in his newspapers and on his radio networks. Sixty years later, the *Lava Jato* prosecutors, Rede Globo's media network, and a furiously anti-PT Congress had conspired to repeat history. On both occasions, of course, Washington was a passive partner in the crime. "Petrobras is the common denominator between the Getúlio story and the Lula story," said Ribeiro over a *bacalhau* cod dinner in Curitiba.

Another delusional conspiracy theory? Perhaps. But I now realized that, in democracies so fragile at a time of growing geopolitical tension, little could be understood in Latin America without injecting a dose of conspiracy into the analysis. This was not a plot hatched by a group of powerful oligarchs behind closed doors in one of those subterranean meeting rooms in the futuristic Niemeyer-designed Congress building in Brasília. Nor in the US embassy in the diplomatic district. Rather, it was the result of a common reading of the Brazilian crisis and the PT government's role in it, under guidelines set by those very same Davos men who had smiled admiringly at Gabrielli in 2008.

When the bonanza ended so did Davos's tolerance for the Lulaist historical compromise. The new consensus extended from the offices of the *Lava Jato* prosecutors in Curitiba to the editorial boards of the major Brazilian and international media (remember that *Economist* cover that threatened: "Time to Go"). It covered Washington think tanks and debt-rating agencies like Standard & Poor's in New

York and São Paulo. It extended from the State Department in Washington to Chevron's legal department in California. PricewaterhouseCoopers even slashed the book value of the company's assets in 2014 by almost $20 billion, blaming its decision on the corruption scandal. This helped weave the new narrative of what Felipe Coutinho described as "the myth of the Petrobras bankruptcy." A company that was said to be on the verge of filing for bankruptcy protection was actually the second most profitable oil corporation in the world.

In truth, the cost of corruption was a drop in the ocean compared with the value of the *pré-sal* crude that the Petrobras geologists had discovered twenty years before and which was now considered the most valuable new oil reserve on the planet. Gabrielli had explained the facts during the Salvador *moqueca* meal: "According to the *Lava Jato* prosecutors, three percent of Petrobras contracts were subject to bribes. That is around six billion reais. It seems like a lot. But the Petrobras turnover in those years was three hundred and fifty billion reais. So the bribes were a relatively small amount. But *Lava Jato* has had a brutal impact. Of the fifteen engineering companies in the Petrobras group, nine are under investigation. That means they have no access to the credit market, nor can they compete for Petrobras business. Or for any government contracts. So the result is inevitable: foreign competition will arrive and take it all."

Mexico

In the swamps and lagoons of the Mexican oil state Tabasco, where Graham Greene set *The Power and the Glory*—a passionate defense of blind faith when persecuted by cold reason—something became transparently clear. While the experts in Mexico City and Washington saw no sense whatsoever in the decision of President Andrés Manuel López Obrador (AMLO) to build a new refinery in the nearby port of Dos Bocas, the *tabasqueño* in the street did not agree.

The new refinery formed part of AMLO's plans to abandon the previous government's liberalizing energy reform and halt the privatization of state-owned oil company, Pemex. For the think tanks in the Mexican capital, it was all madness. Only a fool would wish to nationalize gasoline production rather than refine Mexican crude in the United States. "Building a refinery just doesn't make sense. Refining is not good business," Jorge Andrés Castañeda, a young economist at the Mexican Institute for Competitiveness (IMCO), told me. He was co-author of a damning report which had filled the headlines that week.

Analysts felt the same in the new Richard Rogers-designed multicolor BBVA tower, one of the tallest buildings in the capital, where the Mexican subsidiary to the Spanish bank was headquartered. AMLO's decision to review concessions in the Gulf of Mexico that had benefited Big Oil multinationals such as Shell, Total, Chevron, or Repsol was another disastrous move. "We insist that the business model based on farmouts be reactivated," warned the BBVA oil-analysis team, using the Houston-coined English term to refer to the concessions, although in Tabasco few understood what it meant.

The frustration was palpable in the business districts of the Mexican capital. Just when Mexico had finally come to terms with the reality of the twenty-first-century globalized economy, resource nationalism had reared its ugly head. Overcoming resistance to the privatization of Pemex had been a daunting task for both Mexican and global elites.

Former president Lázaro Cárdenas, like Vargas in Brazil, had created a myth by nationalizing the oil industry in 1936 despite the protests of Standard Oil. And myths were so fiendishly difficult to erase in Mexico. It was AMLO's immediate predecessor Enrique Peña Nieto, a Davos Young Global Leader just like his close friend the Pemex chairman Emilio Lozoya, who had managed to push through the reform. Reason had prevailed over populism. But now López Obrador, after his resounding victory in the 2018 presidential elections and a campaign dotted with references to Cárdenas and the Mexican Revolution, planned to roll it all back. It was a terrible setback for the masters of rationality in Mexico.

Analysts at Moody's invited reporters to a briefing in the financial district of Polanco, surrounded by starchitect-designed skyscrapers, enormous suburban SUVs, and Starbucks franchises, and warned that the deprivatization of Pemex and the Dos Bocas refinery would lead to "a suboptimal tax position" at Pemex, the principal source of income for the Mexican federal state. Inevitably, the fear of a possible downgrade for Mexico's sovereign rating accelerated a stock-market collapse, rising interest rates, and the depreciation of the peso. Everybody knew how destabilization worked in Latin America. But now, with the new socially aware Washington consensus in place at the Lagarde-run International Monetary Fund, the leftist president was told he did not even represent the neediest Mexicans. "Peña Nieto's reform was a total success. AMLO must maintain it and focus on robust social programs to combat inequality in Mexico," explained David Goldwyn, an oil expert at the corporate-financed Atlantic Council in Washington when we spoke by telephone.

IMCO even calculated the exact probability that the new refinery in Tabasco would be a failure: 98 percent. But after decades of neoliberal reforms that had ended with stagnant wages and even more extreme inequality, the exact percentages of the experts meant little to the average Mexican. A year after his inauguration, López Obrador was still supported by two out of every three Mexicans. And in Tabasco, the president's home state, he was a popular hero. "Here Andrés Manuel has one hundred percent support!" exclaimed René Méndez Arjona, who sold delicious *tacos de guiso* in a taqueria in Villahermosa's central market. "And if he does what he promises, he will have even more."

I spent the next few days in Tabasco chuckling at the contrast between IMCO's 98 percent failure rate for the refinery, precisely calculated in the land of Starbucks, and Méndez Arjona's "more than one hundred percent" forecast while he prepared those delicious corn-tortilla tacos filled with crackling *chicharrón* and green chili sauce. It was as if another logic had taken over in Mexico, after thirty-six years swallowing the Kool-Aid hypotheses of efficient markets. Like the tragic whisky priest in Greene's novel, a drunkard who rebels against a police chief's cold positivist logic, the Mexicans seemed to have collectively realized that behind the experts' reason lurked a murderer.

In Villahermosa, López Obrador's irrational defense of energy sovereignty–that a producer country like Mexico should not depend on the United States for its gasoline–seemed like common sense. Perhaps collective memories lingered of US invasion of the neighboring state of Veracruz in 1917, or the gunboat diplomacy that in those years dispatched American, British, and occasionally Spanish warships to the Tabasco coast. In Villahermosa, energy independence had a clear logic, just as it had for Sergio Gabrielli at Petrobras. And, as in Brazil, the Jack the Ripper–style gutting of Pemex under Peña Nieto's energy reform was seen in the Mexican streets as a threat to energy security.

There was an instinctive feeling in Tabasco that what was rational for Moody's, the BBVA, or the Atlantic Council was probably not rational for them. "If it is such a bad idea, why are there so many refineries in the United States?" added Méndez Arjona, with the irrefutable logic of the *taquero.*

Luis Guillermo "Luigi" Pérez, an old friend of AMLO's and the main mover and shaker in the Tabasco branch of López Obrador's Morena party, explained the plan. "What does not make sense is what we have been doing with our oil up to now. The oil from offshore platforms in the gulf is cleaned and desalinated here in Tabasco, put on a ship, and taken to Texas for refining. Then it comes back to Mexico as gasoline with higher prices than in Texas. Sixty percent of the country's gas and crude oil comes from Tabasco, but look at the poverty here!" explained Pérez, whose retired-boxer features would have unsettled many in Polanco. "Andrés Manuel says: 'No! I'm going to build a new refinery, and I'm going to fix the other six that we have in the Republic. And we are going to refine our own oil. We are not going to sell crude oil anymore; we are going to sell gasoline.'"

AMLO had announced in his election campaign that what he dubbed the "Fourth Transformation" would give priority not only to energy self-sufficiency, but also to autonomy in food supply despite the North American Free Trade Agreement (NAFTA) that he had ratified in its new format after the threat of trade war from Trump. This also left the experts scratching their heads. AMLO had also suspended a project already underway to build a new international airport in Mexico City, despite the millions of dollars already spent on construction and millions more that would have to be paid in compensation. It made no sense to economists. But only three in ten Mexicans had ever been to an airport.

Even AMLO's treasury secretary, Carlos Urzúa, a Keynesian who had worked for the progressive United Nations Economic Commission for Latin America and the Caribbean (CEPAL), could see no logic in the construction of the refinery or the deconstruction of the airport. When he finally resigned, AMLO branded him a "neoliberal."

"For López Obrador, anyone who questions him is neoliberal," Urzúa hit back in an interview published in the magazine *Proceso*. And so it was. López Obrador represented a new economic nationalism that was challenging elements of the neoliberal model of globalization after forty years of dominance. The Mexican president sought to recover the vigor of the national state development policies of the 1960s and '70s, when Mexico posted GDP growth rates of 6 or 7 percent.

The new Pemex rationalization plan, presented in the summer of 2019, included the phrase: "For the first time in the history of Mexican democracy, a government has been formed to give the public administration a nationalist vision." Mexico, the country where the "neoliberal era" had failed in the most resounding fashion, with fifty-seven million people living in poverty after thirty years of stunted GDP growth, was perhaps the perfect laboratory to search for a new formula. Although it was not clear what alternative AMLO had in mind, he clearly understood the depth of the popular rejection of the Peña Nieto privatizers and their corrupt public-private partnerships. That 50 percent of the Mexican workforce that earned less than $300 a month saw reason in the AMLO madness.

International-media editorial writers and BBVA macro reports branded López Obrador a populist. "Some investors and analysts fear that in pursuing the mirage of a return to the golden era of growth of half a century ago, with the state firmly in the driving seat, the silver-haired shopkeepers' son is flirting with the sort of demagoguery that could take Mexico down a dangerous populist path," Jude Webber warned in the *Financial Times*. But the truth was that sometimes AMLO's commitment to a national development plan actually involved decidedly unpopulist public sacrifices. The new president was as keen a believer in fiscal conservatism, the only reliable cure for corruption, he claimed. The new rescue plan for indebted Pemex, for example, was the first time that a Mexican government had actually decided to turn down the income of the state oil monopoly. It was AMLO's great political innovation. Austerity became a radical demand of the left. State spending in Mexico was so closely identified with corruption that the idea was a vote-winner, though many progressive economists, including Carlos Urzúa, wondered after the coronavirus-driven depression how a recovery could be engineered given the president's relentless insistence on budget cuts.

Pemex had provided between 30 percent and 44 percent of the state's income during the six-year terms of Felipe Calderón and Enrique Peña Nieto. This coincided with a disastrous divestment in the company's exploration activities: oil production fell 50 percent between 2010 and 2019, to just 1.8 million barrels a day. Meanwhile, Pemex's debt had doubled to two billion pesos ($100 million). AMLO announced that austerity could create space for productive investment at Pemex.

The Pemex plan promised to reduce the transfers from the oil company to the state by almost six billion euros. With this reduction in the tax burden on Pemex, capital could be freed up for investment and exploration in twenty-two new oil fields. It was a major break with the past. Pemex had transferred no less than twenty-nine trillion pesos ($1.5 trillion) to a wasteful and corrupt Mexican state during the three decades that López Obrador described as the neoliberal era. While Peña Nieto and Pemex chairman Emilio Lozoya had justified their plans to dismantle the state monopoly by arguing that Pemex was bankrupt, the López Obrador government set out to make the company viable by suspending the practice of using Pemex revenues to finance costly megaprojects with money funneled from contractors to the political elite. It seemed like an argument that might persuade even the IMF. But like everything the new president proposed, the bailout plan was soon vilified as populist by the experts.

In the street, though, the reaction was different. When Lozoya was extradited from Spain in 2020, accused of corruption and money laundering in the Mexican chapter of the Odebrecht bribes scandal, AMLO's plans seemed vastly preferable. Lozoya would implicate both the former president Peña Nieto and his chancellor Luis Videgaray (Jared Kushner's close friend) as accomplices in the Pemex-Odebrecht bribes scandal. Predictably, little attention had been paid by the US Justice Department or the international media to Lozoya's corruption during his days at Pemex, in stark contrast with Petrobras in Brazil. *The Economist* had published no cover story about Peña Nieto under the headline "Time to Go."

This is not to say there was not indeed an element of old-fashioned populism in AMLO's refinery plan. Tabasco was López Obrador's territory, down the road from his birth place of Tepetitán. He ordered a monthly consignment of delicious Catalan-style *butifarra* sausages from the Tabascan town of Jalpa de Méndez and owned a ranch on the border between Tabasco and Chiapas, which he called *La Chingada* (The Fucked One). One of his main electoral commitments was to promote development in the poor, underdeveloped Mexican southeast through public works such as the Mayan train–a railroad that would run from the beaches of Cancún to the poor interior of Chiapas–and the Trans-Isthmus Corridor, a highway that would connect the Pacific and the Gulf to compete with the Panama Canal. Likewise, the construction of the refinery was expected to generate thirty thousand direct and indirect jobs, vital in Villahermosa, a city devastated by the drastic decline in oil production since 2004.

When I visited Tepetitán, people's belief that AMLO could deal with Mexico's deep-seated problems was palpable, although Mexico's caustic sense of humor helped prevent a personality cult. "Let's see if he brings us more fish," joked a local, smiling after one drink too many as he waited in front of the old grocery store founded by López Obrador's grandparents, now a ruin on the banks of the fast-flowing but overfished river Tulijá. Opposite, a naive mural with the portrait of the new president read: *Soy peje pero nunca lagarto* (I am a *peje* fish but never a lizard), referring to the Tabascan lagoon fish from which López Obrador got his affectionate nickname: El Peje.

Irrational as his program was from the experts' perspective, López Obrador was well-liked in the local villages that struggled to survive in the swamps south of Villahermosa. "I remember seeing Peje when the police broke his head open," recalled thirty-six-year-old José Manuel Reyes in Guatacalca, a community of small farmers from the Chontal ethnic group (a subgroup of the Maya), the first indigenous people that Hernán Cortés had encountered when he set foot in the region exactly five hundred years before.

Reyes was referring to the 1989 protest against Pemex, in which the young López Obrador participated. "In those years, Pemex arrived with large trucks and began to extract oil, but the people here were completely ignored, forgotten. We used to move around on donkeys," he explained as he hosed the street in front of his fish store to settle the dust.

A few years before that pitched battle with the police, López Obrador had been appointed director of the Tabasco Indigenous Institute and settled with his wife and son in the mosquito-infested, malaria-ridden swamps of Guatacalca. He coordinated a project to build islands of mud in the lagoons to recover land from the water for cultivation. The inspiration were the chinampas of the Aztec in the lakes of Xochimilco around Mexico City, then Tenochtitlán. In these Chontal villages, the letter that AMLO had just sent to King Felipe VI of Spain asking the monarch to apologize for the conquest and plunder of Mexico did not cause embarrassment as it did in Polanco, but ironic chuckles.

Yet, as I drove through the Chontal villages once bypassed by Pemex-driven developmentalism in the golden age of the Institutional Revolutionary Party (PRI), a more cogent critique of AMLO's bid for fossil fuel energy self-sufficiency seemed to emerge from the oil-polluted swamps. The environmentalist left, grouped around the Zapatistas in Chiapas, questioned AMLO's reasons not from the stance of the Atlantic Council but that of the future of the planet. Why not build an energy-security strategy in Mexico based on renewables? Mexico was responsible for only 2 percent of greenhouse gas emissions but it was highly exposed to the impacts of the climate crisis as rising temperatures and drought threatened the northern deserts and cyclones and record rainfall flooded the south east. López Obrador had rightly identified as corrupt the market-driven strategy to develop alternative energy sources developed by Peña Nieto with the help of Spanish energy multinationals. But the new president's commitment to state-driven energy policy in the oil sector crowded out solar and wind. The young López Obrador, fighting Pemex alongside the Chontal, seemed a better role model for the age of climate change than the cantankerous veteran of the Mexican left now in the presidential palace and intent on reinventing Cárdenas's petronationalism. When, in the fall of 2020, massive floods left hundreds of thousands homeless in Tabasco in the wake of Hurricane Eta and unprecedented rainfall, the dangers of reverting to the old model in times of climate change became tragically clear. Even the ruins of the López Obradors' grocery store in Tepetitán were flooded.

As the sun set on the Tabasco wetlands, it occurred to me that, dismissed from all sides as unbalanced, irrational, stubborn, and uncompromising, AMLO somehow resembled those conquistadores whom he so despised. Such are the ironies of history. To wit, a quote from Galeano's other masterpiece, the *Memory of Fire* trilogy, describing the epoch-making arrival of Cortés off the Tabascan coast: "Eleven ships are burning up; burning, too, the rebel soldiers who hang from the yardarm of the flagship . . . now there is no going back, no more life than what is born tomorrow." The phrase "now there is no going back" could perhaps illustrate AMLO's promise to end the neoliberal era with no possible return, although nobody, least of all he, knew exactly what would come next.

But, when I mentioned the idea to López Obrador's old friend Pérez, he shook his head. The Galeano quote was not at all suitable for a story on Tabasco. Cortés had actually ordered the burning of his ships in Veracruz, several hundred miles north, in March 1519, months after he made his first sighting of land at the mouth of the Grijalva River.

"We are proud to believe that the story of the conquest of Mexico began here in Tabasco, because the first naval battle took place on the Grijalva River," explained Pérez, with visible pride spreading across his roughly hewn features. He began to reconstruct the events using the present tense, just like Galeano: "Cortés lands at the Point of the Palms on the Grijalva River. The Spaniards descend in brigantines and the battle begins . . . Seven hundred Spaniards versus forty thousand indigenous. The fighting lasts a week and then the Spanish return to the *caravelas*, while the Chontal prepare for guerrilla warfare in the mangroves. Despite their steel swords and blunderbusses," Pérez continued, ratcheting up the narrative tension. "The Spanish only win the battle when they return on horseback. The Chontal think that horse and man are one. They think the Spanish are gods!" It was yet more evidence that battles in Mexico would not be won by reason alone.

CHAPTER SIXTEEN

Hydro (Pará, Brazil)
The Maps of the Munduruku

They had been killing time for more than nine hours at the tiny river port of Buburé, a respite from the dust clouds or, depending on the season, the knee-deep mud of the Trans-Amazonian Highway. The *guerreiro* warriors sported Neymar hairstyles and navy-blue hash-design body paint with black and orange horizontal streaks across their faces. They wore Ipanema-style Havaianas flip flops, white cotton sports socks, and T-shirts stamped with slogans like HARD STREET, URBAN PEOPLE. One brandished a bow but no arrows. Others checked their cell phones though coverage was patchy. They had arrived by launch on the Tapajos River from the Munduruku village of Sawré Muybu, fifteen miles upriver, where they were working on the demarcation of their territory, an essential first step for the coming battles. A second launch was expected in Buburé that evening to transport them to the next demarcation point in the dense Amazon rain forest. "We have been working for three weeks to clear a thirteen-foot-wide boundary in the undergrowth, with machetes and GPS, closely following the FUNAI [National Indian Foundation] *croquis*," said Bruno Kapa Munduruku, the oldest of the warriors, whose face was crisscrossed with mauve-red brushstrokes, the Munduruku war paint.

A few years earlier, FUNAI had mapped out the Munduruku territory, some 178,000 hectares that stretched for several hundred miles along the banks of the Tapajos. The institute's constitutional mandate required the demarcation of indigenous land to protect the territorial rights of more than two hundred native communities. But the official FUNAI report had been suppressed by Dilma Rousseff's government, whose commitment to the indigenous struggle had lost momentum, to say the least, under relentless pressure from the soy and beef, and mining and energy, lobbies. A plan dating from the years of the military junta to dam and tame the Tapajos for hydropower and the transportation of soy to Santarém 150 miles downstream now had the support of the Workers' Party (PT) administration. The warriors, however, appeared to draw on inexhaustible reserves of resistance and guile. They had persuaded some FUNAI dissidents to leak copies of the drafts of maps that the foundation had sketched for the Munduruku demarcation. These would guide the work now being done by Bruno Kapa and his warriors. Once the mapping and boundary clearing was completed, they could launch the legal defense against the dam and the transformation of the Tapajos based on article 231 of the Brazilian Constitution, which forbade "the displacement of indigenous groups from their lands except in the case of catastrophe or epidemic."

The warriors and their GPS-equipped cell phones upheld a tradition of political cartography in the Amazon that dated back to the colonial battles of the nineteenth century–with the significant difference that, in most cases, the maps had justified plunder in the grab for land and resources, a necessary prelude to the territorial claims of an endless succession of imperial pillagers, notably the United States, France, the United Kingdom, Belgium, and the Netherlands, soon to be joined by the new Latin American republics Brazil, Bolivia, and Peru in the scramble for the Amazon.

The Munduruku's heroic demarcation of their ancestral lands differed radically from the mapmaking of the new Brazilian republic as it marshaled cartography against colonialist grabs for the Amazon. By contrast, the Munduruku's maps were a simple representation of the truth. This was land they had inhabited for millennia, delicately adapting the Amazon's infinitely varied vegetation to their needs. Anyone who doubted the validity of their claims could consult the latest archaeological research that noted a close similarity between the Munduruku body paint and the eighth-century ceramics found in the subsoil of the Tapajos basin.

The GPS-facilitated maps of the Munduruku were weapons in a war for survival. The same was true for those Afro-Brazilians who still farmed the *quilombos*, historic settlements of runaway slaves in the Amazon and beyond whose territory was recognized by the 1988 constitution but not by the *latifundistas* and their gunmen. Some *quilombeiros* had joined the pioneers of the Nova Cartografia Social, a movement of radical cartographers who helped those involved in territorial disputes to compile their own maps and so defend their borders.

"They are teaching communities to learn to use GPS and make maps that illustrate their own stories without relying on technicians," explained Paulo Rogerio, an agronomist who advised *quilomberos* in the Amazonian state of Tocantins, west of the Munduruku territory. The landowners understood the threat posed by these militant cartographers to their plans for deforestation, agribusiness, and mining. Two young Afro-Brazilian *quilomberos* in the state of Maranhão, on the deforestation frontier of the Amazon, had made maps to demarcate the land occupied centuries before by slaves. They were brutally attacked by landowners' thugs. "Their hands were cut off," said Rogerio.

Another map that hung from the timber wall of the solitary store in Buburé, where the guerreiros slumbered, left little doubt as to why the Brazilian government had refused to recognize the sovereignty of the Munduruku land. SÃO LUIZ DO TAPAJOS HYDROELECTRIC DEVELOPMENT, announced the masthead. A list of companies, Brazilian and multinational, occupied the right-hand margin, partners in the first phase of the project to build the next big dam in the Amazon. Prominent were the corporate logos of the state energy monopoly Eletrobras and the São Paulo–headquartered construction giant Camargo Corrêa, both under investigation in the *Lava Jato* corruption scandal. And then, of course, there were the European transnationals: France's Électricité de France (EDF) and GDF Suez (now ENGIE), and Spain's Endesa. The most colorful logo on the map was that of Diálogo Tapajos, the São Paulo–based public relations firm whose job was to prepare public opinion for the 108-foot-high dam and 450-square-mile reservoir that would submerge part of the Munduruku's historic territory. The flooded forest would include a sacred site, Daje Kapap Eipi, the Garden of Eden in the Munduruku's creation myth. Not to mention it would also include many of the homes of the thirteen thousand Munduruku who made up a long chain of vibrant communities along five hundred miles of the Tapajos.

This was a map of destruction. But the cartographic marketing of Diálogo Tapajos had been sabotaged on the timber wall in Buburé. Someone, a *guerreiro* warrior perhaps, had used a fluorescent-blue highlighter to draw a line from Buburé across the river to Bom Jesus and then across the forest to the Jamanxim River, enclosing a large triangle. MUNDURUKU TERRITORY, said the improvised key to the highlighted area. Next to it, in large print, with an arrow pointing to a hypothetical sketch of the hydroelectric project and the megadam, the saboteur had scrawled a message in Portuguese: *NUNCA SERÃO*. Never will be.

* * *

The São Luiz do Tapajos dam was one of forty-three hydroelectric projects that Dilma's PT government planned to build on the Tapajos and Teles Pires Rivers, elements to the so-called Growth Acceleration Program (PAC) that would later be resuscitated by Jair Bolsonaro in the wake of the 2020 pandemic-induced economic slump. Seventy-five percent of the energy consumed in Brazil was generated in hydroelectric plants, and Rousseff hoped to exploit the potential of the enormous Amazon rivers, despite the fact that such slow-moving rivers that meandered ponderously through a landscape as flat as the southwestern Brazilian Amazon were ill-equipped for hydro and required mass flooding to generate even small quantities of energy.

But big dams were not the only drivers of the accelerated growth strategy. Many of the PAC projects—such as the one on the Chacorão River, which would flood 1,870 hectares of indigenous territory—appeared to be designed primarily to open commercial routes, or *hidrovia* waterways, as the Diálogo Tapajos spokespeople called them. These would allow Cargill's green-and-white megabarges laden with soy from the Mato Grosso plains to easily navigate the Amazon rivers to Santarém, with its Cargill soy terminal, and from there to Europe and China. "The idea is simple: to open up the Amazon to agribusiness and large-scale mining," said

Mauricio Torres, a geographer who advised the Munduruku on demarcation, as we wiped beads of sweat from our necks and swatted mosquitos in a bar in Itaituba.

After the extraordinary success of pulling forty million people out of centuries-long exclusion and deprivation, the PT government considered dam-building essential to eliminate poverty altogether in Brazil, as Dilma had promised to do before her 2014 election victory. Only with more energy could Brazil's potential GDP growth be raised. Besides, as Rousseff argued, an economic development strategy focused on hydro-electric power and river freight would mean less deforesta-tion than the alternative of building roads to provide access to loggers and cattle ranchers. Dilma spoke with passion of the need to continue the job of turning Brazil into a developed economy. But on the banks of the Tapajos it was difficult not to feel that the PT had ceased to believe in its own project. The government had bypassed environmental protection regula-tions legislated by its own parliamentary group. Even part of the historic Amazon National Park had been reclassified to clear the way for the São Luiz hydroelectric project.

Many of the companies involved in the hydro scheme had benefited from carbon credits for investing in renewable energy under the Kyoto Protocol Clean Development Mech-anism, despite indications that big dams left a deep carbon footprint and led to rapid deforestation. Two years later, when Jair Bolsonaro was settled into the futuristic presi-dential palace in Brasília, it was easy to long for the Dilma years. But in the land of the Munduruku, the battle against destruction had begun when the PT was still in government.

About an hour upriver from Buburé, on a fifteen-foot motor launch with a young Munduruku *guerreiro* at the helm, we reached the main settlement of Sawré Muybu, where some 120 Munduruku families lived in timber and adobe huts, fed almost exclusively from game hunted in the surrounding forest, a plethora of plants both gathered and cultivated, and fish from the Tapajos. The river at that time of year was a vast, glimmering lake. Snow-white egrets perched motionless on the riverbank while gray cormorants skimmed across the water. Pirarucu fish as big as sharks broke the surface every few minutes and pink dolphins leapt in fleeting arches in the wake of the launch. The albino dolphins, or *botos*, as the Amazons called them, were creatures of magic and myth. The captain of the ferry that had brought me to Itaituba assured without a trace of irony that the dolphins left women pregnant after nocturnal visits to the riverbank villages.

In the Munduruku village, a group of teenagers were playing soccer on a field surrounded by towering andiroba and pau brasil trees as high as one hundred feet. Many were wearing only one Nike cleat with an accompanying sock, leaving the other foot bare. "We share all that we have," explained a fifteen-year-old mother who was watching the match with her baby in her arms. Private property hardly existed in Munduruku society. "In our world there are no high- or low-level people, no rich or poor. We are all the same," explained Jairo Saw Munduruku, a university graduate who, at forty-six years of age, represented the Munduruku in their global fight against the hydroelectric project.

The Munduruku had waged a centuries-long resistance during the first colonization of the Amazon in the seventeenth century, when the warriors demarcated their territory with an unambiguous semiology. They beheaded the Europeans they had killed in battle and nailed their stuffed heads to tree trunks. Four hundred years later, some of the warning signs placed on the newly demarcated Munduruku boundary were appropriately illustrated with a rough sketch of a head nailed to a pole.

"In the past, we Munduruku had a reputation for being ants, warriors who had tirelessly fought the Portuguese for centuries. But now we are not ants; we are people with rights," said Jairo Saw. Although the São Luiz do Tapajos hydroelectric plant would not directly force the town's inhabitants to leave, the impact on fishing and hunting would be devastating, said the tribal chiefs. "We depend on the cyclical variations of the river. There are huge changes to the river between summer and winter; all this will end with the dam and the fish will not be able to swim upstream to reproduce," said Juárez Saw Munduruku, the village *cacique*, when I interviewed him at the communal house.

The Munduruku's struggle was not just a matter of local concern. Ten percent of all the species on the planet were present in this part of Amazon rain forest, and the Munduruku doubted that they would continue to thrive if a living, cyclical river were turned into a descending succession of near-stagnant reservoirs. Furthermore, without the Munduruku, the Tapajos jungle would lose its guardians and sentinels in the constant battle with invading *garimpeiro* miners and loggers as deforestation returned with a vengeance after the brief success of the first Lula government in protecting the Amazon.

Multiple studies had already shown causal links between water shortages in the great metropolises of central and southern Brazil and deforestation of the Amazon. Some scientists now speculated that central and southern Brazil–including the vast metropolises of São Paulo, Rio de Janeiro, and Belo Horizonte–would be desert were it not for the so-called *rios voladores* or flying rivers, air currents loaded with billions of liters of moisture from the transpiration of millions of trees, that moved southward from the Amazon. "The climate is changing. In São Paulo they are cutting the water due to the drought," said Jairo Saw Munduruku, aware that the battle had to be taken to the big cities. "There are no people better prepared to protect the jungle than we are."

Mauricio Torres, the geographer who advised the Munduruku, showed me another map rendered from satellite images provided by the Institute for Space Research (INPE). It revealed the critical importance of the Munduruku and their sister peoples. The Brazilian Amazon (60 percent of the total) was divided in the chart into patches of lime and bottle greens, depicting living forest, and several shades of scarlet, which represented the swathes of deforestation.

Red was already the dominant color in the south and west as the frontiers of cattle and soy advanced. Long red veins stretched out from Brasília toward Belém or from Manaus toward Venezuela, the new Trans-Amazonian Highways with their lateral crosslines of deforestation in the shape of a fish bone. A huge crimson stain spread around the Vale iron mines in the Carajás Mountains, and further north to the Belo Monte hydroelectric project, where an expanding gray stain surrounded by red signaled the demographic explosion in the city of Altamira. But further west and south, green was the predominant color in areas of the map with hardly a pinpoint of red. These were over six hundred indigenous reserves that covered more than 20 percent of the surface of the Amazon.

* * *

When I visited Sawré Muybu and watched the one-cleated Munduruku football match and listened to Jairo and Juárez Saw, I still inhabited a primitive and backward world, ignorant of Amazon history. Every time I saw one of those arresting pictures of uncontacted indigenous tribes–people gazing skyward, perhaps aiming a poisoned arrow at the *O Globo* photojournalist leaning out of a FUNAI helicopter, I naturally assumed that this was a fleeting glimpse of an ancient world that existed before the arrival of Europeans in the sixteenth century, a window onto a distant past. These small groups of nomadic hunter-gatherers were obviously, I thought, the surviving remnants of the forest dwellers who inhabited the Amazon in the millennia prior to colonization and the creation of Brazil after the arrival of Portuguese conquistador Pedro Álvares Cabral in 1500. It seemed simple common sense to extrapolate from those ephemeral images of the uncontacted tribes that the pre-Hispanic Amazonians must have been nomadic hunters living in a state of Rousseauean *bon sauvage* amidst an enormous, sparsely populated virgin forest. For that reason perhaps I had felt slightly shocked, perhaps even a little sad, to witness the Munduruku warriors in Buburé dressed in those HARD STREET, URBAN PEOPLE T-shirts. After all, everybody knew that back to their most remote origins, the Amazonian people were part of nature, the antithesis of an urban people.

A conversation with Reinaldo José Lopes, columnist at *Folha de São Paulo* and author of the book *1499: Brazil Before Cabral*, soon changed my perception of the past in the Amazon and, even more importantly, of the future. More than a vision of Rousseau, Lopes explained, the uncontacted Amazonian tribes might be compared to the protagonists of a *Mad Max* movie. They were survivors of the collapse of complex, densely populated, and, in their own idiosyncratic sense, urban societies. Lopes's book described a pre-Columbian Amazon that Olavo de Carvalho would have denounced as the historical revisionism of cultural Marxism. But this was journalism rigorously based on the latest archaeological discoveries from areas such as the Xingu River, the islands of Marajó, and the Tapajos basin.

The first staggering lesson from the new wave of Amazonian archeology and anthropology concerned population levels. There was now a broad consensus amongst the experts that no fewer than eight million people lived in the Amazon rain forest before the first Europeans headed feverishly upriver in search of El Dorado. To feed themselves, these societies had learned to manage the forest by selecting trees and smaller plants for reproduction and modifying other vegetation. Complex social structures arose in mass societies that produced highly sophisticated ceramic art. After the arrival of the Europeans, just like in other parts of the New World, the Amazonian societies rapidly collapsed, annihilated by systemic violence, mass enslavement, and hitherto unknown contagious diseases such as chicken pox. The forest's population was decimated and survivors of the apocalypse were forced to revert to much more rudimentary methods of subsistence based on nomadic migration, hunting, and the gathering of wild fruits and vegetables. Of course, they still made use of a vast bank of environmental knowledge acquired over centuries of collective management of nature. It was the only way to survive.

Before the collapse, the inhabitants of the Xingu region lived in communities with hundreds of thousands of inhabitants, structured around "a peculiar form of urbanism: wide avenues, monumental squares, and a subtle and gradual integration between inhabited areas, parks, and forested landscape," Lopes explained to me as my jaw dropped. Conceptually, "you might say it's a bit like Brasília but without the reinforced concrete," he went on, referring to the modern capital of Brazil, designed in the mid-twentieth century by Lúcio Costa and Oscar Niemeyer. Perhaps it was irony. Perhaps not.

By "parks," Lopes meant areas that anthropologists in the United States, like Michael Heckenberger at the University of Florida, called "cultural parklands": areas of managed forest that served as a source of food, medicine, construction materials, or an inspiration for art, sculpture, and worship. Large areas of the Amazon jungle in the early twenty-first century, far from being virgin nature, were in fact "the result of a complex relationship between the raw material of biodiversity and human culture," said Lopes. This explained the concentration of particular types of vegetation in what appeared to be a virgin forest. While in 2018 there were more than twelve thousand species of tree in the Amazon, twenty kinds of semidomesticated trees are found in 70 percent of the forest, from cocoa to walnut to rubber, all of them of great utility to human settlements. This is not accidental, but rather the result of the management of nature by pre-Columbian societies. Carolina Levis, one of the researchers on whose work Reinaldo's book is based, summed up the revelation succinctly in an article published in *Science*: the Amazonian flora is to a significant extent "a surviving heritage of its past inhabitants."

So the ancient Munduruku and the other indigenous societies in the pre-Cabral Amazon designed an innovative system of managed natural resources and biodiversity that was necessary to make their densely populated societies viable and, at the same time, to guarantee environmental sustainability. They devised techniques of natural fertilization and crop rotation where wild plants were managed and rotated to create vast areas of fertile *terra preta* or "black earth." This human-made but natural fertilizer still remained in the soil around the Xingu, and was a sad reminder of alternative worlds in Altamira, now a boom-town of murder, prostitution, and urban slums that fol-lowed in the wake of the Belo Monte megadam.

Not only were the forest and its plants carefully man-aged to guarantee the supply of large semi-urban and mass-populated communities in the Amazon. The forest dwellers also developed expertise in agriculture. Cassava, a tuber that in its wild state is poisonous to humans due to the cyanide it contains, was a ubiquitous crop. Amazon dwell-ers developed species of cassava that were not toxic through selection over centuries, but they continued to grow the poisonous variety. Why? Because the cyanide increased the resistance of the tuber to parasites and other plagues. When insects or bacteria destroyed the edible crops, the toxic cas-sava could be harvested and processed to remove its toxic substances and transform it into flour.

When, half a millennium later, I visited Tururcari Uka, a Kambeba community sixty miles from Manaus, which was threatened by a luxury tourist development called Amazonia Towers where Bill Gates, Arnold Schwarzenegger, Queen Beatrix of the Netherlands, and Charlton Heston had all spent vacations, we ate a paste made from cyanide-laced cassava. "We soak it to extract the poison, and then make flour," said Larissa Kambeba as a wide-eyed spider monkey clambered from her shoulder to perch on top of her head.

"Everything in the Kambeba universe is circular, including the music, including time," said Márcia Kambeba, a member of the tribe who had graduated and made a rep-utation as a poet and singer. She would soon become one of a new generation of indigenous women elected as political representatives, in Marcia's case, for the leftist grouping the Socialism and Liberty Party (PSOL), which took control of the Belém city council in late 2020.

The revolutionary revision of Amazon prehistory that Lopes had popularized in his bestselling book was critically important at a time in which Bolsonaro pledged to end the policy of "keeping prehistoric men in zoos" and to "demarcate not one more centimeter" of the Amazon. Not only did it challenge the idea that progress had arrived along with the smallpox and the blunderbuss in the Spanish and Portuguese caravels. It also provided crucial lessons for the epic battle now underway to save the planet.

Unlike the soy monoculture or the invasion of those ghostly white zebu that were destroying an area equivalent to three thousand soccer fields every day, the agriculture and management of the forest by the pre-Columbian Amazonians "was based on hundreds of different species and excellent land management," said Lopes. The egalitarian orchard cities and cultural parklands that spread through the Amazon under collective land management and communal property before the arrival of the Europeans should be models even today, he continued. "The first inhabitants of the Xingu de Altamira and Marajó Island found ways to transform the environment in which they lived instead of destroying it. There is much that we should learn here."

* * *

The use of GPS technology in mapping and the demarcation of the Munduruku territory in the Tapajos basin, along with those HARD STREET, URBAN PEOPLE T-shirts, reminded me of a crucial scene from Ciro Guerra's movie *The Embrace of the Serpent*, a thought-provoking analysis of the clash of cultures between Amazonian natives and Western explorers at the beginning of the twentieth century. In it, the ethnographer Theo von Martius travels through the Amazon rain forest guided by a shaman, Karamakate. In one scene von Martius tries unsuccessfully to recover a compass that a tribal leader has stolen from his luggage. "If they learn to use the compass, their knowledge of the stars and the winds will be lost," says the German, trying to justify an angry outburst in which he grapples with the tribal *cacique*. Karamakate responds: "But you cannot forbid them from learning. Knowledge belongs to everyone."

Like everything else in this fascinating film by the Colombian filmmaker, the scene posed a very relevant question for the Munduruku's battle not only against the Tapajos dam or the mining and agribusiness lobbies that pushed for new highways or water ways, but also against romantic perceptions of the exotic "noble savage" whose life is incompatible with modern life. The idea fueled Bolsonaro's racist characterization of subhumans trapped in the Stone Age in order to fulfill the agenda of international NGOs, typified by his remark that "the Indians are now becoming human beings," made in a speech delivered in the Amazon in 2019. But the idea of the natural state also filtered through some of the arguments of Western NGOs like Survival International.

I asked Guerra what he thought during an interview held soon after the film was released. "The idealized image of indigenous people in their pure state is our idea; it is not theirs. They do not want to live like they did a hundred years ago," he replied. But when the question arose as to which development model and which technologies are worth adopting, he was no less forthright: "The communities that inhabit the territory should be the ones to decide. They have been there for centuries without overpopulation, without polluting, without depleting resources. They have knowledge that should be respected." The Munduruku formula for adopting technological knowledge without destroying their own culture might offer suggestive ideas for the rest of us. After all, in *Embrace of the Serpent* it is the shaman Karamakate who guides the two European explorers along the river on a journey of inner discovery.

In their fight against the hydroelectric project in Tapajos, the Munduruku fully understood the epic importance of their example. Jairo Saw Munduruku and other leaders had traveled to Germany, Austria, and the United States to meet with the engineers of the multinationals involved in the hydroelectric project. These companies "talk about development and sustainable technology, but the turbines they manufacture will destroy the Amazon," said Jairo Saw during a second interview at the Museum of the Indian in Rio before he set off for Los Angeles for the meeting with General Electric.

While he confronted the enemy in California, back on the banks of the Tapajos Fernanda Moreira, a young anthropologist from São Paulo who had moved to Itaituba to learn from the Munduruku and finish her doctoral thesis, had staged a screening of *The Embrace of the Serpent* in the middle of the self-demarcated territory. Dozens of residents of the Munduruku *aldeias* attended and enjoyed the film, she told me after the screening. They all agreed on one thing: "Technology is neither good nor bad; it all depends on who controls it."

ABOUT THE AUTHOR

Andy Robinson is a roving reporter for *La Vanguardia*. A graduate of the London School of Economics, he is a contributor to *Business Week*, *City Limits*, *The Guardian*, *Ajoblanco*, and *The Nation*.

INDEX

Abaco Quispe, Rodolfo, 165
Abertis, 179
ACI Systems, 194, 198, 202, 204
Acosta, Alberto, 8
Acuña, Máxima, 166
Acurio, Gastón, 149
AgroSB, 267
Agüero, Félix, 161
Aguilera, Dalila, 219–20
Aguirre, Lope de, 92
Albuquerque, Bento, 54
Alcoa, 30–31
Alencar, Ane, 272
Allegheny Technologies Inc., 57
Allende, Salvador, 169
Almagro, Luis, 129, 177, 198
Alonso, Fernando, 221
Álvares Cabral, Pedro, 328
Álvarez, Bernardo, 121
Amalfi, Colombia, 77–85
Amazon Environmental Research Institute (IPAM), 272
Amazônia (de Souza Marques), 34
American Principles Project, 98
Anaconda, 168
Andean Community (CAN), 214
Andrade Gutierrez, 106, 109, 110
Añez, Jeanine, 200–201, 203
AngloGold Ashanti, 82
Apurímac, Peru, 158–67
A queda do céu (The Sky Is Falling) (Kopenawa), 55

Araújo, Ernesto, 270, 274
Arauz, Andrés, 10
Árbenz, Jacobo, 120
Arce, Luis, 203–4, 215
Archer-Daniels-Midland (ADM), 249
Aria, Ze, 278
Artaud, Antonin, 220, 228
Association of Rural Education, 136
Astrid y Gastón (Lima restaurant), 149, 156
Astudillo, Mirko, 153
Atacama Desert, 167–72, 182, 192, 196
Atlantic Council, 309, 311, 316
Austrian Freedom Party, 126
Ávila, Keymar, 61
Avocado Producers and Packers/Exporters Association of Mexico (APEAM), 240–41
Aymara people, 132–33, 144–54, 185, 189, 193, 200, 203, 206–8, 211–12
Ayotzinapa students, 226–27
Azevedo Antunes, Augusto, 25
Aznar, José María, 76

Bachelet, Michelle, 176, 180
Bachmann, Michele, 98
Bahia, Brazil, 256–65
Las Bambas mine (Peru), 158–67
Banco Itaú, 43–44
Banco Santander, 174–75

Bannon, Steve, 23
Barbosa, Nelson, 26
Barrick Gold, 76, 90, 101
Batiste, Eike, 30
Bautista, Hugo, 207–8, 214, 215–16
Bautista Huanca, Jorge, 216
BBVA México, 308, 311, 312–13
Beck, Glenn, 98
Belmond, 7, 132–36, 150, 151–52
Belmond Hiram Bingham, 132, 136, 151
Belo Monte hydroelectric project, 31, 46, 327, 331
Bento Rodriques, Brazil, 17–18, 36–38
Bernstein, Peter, 71–72, 74
Bethlehem Steel, 25
BHP Billiton, 18–19
Biden, Joe, 50–51, 78, 120, 294
Bingham, Hiram, 132
BlackRock, 260
BNDES, 24, 26, 35, 121, 252, 295
Bolivarian Alliance for the Peoples of Our America (ALBA), 118, 121, 201
Bolivarian Revolution, 58, 62–63, 281–82, 287
Bolivia, 12, 135, 183–204, 205–17
Bolm, Barbara, 126
Bolsa Família, 28, 34, 255
Bolsonaro, Eduardo, 52
Bolsonaro, Jair, 4, 11, 22–23, 39, 49–57, 58, 63, 107–8, 113, 175,

182, 195, 201, 257–58, 266–79, 270–79, 303–5, 323–24, 332, 333
Bolsonaro, Percy, 107–8
Bolton, John, 49–50, 284, 292–94
BP, 291, 302
Branson, Richard, 67, 287, 288
Brazil, 1–14, 17–39, 40–57, 103–13, 215, 247–65, 266–79, 294–307, 310–11, 319–34
Brazilian Agricultural Research Corporation (EMBRAPA), 252
Brazilian Institute of the Environment and Renewable Natural Resources (IBAMA), 19, 275–76
Brazilian Social Democracy Party (PSDB), 110, 112–13
Brazilian Workers' Party (PT), 1, 4, 7–8, 23, 26–28, 35–38, 48–49, 103, 107, 110, 112–13, 278, 297, 300–302, 304–6, 320, 323–24
Bresser-Pereira, Luiz Carlos, 28–29
BRICS, 29, 32
Brilhante Ustra, Carlos Alberto, 22–23
Brito, Jeison, 68
Brodie, Fawn, 99
Bulnes, Amílcar, 118
Bunge, 2, 249–50, 254, 258, 265
Burger King, 11, 42, 242, 259, 269, 279
Bush, George W., 59

Los Caballeros Templarios, 238–39
Cabbages and Kings (O. Henry), 119
Cabral, Sergio, 109
Cáceres, Berta, 123, 127
Calama, Chile, 167–72, 181–82
Calderón, Felipe, 223, 313
California Seasteading Institute, 126

Camacho, Luis Fernando "Macho," 195, 197–99, 203, 210
Camargo Corrêa, 322
Cameron, James, 46
Camino, Guiomar, 288
Campos, Elmer, 166
Campos, Marcelo, 19, 36
Carajás iron mines (Brazil), 30–34, 327
Cárdenas, Lázaro, 12, 239, 309, 317
Cardoso, Fernando Henrique, 25–26, 29, 267
Cargill, 247–65, 323
Castaneda, Carlos, 220
Castañeda, Jorge Andrés, 308
Castello Branco, Roberto, 303
Castelo, Manuel, 152–53
Castelo Branco, Humberto, 21–23
Castilla de Oro Foundation, 88
Castro, Fidel, 24, 168
Cattelan, Maurizio, 72–73, 76
Catur, Juan Tomás, 205
CBMM, 44
Cerrado ecosystem, 256–65, 274, 276
Cerro Rico (Bolivia), 184–85, 192, 195, 202, 203
Chacaltaya glacier, 135
Chahuallo, Berto, 163–64
Chateaubriand, Assis, 306
Chávez, Gonzalo, 199
Chávez, Hugo, 5, 59–66, 69–70, 118, 121, 130, 156, 281, 286–93, 296
Cheasty, Adrienne, 157–58, 159
Chevron, 284, 291, 302, 304, 307, 308
Chiapas, Mexico, 91, 95–97, 226, 315, 316
Chicago Boys, 173–75, 179–81, 301
Chile, 6, 10, 94, 167–82, 191, 192, 196, 243
China, 3, 26–29, 31–33, 44–45, 49–51, 160,

194, 202, 251–52, 259, 282–83, 292, 304
China Molybdenum, 44–45
Chiquita (United Fruit Company), 117–23
Chomsky, Noam, 59
Chontal people, 224, 226, 315–18
Choquehuanca, David, 203
Choquehuanca, Zenón, 136
Chrétien, Jean, 232
Christmas, Lee, 118–19
Chuquicamata mine (Chile), 167–71, 182
CIA, 24, 60, 120, 300
Cinta Larga people, 108
CITGO, 282, 284
Clariant, 19
Claver-Carone, Mauricio, 50, 51
Clinton, Bill, 78, 81, 232
Clinton, Hillary, 120
Clinton Giustra Sustainable Growth Initiative, 81
CNN, 49–50, 66, 67, 164
CNPC, 283
Coclesito, Panama, 86–89
Codelco, 167–68, 181
Colombia, 9, 12, 24, 66–67, 71–102, 120, 243, 285
Colque, Juan, 185
Coltan (Nest), 69
Columbus, Christopher, 71, 89–91, 100, 145
Companhia Vale do Rio Doce, 18–19, 25–26. See also Vale
Comstock Mining Inc., 101
Comstock Residents Association, 101–2
Conan Doyle, Arthur, 40–41
Confederation of Indigenous Nationalities of Ecuador (CONAIE), 10
La Conga mine (Peru), 162, 166
Conoco, 302

Continental Gold, 85
Cooperacción (Peruvian
NGO), 163
Cordillera Blanca, 135
Cornejo Velázquez,
Hernán, 149
Correa, Rafael, 5, 8, 10,
155–56, 167, 225, 305
Cortés, Hernán, 71, 76,
96, 231, 315, 317–18
COSIBAH, 117, 126
Cotacachi glacier, 135
Coutinho, Felipe, 303,
304, 307
COVID-19 pandemic, 5,
10, 49, 51, 55–56, 75,
141, 204, 261, 273,
290, 323
Cuenca, Lucio, 180
Curcio, Pasqualina, 287

da Cunha, Euclides, 106–7
Dantas, Daniel, 267–68,
276, 279
da Silva, Marina, 279
da Silva, Paulino ("Paulino
do PT"), 277–78
Dávila, Miguel, 119
Davis, Tammy, 101–2
Davos World Economic
Forum, 34, 294–307
de Aguiar, Danicley, 47
de Alcalá, Jerónimo, 235,
245
de Bolle, Monica, 9
de Castro, Sergio, 174
de la Masa, Gregorio,
219–20
de Montaño, Francisco,
236
de Resende Costa, José,
105
de Souza, Ana, 274–75,
276
de Souza Marques,
Gilberto, 34
Diálogo Tapajos, 322–23
Diamantina, Brazil,
105–13
Díaz, Porfirio, 219–20,
223
DiCaprio, Leonardo, 55
Didion, Joan, 122–23
DINA (Chile), 173
Dolar Today, 286–90

Dole (Standard Fruit),
118–19
Duque, Iván, 9, 83, 85
Duque, Raúl, 77–78
Dúrcal, Rocío, 129–30
"Dutch disease," 28–29,
297
Dynacor, 81

Eating Up the Amazon
(2006 Greenpeace
report), 253
Echave, José, 166, 167
Echazú, Alberto, 193–94
Eclipse of the Huichol
World (López Pinedo),
228
The Economist, 6, 28, 29,
35–36, 306, 314
Eco Oro, 81
Ecuador, 8–10, 135, 167,
206, 225, 305
El Dorado (film), 92
Électricité de France
(EDF), 322
Eletrobras, 322
El Salvador, 93–94, 118,
122–23, 127
The Embrace of the
Serpent (film), 332–34
Empire's Workshop
(Grandin), 120
Endesa, 322
Escobar, 84
Escobar, Loyola, 150, 151
Escobar, Pablo, 85, 139
Espiritu Santo, João, 106
European Commission, 51
Exxon, 50, 280, 291, 299,
302, 304

Facussé, Miguel, 126
Falchetti, Ana María, 79
FARC, 80, 83–85
Fazenda Estrondo (Brazil),
261–65, 268
Federal Reserve, 98
Federation of Industries of
the State of São Paulo
(FIESP), 302
Ferraz, Daniel, 264–65
Ferreria, Fernando,
261–62
Ferrovial, 179
FETAGRI, 277

Fifer, Richard, 88
First Majestic Silver,
219–21, 222–23, 226
Flores Bautista, Francisco,
234–35, 237, 242
Fonsi, Luis, 67
Ford, Henry, 13, 249–50
1499: Brazil Before Cabral
(Lopes), 328–29
Fourth Transformation
(Mexico), 223–24,
311–12
Fox News, 67, 98
Franco, Francisco, 180
Frank, Andre Gunder, 5
Freitas, Robert, 34
Friedman, Milton, 126,
173–75, 176, 179
Friedman, Thomas, 44
Frito-Lay, 11, 137–54, 214
Frontin (cooperative), 82
Furtado, Celso, 5, 25

Gabrielli, Sergio, 294–307,
310
Galeano, Eduardo, 1–11,
20, 22–26, 34, 36,
42–43, 59–60, 70,
82, 91, 119, 123, 133,
160–61, 171, 177,
183–85, 195, 212, 246,
317–18
Galvez, Brad, 97, 100
Gálvez Pinillos, Carlos,
165, 167
García, Alan, 166
García Linera, Álvaro, 201
García Márquez, Gabriel,
38, 120
Garrett, David, 97
Gavito, Mayra Elena,
241–42
GDF Suez (now ENGIE),
322
Geglia, Beth, 119, 131
Geneva Convention, 62
Gingrich, Newt, 126
Giustra, Frank, 81, 93,
227
Glencore Xstrata, 163
Goldcorp, 81, 93–94, 227
Goldex, 84
Gold Museum (Bogotá), 79
Gold Reserve, 69–70
Gold Standard 2012, 98

Goldwyn, David, 309
Gómez, Juan Vicente, 69
Gómez-Tagle, Alberto, 242–44
Góngora, Paco Chapa, 140, 153
Gonzalez, Fredy, 94
Gore, Al, 46
Goulart, João "Jango," 21, 24
Goya, Francisco, 66, 67, 96
Gran Colombia Gold, 81–83
Grandin, Greg, 120
Gran Sabana, Venezuela, 58–70
Graystar, 81
Green Blood campaign, 164–65
Greene, Graham, 136, 307–8, 310
Greenpeace, 47, 253–54, 258, 275–76
Grice, Dylan, 74–75
Griffith-Jones, Stephany, 181
Growth Acceleration Program (PAC), 1, 323
Grupo Delfin, 263
Guaidó, Juan, 61, 62, 64, 70, 200–201, 284, 288, 292–94
Guardiola-Rivera, Oscar, 90, 97, 180n
Guatemala, 92–95, 101, 120, 127–28
Guedes, Paulo, 52, 175
Guedes de Souza, André, 261–62, 264
Guerra, Ciro, 332–34
La guerra que nos ocultan (Cruz et al.), 226–27
Guevara, Ernesto "Che," 24, 168–69, 182
Guide to the Perfect Latin American Idiot (Vargas Llosa), 6
Guillermoprieto, Alma, 9
Gustu (La Paz restaurant), 216–17
Guzmán, Alisandro, 80
Guzmán, Jaime, 179–80

Hanna Mining

Corporation, 20–22, 25, 301
Harvard International Human Rights Clinic, 200
Harvard University, 142, 260
Harvey, David, 65
Hebda, John, 57
Hecht, Susanna, 259–60
Heckenberger, Michael, 330
Heleno, Augusto, 54, 274
Henry, O. (William Sydney Porter), 119, 130–31
Hernández, Juan Orlando, 125, 126, 128–31
Herrera, Fausto, 8
Hickel, Jason, 12–13
Hilton, Larry, 97–100
Historic Memoir of the Diamond (de Resende Costa), 105
Honduran Council of Private Enterprise (COHEP), 117–20
Honduras, 117–31
Horowitz, Glen, 256
Huamaní, Suyana, 135–36
Huayllani, José Luis, 187–88
Huichol people, 11–12, 91, 218–28
Humala, Ollanta, 156–57, 160, 166, 209
Humphrey, George, 20
Hurricane Mitch, 118

Illanes, Rodolfo, 197
Inca Empire, 89, 132–35, 144, 153, 154, 156, 158
Institutional Revolutionary Party (PRI), 316
Inter-American Commission on Human Rights, 36, 37
Inter-American Development Bank (IDB), 50, 142, 191
International Centre for Settlement of Investment Disputes, 70

International Crisis Group, 67
International Development Finance Corporation, 50
International Financial Corporation, 165
International Monetary Fund (IMF), 7, 10, 75, 119, 155–67, 171, 173, 191, 309, 314
International Potato Center (CIP), 145, 146, 152
Itaituba, Brazil, 1–14, 249, 275, 324–25, 334

Jameson, Fredric, 8–9
JBS, 48, 110–12, 251, 256, 268, 275–76, 279
Jucá, Romero, 45–46, 48, 55

Kambeba, Larissa, 331
Kambeba, Márcia, 331
Kapa Munduruku, Bruno, 319–20
Kelly, John, 130
Kennecott, 168
Keynes, John Maynard, 98
Klare, Michael, 44–45
Klein, Naomi, 298
Klugmann, Mark, 125–26
Kopenawa, Davi, 55
Krenak, Ailton, 19
Kubitschek, Juscelino, 20–21
Kyoto Protocol Clean Development Mechanism, 324

La Cruz, Marciano, 218, 220–21
Lagarde, Christine, 7, 155–57, 159, 165–67, 173, 309
Lagos, Ricardo, 180
Laguarta, Ramon, 142
Larrazábal, Hernando, 191
Lasso, Guillermo, 10
Latin American Observatory of Environmental Conflicts, 180

Lava Jato corruption scandal, 109–13, 157, 298, 300, 304–7, 322

Lazo, Carmen, 172

Le Clézio, J. M. G., 89, 222

Lemann, Paulo, 279

Levinsohn, Ronald Guimarães, 262–65, 268

Levis, Carlina, 330

Levy, Joaquim, 301

Leyland, Andy, 204

Lippaus, Eutimio, 276–78

Lobato, Joel, 270–71

Lobo, Porfirio "Pepe," 123, 125–26

Lopes, Reinaldo José, 328–30, 332

López, Leopoldo, 287, 294

López, Raimunda, 93

López Obrador, Andrés Manuel (AMLO), 12, 141, 199, 223–26, 308–18

Louis Dreyfus, 249

Lozoya, Emilio, 309, 314

Lula da Silva, Luiz Inácio, 3, 5, 23, 26–29, 33–37, 39, 41, 47–48, 103, 105, 107, 112, 157, 172, 209, 215, 253, 255, 261, 275, 297–98, 300, 305–6

LVMH Moët Hennessy Louis Vuitton, 7, 72, 133, 151, 158

Machicao, Jimena, 193

Machu Picchu, 7, 132–35, 145, 151, 158, 165, 186

Macron, Emmanuel, 266, 270, 273

Macuxi people, 40–42, 52–56, 58

Maduro, Nicolás, 60–70, 281–94

Magassa, Madi, 105

Mam people, 93–95

Mandetta, Luiz Henrique, 51

Mansilla, Edwin, 135

Mara Salvatrucha (MS-13), 92, 124, 128–30

March of the Family with

God for Freedom, 21, 36

Marfrig, 256, 275–76, 279

La Marlin mine (Guatemala), 93–94

Márquez Marín, Gustavo, 64–65, 69, 70

Martineau, Jean, 81

Martinelli, Ricardo, 88

Martins, Jeremías, 106

Mato Grosso, Brazil, 48–49, 248–56, 257, 323

MATOPIBA program, 260

Matta, Roberto, 178

Mayan people, 76, 86, 89, 93–96, 122, 315

Mayr, Martin, 260–61, 265

McCabe, Andrew, 292

McDonald's, 44, 122, 250, 253, 255

Medellín, Pedro, 228

Mejía, Bonifacio, 94

Memory of Fire trilogy (Galeano), 317

Méndez Arjona, René, 310–11

Men with Guns (film), 93

Messa, Carlos, 203

Metabase, 38

Metalor, 85

MetLife, 175

The Mexican (film), 228

The Mexican Dream (Le Clézio), 89, 222

Mexican Institute for Competitiveness (IMCO), 308, 309–10

Mexico, 11–12, 27, 95–97, 128, 140–43, 218–28, 231–46, 307–18

Meyer, Claus, 216

Micheletti, Roberto, 120

Michell Group, 132

Michoacán, Mexico, 11, 231–46

Mighty Earth (NGO), 256

Miller, Todd, 128

Minas Gerais, Brazil, 5, 17–39, 43–44, 105–11, 168

Mireles, José Manuel, 239

Miterhof, Marcelo, 24

MMG, 161, 163

Molano Bravo, Alfredo, 84

Molony, Guy "Machine Gun," 119, 121

Monroe, James, 50

Moody's, 33, 175, 309, 311

Morales, Evo, 4, 5, 8, 12, 155–56, 167, 182, 185–86, 188–204, 205–15, 225, 305

Moreira, Fernanda, 334

Morel, Cecilia, 177

Moreno, Lenín, 9–10

Moreno, Luis Alberto, 142

Mormonism (Church of the Latter Day Saints), 97–100

Moro, Sergio, 113, 157, 304–5

Moss, Michael, 138, 141, 142–43

Motorcycle Diaries (Guevara), 168

Movement Toward Socialism (MAS), 4, 193, 198, 203, 215

Movistar, 178–79

Mubadala, 83

Mujica, José "Pepe," 170

Munduruku community, 1–2, 14, 275, 319–34

Munguía, Iris, 117, 120

Muñoz, Diego, 151

Muñoz, Maria, 88

Muraña Huanca, Emilio, 205

Museum of the Americas (Madrid), 79, 86, 96

Musk, Elon, 201

Nasralla, Salvador, 129

National Agrarian Institute (INA), 122

National Football League (NFL), 231–32, 233

National Indian Foundation (FUNAI), 45, 48, 54, 319–20, 328

National Institute for Colonization and Agrarian Reform (INCRA), 277

National Institute for Space Research (INPE), 270, 327

National Liberation Army
(ELN), 66–67
National Society of
Mining, Petroleum, and
Energy, 165
National Wildlife
Federation, 271
Navia, Patricio, 181
Neruda, Pablo, 90
Nest, Michael, 69
Nevada, 100–102
Neves, Aécio, 109–13
Neves, Tancredo, 112
Newmont Mining, 90
Niemeyer, Oscar, 21, 306,
330
Nobre, Carlos, 274
Nooyi, Indra, 142
Norquist, Grover, 126
North American Free
Trade Agreement
(NAFTA), 232, 311
Nova Cartografia Social,
321
Núñez de Balboa, Vasco,
89

OAS (Brazilian company),
109
Obama, Barack, 5, 59–60,
120, 126–27, 300
Odebrecht, 109–10, 268,
298, 314
Olavo de Carvalho, 22–23,
51–53, 270, 301,
328–29
Olvea, Edilesa, 144–45,
151
One Hundred Years
of Solitude (García
Márquez), 8–9, 120
Open Veins of Latin
America (Galeano),
1–7, 11, 20, 23–24, 43,
59–60, 70, 119, 160,
183–85, 223, 225, 301
Operation Brother Sam,
24–25, 301
Opportunity Fund,
267–68, 279
Organization of American
States (OAS), 129, 177,
198, 201, 203
Organization of the
Petroleum Exporting

Countries (OPEC), 194,
291
Orinoco Mining Arc,
61–69
Orinoco Petroleum Belt,
65, 280–94
Ortiz Pinchetti, José
Agustín, 226
Osorio, Raissa Macedo
Lacerda, 253
The Other Side of Paradise
(telenovela), 103–5,
110, 111
Ouro Preto, Brazil, 38–39,
52

Panama, 86–92, 101
Paniagua, Carlos, 241
Pará, Brazil, 2, 30, 34,
252–53, 266–79,
319–34
Pastoral Land
Commission, 274–75
Paul, Ron, 98
Pemex, 308–18
Pemon people, 58–59, 290
Peña Nieto, Enrique, 219,
222–24, 227, 309, 311,
312–14, 317
PepsiCo, 11, 137–54, 214
Peralta Escobar, Nélida,
148, 149, 150–51
Pérez, Luis Guillermo
"Luigi," 311, 317–18
Pérez de Holguín,
Melchor, 183–84
Peru, 7, 132–54, 155–67,
208–9, 212–13
Petaquilla Gold, 86–88, 92
Petro, Gustavo, 9, 83
Petrobras, 29, 35, 109,
269, 294–307
Petroleum of Venezuela,
S.A. (PDVSA), 281–82,
283, 291, 293
Pieth, Mark, 73–74
Piñera, José, 175
Piñera, Sebastián, 168,
171–81
"pink tide," Latin
American, 3, 6, 8, 70,
165, 167, 209, 297, 300
Pinochet, Augusto, 27,
169, 170, 171, 173–76,
178, 179–80, 192, 196

Pizarro, Francisco, 71, 90,
92, 212
Plan Colombia, 78
Plan País (Venezuela), 293
Pompeo, Mike, 284
Potato Park (Peru), 152
Potosí, Bolivia, 146,
183–204, 206–7, 212
Potosínista Civic
Committee, 195
The Power and the Glory
(Greene), 307–8, 310
Pradal, Patricia, 304
Proyecto Cucara (Project
Spoon), 142
Pumari, Marco, 195–200,
202–3
Puno, Peru, 135–36,
144–54, 237
Purépecha civilization,
11, 231–46

Quadros, Jânio, 21, 24
Quagliato brothers,
266–67, 274, 276
QuantumScape, 194,
195–96
Quechua people, 9–10,
145–54, 159–66, 187,
193, 195, 199, 203,
205–16
Quimbaya collection,
78–79, 86, 96
Quiñones, Marco Aurelio,
70
Quiroga, Alejandro, 175
Quispe, Daniel, 162, 163
Quispe, Jorge, 213–14

The Race for What's Left
(Klare), 45
Ramírez, Edgar, 147–48,
151
Ramírez, Jorge, 128
Ramírez, Rafael, 281
Ramseier, Cornelia Ruth,
227
Raposa Serra do Sol
(Brazil), 40–57, 58, 201
Raudales, Julio, 125, 131
Reagan, Michael, 126
Reagan, Ronald, 93, 125,
173–74
Real de Catorce, Mexico,
218–28

Rede Globo, 104, 105, 110, 111, 112, 305, 306
Reid, Michael, 6–7, 9
Relación de Michoacán (de Alcalá), 235, 245
Un reportero en la montaña mágica (Robinson), 34
Reyes, José, 129–30
Reyes, José Manuel, 315–16
Ribeiro, José "Ze" Augusto, 305–6
Rights, Environment, and Natural Resources (Lima NGO), 136
La Rinconada mine (Peru), 73–74
Rio de Janeiro Olympics (2016), 4, 18, 109, 302
Rio Doce, 17–39
Robertson, Geoffrey, 112
Rodríguez, Francisco, 284–85
Rogerio, Paulo, 321–22
Rojas Rabiela, Teresa, 236
Rojo, Wilfredo, 201
Romer, Paul, 124–25, 127, 130–31
Rondônia, Brazil, 48–49, 108
Roof (Salt Lake City restaurant), 97–100
Roosevelt, Franklin, 20, 24
Roosevelt Indigenous Reserve, 108
Roraima Mountains, 40–57, 58, 65
Rosneft, 282, 283
Rousseff, Dilma, 1, 23, 29, 33, 35–37, 39, 45, 47, 49, 112, 155–56, 172, 209, 215, 225, 261, 299–302, 304, 320, 323–24
Rubio, Marco, 49–50, 51, 63, 284, 294
Russia, 282–83, 292, 300

Saavedra, Dario, 88
Sachs, Jeff, 284–85
Salar de Uyuni, Bolivia, 12, 183–204, 207, 213–15

Salas, Alberto, 145, 146–47, 152, 154
Salas, Luis, 293–94
Salcedo, Doris, 84
Sales, Ib, 254
Salgado, Sebastião, 77, 108
Salinas de Gortari, Carlos, 232, 241
Salles, Ricardo, 273–74
Salles, Walter, 43–44, 168
Salt Lake City, Utah, 97–100
Salt Sugar Fat (Moss), 138
Salvador (Didion), 122–23
Samarco mine (Brazil), 17–19, 36
San Luis Potosí, Mexico, 11–12, 185–86, 218–28
San Marcos, Guatemala, 92–94
San Miguel Ixtahuacán, Guatemala, 93–94
San Pedro Sula, Honduras, 117–31
Santa Cruz, Bolivia, 189, 192, 195, 197–98, 209, 210–12
Santarém, Brazil, 1–2, 7, 247–54, 261, 320, 323
Santiago de Chile, 5, 27, 155, 167–70, 171–82
Santos, Juan Manuel, 80, 84, 85
Santos, Vivienne, 110–12
São Luiz do Tapajos hydroelectric dam, 1, 14, 323–26
Saura, Carlos, 92
Saw Munduruku, Jairo, 14, 325–27, 334
Saw Munduruku, Juárez, 326, 327
Sayles, John, 93
Sembrando Vida (Sowing Life), 225–26
Sena, Edilberto, 7, 255, 260–61
Serdarevi, Masa, 72
Shell, 299, 302, 308
Las siembras de ayer (Rojas Rabiela), 236
Singer, André, 35
Sinopec, 304

The Skeleton of Tatewari (Benítez), 228
Smith, Joseph, 97, 99–100
Socialism and Liberty Party (PSOL), 331
Sociedad Química y Minera de Chile (Soquimich), 196
Socorro Castillo, José, 244–45
Solón, Pablo, 196, 209–11, 214–15
Southern Command of the US Armed Forces, 130, 287
SpaceX, 43
Spain, 76, 79, 96–97, 137–38, 140, 145–46, 178–80, 251, 316, 317
Spector, Nancy, 76
Standard Fruit, 118–19
Standard Oil, 309
Stanley, Leonardo, 76
Statoil (now Equinor), 299, 302
Stiglitz, Joseph, 181
Storming the Wall (Miller), 128
Summit of the Americas in Lima (2018), 49, 292
Summit of the Americas in Trinidad (2009), 59
Surat, India, 11, 108
Survival International (NGO), 333

Tabasco, Mexico, 226, 307–18
Tabasco Indigenous Institute, 316
Taha, Marsia, 217
Tapajos River, 1–2, 14, 247–48, 250, 254, 319–34
TBEA, 194
TechMet, 50
Temer, Michel, 36–37, 39, 45, 47–48, 298, 304, 305
Tesla, 194, 201–2
Tett, Gillian, 75
Thatcher, Margaret, 173–74
Theroux, Paul, 221
Thiel, Peter, 74–75

Tillerson, Rex, 50, 291
Toro, José, 293
Toronto Stock Exchange, 73, 81, 223
Torres, Mauricio, 324, 327
Total, 291, 302, 308
Toufic, Gaby, 110
Trans-Amazonian Highway, 2, 56, 296, 319, 327
Treasure of the Sierra Madre (film), 227–28
Trump, Donald, 23, 49–51, 59, 61–62, 72–73, 74, 76, 85, 98–99, 128–29, 139, 177, 193, 200–201, 282–85, 291–92, 300, 311
Túpac Amaru uprising, 91
Twain, Mark, 102
Tyndall Centre, 135

Union of South American Nations (UNASUR), 201
United Fruit Company, 117–23
United Nations, 98, 196, 281
United Nations Economic Commission for Latin America and the Caribbean (CEPAL), 26–27, 34, 223, 312
United Nations Food and Agriculture Organization (FAO), 145, 212, 269
United States Agency for International Development (USAID), 284
United States-Mexico-Canada Agreement (USMCA), 232
Upside Down: A Primer for the Looking-Glass World (Galeano), 60
Los Urbanos, 84–85
Uribe, Ávaro, 80–82, 84–85
Uribe, Sergio, 227
Uruapan, Mexico, 234, 240–43
Urzúa, Carlos, 312, 313

US Department of Defense, 45
US Department of Justice, 300, 304, 314
US Department of State, 121, 304, 307
US Geological Survey, 42, 43, 57
US Steel, 20, 25, 30, 33–34, 301
Utah, 97–100
Uyuni region of Bolivia, 205–17. *See also* Salar de Uyuni, Bolivia

Vale, 25–38, 327
Valentín, Félix Omar, 126
Valenzuela, Iván, 181–82
Vargas, Getúlio, 20, 25, 296, 305–6
Vargas, Guillermo, 238–39, 245–46
Vargas Llosa, Álvaro, 6
Vargas Llosa, Mario, 262–63
Vásquez, Henry, 163
Velásquez, Esteban, 169–70, 172
Vélez, Julio, 287
Venezuela, 6, 58–70, 118, 121, 202, 280–94, 300, 302, 303–4
Venezuela Aid Live (2019), 67, 287, 288
Ventura Colindre, Santos, 122
Los Viagras, 238–39
Videgaray, Luis, 314
Villa, Pancho, 220
Villarroel, Gualberto, 199
Vips cafeteria chain, 242–44
Virginia City, Nevada, 100–102
Voluntad Popular, 70
von Martius, Theo, 332–33

Waiapi, Emyra, 55
Walker (British chip-maker), 143
Wallerstein, Immanuel, 5
Walmart, 242, 244, 253, 259
Wapichana, Joênia, 56

Warao people, 65–66, 67
The War of the End of the World (Vargas Llosa), 262–63
Washington Center for Strategic and International Studies, 292
Waxman, Henry, 256
Webber, Jude, 313
Weisbrot, Mark, 285
What If Latin America Ruled the World? (Guardiola-Rivera), 90
Winfield, John, 101
World Bank, 26, 70, 124–25, 155, 165

Xinguara agricultural fair (Pará, Brazil), 266–79

Yacimientos de Litio Bolivianos (YLB), 192
Yangüez, Carmelo, 86–87
Yanomami people, 45–46, 53, 55, 58
Yao, Julio, 92
Yasuní National Park (Ecuador), 167
Yellen, Janet, 98
Yeltsin, Boris, 174
YLB, 194, 198, 201
Yo lo vi (I Saw It) (Goya), 66, 67

Zacatecas, Mexico, 5, 224–25, 226, 239
Zapata, Emiliano, 96–97, 220
Zapatista National Liberation Army (EZLN), 91, 95, 96–97, 316
ZEDEs Project (Honduras), 123–31
Zelaya, Manuel "Mel," 117–31
Zemurray, Samuel, 118–19
Zika virus, 4, 18, 56